Advanced SQL
Fourth Edition

Lucy Scott

ISBN-13: 979-8-8689-0022-8

DEDICATION

TO LISA

Copyright © 2023 Lucy Scott

All rights reserved.

ISBN-13: **979-8-8689-0022-8**

CONTENTS

DISCLAIMER

NOTICE OF LIABILITY

ACKNOWLEDGEMENT

Gratefully acknowledge the assistance of Dr. Youlong Zhuang who reviewed this edition of the book.

CHAPTER 1: VIEWS AND INDEXES

Chapter Learning Objectives

1.1 Demonstrate the practical ability to create, modify, and delete views within a relational database.
1.2 Apply the knowledge to effectively create both clustered and nonclustered indexes.
1.3 List and describe the function of indexes in a relational database.

1.1 View Definition

In a relational database, a view is a conceptual construct akin to a virtual table. In contrast to the fundamental tables introduced in our first database textbook, which are often referred to as base tables, a view derives its existence from an SQL query. For instance, consider the "Student" table, which houses student identifiers, first names, last names, social security numbers, dates of birth, and class associations. A view named "classof2025_view" can be established through a query like "SELECT * FROM Student WHERE Class = '2025';."

At first glance, it might seem that the "Student" table encompasses all students within the school, while the "classof2025_view" encompasses solely those set to graduate in 2025. This perspective is somewhat accurate. You are correct in thinking that "classof2025_view" can be treated as if it were a table housing all students graduating in 2025. However, it is essential to clarify that the "classof2025_view" is devoid of any actual data. Instead, it solely encapsulates the SQL statement referenced above.

You might wonder how a view can function as a table when it contains no data. The answer lies in its dynamic nature. When you interact with the view, it dynamically retrieves data from the underlying base table, providing the illusion of interacting with a complete and separate table.

Review Question 1.1
In a database, a view is ______ .
a. a table
b. a table with a different view
c. a virtual table
d. a table used for displaying only

Review Question 1.2
In a database, a view is defined by ______.
a. an SQL query
b. a programmer
c. a table
d. a database administrator

Review Question 1.3
In a SQL Server database, most data are held in ________.
a. views
b. tables
c. base tables
d. base views

Review Question 1.4
In a SQL Server database, _______.
a. you cannot retrieve data from a view because it contains no data
b. you can retrieve data from a view because a view is defined by an SQL query
c. you cannot retrieve data from a view because of security concerns
d. you can retrieve data from a view because a view is the same as its base table

Review Question 1.5
How is a view different from a base table?
a. A view contains more data.
b. A view is created using SQL queries, while base tables are not.
c. A view is a physical table, and a base table is a virtual table.
d. A view is dynamic, while a base table is static.

Review Question 1.6
What kind of data does a view like "classof2025_view" contain?
a. Data of all students in the school
b. Data of students graduating in 2025
c. Part of a larger table like Student
d. No data, just an illusion

Review Question 1.7
What is the purpose of creating a view in a relational database?
a. To store and manage large datasets
b. To organize data into categories

c. To encapsulate complex SQL queries
d. To physically store data

Review Question 1.8
Why is a view described as dynamic in nature?
a. It can be modified easily.
b. It retrieves data from the base table on demand.
c. It contains constantly changing data.
d. It can be accessed by multiple users simultaneously.

Review Question 1.9
What is the primary role of an SQL query in creating a view?
a. To define the view's data structure
b. To insert data into the view
c. To delete records from the view
d. To specify view permissions

1.2 View Purposes

When considering the utility of views in a relational database, it's essential to recognize the specific purposes they serve, particularly when they need to retrieve data from the base table. There are three primary reasons why utilizing a view may be more appropriate than working directly with a base table or even the sole choice:

1. Simplification of Data Access:

Views offer a simplified and tailored perspective of data. In scenarios where a base table is extensive, containing numerous columns and rows, views enable the creation of more focused, compact datasets. For example, consider a "student" table with extensive information, but the alumni office may only require data pertaining to graduated students, including names and contact information. In this case, a specialized view can be crafted exclusively for the alumni office's needs. Furthermore, views can consolidate data from multiple tables, presenting a unified and simplified source for queries, which is far more manageable than working with multiple base tables.

2. Enhanced Data Security:

Views can be employed to bolster data security and privacy. For instance, instructors might need access to student data but have no legitimate reason to access social security numbers. Views offer a layer of abstraction between users and the base table, effectively concealing sensitive data. This additional layer enhances data protection. With well-defined access control mechanisms, users with view access can be restricted from directly accessing the base table, ensuring data integrity and security.

3. Support for Backward Compatibility:

Views play a pivotal role in maintaining backward compatibility when dealing with evolving database structures. If an application relies on a base table, any alterations to the table's schema may necessitate corresponding adjustments in the application's code. However, when a view is utilized within the application, changes to the base table structure do not impact the application. This is particularly useful in scenarios where different views are created for various applications, all drawing data from the same base table. For instance, a "student" table can serve as the source for one view tailored to the admission process and another designed for financial aid. These distinct views can provide different datasets and formatting while preserving the stability of the underlying base table.

Review Question 1.10
Which of the following is a reason for using views over tables?
a. A view can be faster for retrieving data than a base table.
b. A view can be simpler for retrieving data than a base table.
c. A view can store more data than a base table.
d. A view can be more reliable than a base table.

Review Question 1.11
Which of the following is a reason for using views over tables?
a. A view can be more reliable than a base table.
b. A view can be created for security purposes.
c. Attackers are not interested in a view because it does not store any data.
d. Views are more secure because it does not store any data.

Review Question 1.12
Which of the following is a reason for using views over tables?
a. A view can store more data than a base table.
b. A view can be used for backward compatibility.
c. A view contains data that are more volatile than a base table.
d. A view is easier to set foreign keys than a base table.

Review Question 1.13
What is the primary function of views in a relational database?
a. To complicate data access.
b. To replace base tables entirely.
c. To simplify and tailor data access.
d. To create additional data tables.

Review Question 1.14
In which situation is a view particularly advantageous?
a. When you need a complex schema with many tables.
b. When you require an identical copy of the base table.

c. When you need to consolidate data from multiple tables.
d. When you need data exactly as it exists in the base table.

Review Question 1.15
How can views enhance data security in a database?
a. By directly exposing sensitive data to all users.
b. By restricting access to base tables.
c. By making social security numbers available to all users.
d. By eliminating the need for access control mechanisms.

Review Question 1.16
Which of the following best describes the concept of backward compatibility with views?
a. It requires no changes when the base table's schema changes.
b. It always necessitates application code adjustments.
c. It makes views incompatible with any application.
d. It prevents the use of multiple views with a single base table.

Review Question 1.17
How can views benefit different applications using the same base table?
a. By ensuring that all applications use identical data.
b. By eliminating the need for views altogether.
c. By allowing the base table's schema to change freely.
d. By creating different views tailored to each application's needs.

Review Question 1.18
What is the purpose of a specialized view for the alumni office, assuming alumni are students and stored in a Student table?
a. To provide extensive student information.
b. To protect sensitive student data.
c. To offer backward compatibility.
d. To offer a simplified dataset for the alumni office's needs.

Review Question 1.19
How do views enhance data protection in the context of security?
a. By exposing sensitive data to all users.
b. By eliminating access control mechanisms.
c. By acting as an additional layer between users and the base table.
d. By granting unrestricted access to the base table.

Review Question 1.20
When changes occur in the schema of a base table, how do views help in maintaining application stability?
a. By making the application code immune to any changes.
b. By requiring all applications to be rewritten from scratch.
c. By allowing changes to the base table schema without impacting the application.
d. By preventing the use of views in any application.

1.3 Creating Views

In this section, we will explore the creation of views in a relational database. Views offer a convenient way to access and manipulate data based on specific criteria. We'll be using the same database as in our previous book. If you don't have it, you can download the script from this link (goo.gl/ftzOxl) and execute it to set up the necessary database for the examples and exercises in this book.

To create a view, use the following syntax:

```
CREATE VIEW ViewName
AS
SELECT Column1, Column2, ...
FROM OneOrMoreBaseTableName
WHERE conditions;
```

Now, let's look at a few examples to understand the practical application of creating views:

SQL Example 1.1

Suppose you want to create a view named "DomesticContact" containing contact information for domestic customers. You only need the contact name and email.

SQL Example 1.1 Analysis

This is an example where you can directly apply the CREATE VIEW syntax. Pay close attention to the SELECT statement within the CREATE VIEW. It's recommended to write the SELECT statement first to ensure that the correct data is retrieved. Although not strictly necessary, we've included the DROP VIEW command. This line can be helpful for beginners to start with a fresh view each time the code is executed.

SQL Example 1.1 Statement

```
DROP VIEW IF EXISTS Sales.DomesticContact;
CREATE VIEW Sales.DomesticContact
AS
SELECT Contact, Email
FROM Sales.Customers
WHERE Country = 'USA';
```

After executing these statements,

```
Command(s) completed successfully.
```

You can use the "DomesticContact" view as if it were a table in the database, like this:

```
SELECT *
FROM Sales.DomesticContact;
```

The result will be:

	Contact	Email
1	John White	jwhite@je.com
2	Scott Green	green@beil.com
3	Alice Black	black1@be.com
4	Ben Gold	bgold@efun.com
5	Daniel Yellow	dy@os.com

SQL Example 1.2

Create a view called "Customer1Orders," which includes order dates, employee IDs, product IDs, prices, and quantities for all orders placed by Customer 1. The SQL statement involves joining data from multiple tables:

SQL Example 1.2 Analysis

Creating the view is a straightforward task, but crafting the SELECT statement may pose a challenge for some readers. This could be a good opportunity for those in need to revisit the SELECT skills they acquired in our first database book.

When extracting data from multiple tables, using JOIN is often the preferred approach. In this scenario, we need to gather information from different sources. For instance, Employee ID and order dates can be obtained from the Sales.Orders table, while Product ID, price, and quantity data are stored in the Sales.OrderDetails table.

To begin, issue a SELECT statement to retrieve all orders placed by Customer 1, including details of all the products within each order:

```
SELECT *
FROM Sales.Orders JOIN Sales.OrderDetails
ON Orders.OrderId = OrderDetails.OrderId
WHERE Orders.CustomerId = 1;
```

The output should resemble the following:

	OrderId	CustomerId	EmployeeId	OrderDate	OrderId	ProductId	Price	quantity
1	1	1	5	2017-01-03	1	1	1499.99	1
2	1	1	5	2017-01-03	1	3	149.99	2
3	2	1	3	2017-03-05	2	1	1499.99	1
4	2	1	3	2017-03-05	2	2	1599.99	1
5	2	1	3	2017-03-05	2	4	99.99	6
6	2	1	3	2017-03-05	2	6	189.99	5
7	5	1	4	2017-05-03	5	3	149.99	6
8	5	1	4	2017-05-03	5	6	199.99	3

Subsequently, replace the asterisk (*) in the SQL statement above with specific column names to complete the "Customer1Orders" view.

SQL Example 1.2 Statement

```
DROP VIEW IF EXISTS Sales.Customer1Orders;
CREATE VIEW Sales.Customer1Orders
AS
SELECT O.OrderId, O.EmployeeId, O.OrderDate, OD.ProductId, OD.Price, OD.quantity
FROM Sales.Orders AS O JOIN Sales.OrderDetails AS OD
ON O.OrderId = OD.OrderId
WHERE O.CustomerId = 1;
```

After creating the view, you can retrieve data from it by executing the following SQL statement:

```
SELECT *
FROM Sales.Customer1Orders;
```

This will provide you with the expected result:

	OrderId	EmployeeId	OrderDate	ProductId	Price	quantity
1	1	5	2017-01-03	1	1499.99	1
2	1	5	2017-01-03	3	149.99	2
3	2	3	2017-03-05	1	1499.99	1
4	2	3	2017-03-05	2	1599.99	1
5	2	3	2017-03-05	4	99.99	6
6	2	3	2017-03-05	6	189.99	5
7	5	4	2017-05-03	3	149.99	6
8	5	4	2017-05-03	6	199.99	3

SQL Example 1.3

Create the "Customer1OrderTotal" view, similar to "Customer1Orders," but with some enhancements. It includes employee names, product names, and the total value of each order. The SQL statement is more complex and involves joins and aggregation.

SQL Example 1.3 Analysis

To include the customer name, you need to join the Sales.Customers table with Sales.Orders. To include the product name, you should join the Purchasing.Products table with Sales.OrderDetails. To calculate the total value of each order, you'll use the SUM() aggregate function. The total value of each product in an order is calculated as Price multiplied by Quantity. Since an aggregate function is in the SELECT clause, you must use GROUP BY to include all non-aggregate columns. Before creating the view, you can practice by executing the following SELECT statement:

```
SELECT *
FROM HR.Employees AS E JOIN Sales.Orders AS O
ON E.EmployeeId = O.EmployeeId
JOIN Sales.OrderDetails AS OD
ON O.OrderId = OD.OrderId
```

```sql
JOIN Purchasing.Products AS P
ON OD.ProductId = P.ProductId
WHERE O.CustomerId = 1;
```

The result table may contain too many columns, likely resulting in eight rows. To complete the task, replace the asterisk (*) with specific column names and add the CREATE VIEW statement.

SQL Example 1.3 Statement

```sql
DROP VIEW IF EXISTS Sales.Customer1OrderTotal;
CREATE VIEW Sales.Customer1OrderTotal
AS
SELECT E.FirstName + ' ' + E.LastName AS "Employee Name",
    O.OrderId, O.OrderDate, P.ProductName,
    SUM(OD.Price*OD.Quantity) AS "Order Total"
FROM HR.Employees AS E JOIN Sales.Orders AS O
ON E.EmployeeId = O.EmployeeId
JOIN Sales.OrderDetails AS OD
ON O.OrderId = OD.OrderId
JOIN Purchasing.Products AS P
ON OD.ProductId = P.ProductId
WHERE O.CustomerId = 1
GROUP BY E.FirstName + ' ' + E.LastName,
    O.OrderId, O.OrderDate, P.ProductName;
```

To verify the functionality of the "Customer1OrderTotal" view, you can use the following SQL statement:

```sql
SELECT *
FROM Sales.Customer1OrderTotal;
```

The result is:

	Employee Name	OrderId	OrderDate	ProductName	Order Total
1	Alice Law	5	2017-05-03	3200 Lumens LED Home Theater Projector	899.94
2	Alice Law	5	2017-05-03	Color Laser Printer	599.97
3	Black Hart	1	2017-01-03	3200 Lumens LED Home Theater Projector	299.98
4	Black Hart	1	2017-01-03	65-Inch 4K Ultra HD Smart TV	1499.99
5	Maria Law	2	2017-03-05	60-Inch 4K Ultra HD Smart LED TV	1599.99
6	Maria Law	2	2017-03-05	65-Inch 4K Ultra HD Smart TV	1499.99
7	Maria Law	2	2017-03-05	Color Laser Printer	949.95
8	Maria Law	2	2017-03-05	Wireless Color Photo Printer	599.94

Review Question 1.21
If you execute CREATE VIEW command and the view is successfully created, you will see _____ in the output message.
a. all data in the newly created view
b. all data in the base table
c. one row affected.
d. command(s) completed successfully

Review Question 1.22
Your knowledge of SQL _______ is very helpful when writing code for creating a view.
a. SELECT
b. SELECT and UPDATE
c. SELECT, UPDATE, and DELETE
d. SELECT, UPDATE, DELETE, and INSERT

Review Question 1.23
What is the primary purpose of creating views in a relational database?
a. To replace base tables
b. To simplify and tailor data access
c. To eliminate the need for SQL queries
d. To increase database security

Review Question 1.24
What SQL statement is used to retrieve data from the "Customer1Orders" view after it's created?
a. SELECT * FROM Sales.Customer1Orders;
b. CREATE VIEW Sales.Customer1Orders;
c. SELECT * FROM Sales.Orders JOIN Sales.OrderDetails;
d. DROP VIEW IF EXISTS Sales.Customer1Orders;

Review Question 1.25
In SQL Example below, what is the purpose of the GROUP BY clause in the SELECT statement?

```
SELECT E.FirstName + ' ' + E.LastName AS "Employee Name",
    O.OrderId, O.OrderDate, P.ProductName,
    SUM(OD.Price*OD.Quantity) AS "Order Total"
FROM HR.Employees AS E JOIN Sales.Orders AS O
ON E.EmployeeId = O.EmployeeId
JOIN Sales.OrderDetails AS OD
ON O.OrderId = OD.OrderId
JOIN Purchasing.Products AS P
ON OD.ProductId = P.ProductId
WHERE O.CustomerId = 1
GROUP BY E.FirstName + ' ' + E.LastName,
    O.OrderId, O.OrderDate, P.ProductName;
```

a. To filter data based on specific criteria
b. To remove duplicate rows from the result
c. To join data from multiple tables
d. To group rows based on common values for aggregation

1.4 Updatable Views

Views serve not only as tools for retrieving data from table(s) but also as a means to update the underlying base table(s). However, it's important to note that not all views can be updated.

To practice the examples in this section without affecting the original data, we recommend creating a new schema and copying a subset of tables. Here's how you can do it:

```
CREATE SCHEMA Chapter1 AUTHORIZATION dbo;
GO
SELECT * INTO Chapter1.Orders FROM Sales.Orders;
SELECT * INTO Chapter1.OrderDetails FROM Sales.OrderDetails;
SELECT * INTO Chapter1.Customers FROM Sales.Customers;
```

SQL Example 1.4

Create a view called Employee5Orders that includes all orders handled by Employee5

SQL Example 1.4 Statement

```
DROP VIEW IF EXISTS Chapter1.Employee5Orders;
CREATE VIEW Chapter1.Employee5Orders
AS
SELECT *
FROM Chapter1.Orders
WHERE EmployeeId = 5;
```

The Employee5Orders view functions like a table. Any updates, insertions, or deletions made in Employee5Orders will have corresponding effects on the base table, which is the Orders table.

For example, issue the following SQL statement to change Order ID 1 order date from "2017-01-03" to "2018-01-03" on the Employee5Orders

```
UPDATE Chapter1.Employee5Orders
SET OrderDate = '20180103'
WHERE OrderId = 1;
```

Then issue the following SQL statement to retrieve all data from the Orders table (the base table):

```
SELECT *
FROM Chapter1.Orders;
```

The Orders table now looks like this (Note the first row, the year is changed from 2017 to 2018):

	OrderId	CustomerId	EmployeeId	OrderDate
1	1	1	5	2018-01-03
2	2	1	3	2017-03-05
3	3	2	5	2017-02-23
4	4	4	5	2017-04-13
5	5	1	4	2017-05-03
6	6	3	6	2017-05-08
7	7	5	7	2016-11-08
8	8	7	2	2016-12-23

However, not all views can be used to update the base table. For example, if an update view statement involves data from more than one base table, the statement will not execute.

SQL Example 1.5

Create a view called Employee5OrderDetails that will include all orders handled by employee 5, including the product, price, and quantity in each order.

SQL Example 1.5 Statement

```
DROP VIEW IF EXISTS Chapter1.Employee5OrderDetails;
CREATE VIEW Chapter1.Employee5OrderDetails
AS
SELECT O.OrderId, O.CustomerId, O.OrderDate, OD.ProductId, OD.Price, OD.quantity
FROM Chapter1.Orders AS O JOIN Chapter1.OrderDetails AS OD
ON O.OrderId = OD.OrderId
WHERE EmployeeId = 5;
```

If you select all data from the Sales.Employee5OrderDetails view, you get the following result:

	OrderId	CustomerId	OrderDate	ProductId	Price	quantity
1	1	1	2017-01-03	1	1499.99	1
2	1	1	2017-01-03	3	149.99	2
3	3	2	2017-02-23	3	159.99	2
4	3	2	2017-02-23	6	199.99	1
5	3	2	2017-02-23	7	109.99	2
6	3	2	2017-02-23	8	69.99	2
7	3	2	2017-02-23	9	1449.99	1
8	4	4	2017-04-13	4	99.99	2
9	4	4	2017-04-13	8	69.99	1

An update statement to update the orderdate in Sales.Employee5OrderDetails view will also update the orderdate in the Sales.Orders base table because orderdate is from a single table, the Sales.Orders table.

Similarly, an update to both price and quantity of order ID 1 and Product ID 1 will work because they are from the same table OrderDetails. Try the following statement that will double quantity and reduce the price by 10% for the order ID 1 and Product ID 1.

```
UPDATE Chapter1.Employee5OrderDetails
SET quantity = 2 * quantity,
price = price * 0.9
WHERE OrderId = 1 AND ProductId = 1;
```

The following table shows the data in the OrderDetails table after it is updated (the first row):

	OrderId	CustomerId	OrderDate	ProductId	Price	quantity
1	1	1	2017-01-03	1	1349.991	2
2	1	1	2017-01-03	3	149.99	2
3	3	2	2017-02-23	3	159.99	2
4	3	2	2017-02-23	6	199.99	1
5	3	2	2017-02-23	7	109.99	2
6	3	2	2017-02-23	8	69.99	2
7	3	2	2017-02-23	9	1449.99	1
8	4	4	2017-04-13	4	99.99	2
9	4	4	2017-04-13	8	69.99	1

Now, try to update the order date and quantity from the Sales.Employee5OrderDetails view with the following SQL statement:

```sql
UPDATE Chapter1.Employee5OrderDetails
SET OrderDate = '20180103',
quantity = 10
WHERE OrderId = 1 AND ProductId = 1;
```

An error message similar to the following will be displayed:

```
Msg 4405, Level 16, State 1, Line 101
View or function 'Sales.Employee5OrderDetails' is not updatable because the modification affects
multiple base tables.
```

In short, an update to a view with references to columns from more than one base table is not allowed.

Also, if a view with SQL statement contains aggregate function, such as COUNT(), the view cannot be used to update the base table. A view with aggregate functions is not updatable.

SQL Example 1.6

Create a view called Employee5OrderCount that includes all orders employee 5 handled, with order ID, order date, total quantity in each order.

SQL Example 1.6 Statement

```sql
DROP VIEW IF EXISTS Chapter1.Employee5OrderCount;
CREATE VIEW Chapter1.Employee5OrderCount
AS
SELECT O.OrderId, O.CustomerId, O.OrderDate, COUNT(Quantity) AS TotalQuantity
FROM Sales.Orders AS O JOIN Sales.OrderDetails AS OD
ON O.OrderId = OD.OrderId
WHERE EmployeeId = 5
GROUP BY O.OrderId, O.CustomerId, O.OrderDate;
```

See if you can update the Orderdate column in the Orders table via the Sales.Employee5OrderCount view:

```
UPDATE Chapter1.Employee5OrderCount
SET OrderDate = '20180103'
WHERE OrderId = 1;
```

The result will be the following error message:

```
Msg 4403, Level 16, State 1, Line 126
Cannot update the view or function 'Sales.Employee5OrderCount' because it contains aggregates,
or a DISTINCT or GROUP BY clause, or PIVOT or UNPIVOT operator.
```

Even though the update concerns only data from one single table, the view still not be used to update the base table because the use of aggregate functions in the view.

Additionally, if a view has GROUP BY, HAVING, or DISTINCT in its SQL statement, the view is not updatable.

SQL Example 1.7

Create a view called Customers2017 that includes all customers that ever placed an order in the year 2017 with customer name.

SQL Example 1.7 Statement

```
DROP VIEW IF EXISTS Chapter1.Customers2017;
CREATE VIEW Chapter1.Customers2017
AS
SELECT DISTINCT C.CustomerName
FROM Chapter1.Customers AS C JOIN Chapter1.Orders AS O
ON C.CustomerId = O.CustomerId
WHERE YEAR(O.OrderDate) = 2017;
```

If this view is used to update a customer name, such as

```
UPDATE Chapter1.Customers2017
SET CustomerName = 'New E Fun'
WHERE CustomerName = 'E Fun';
```

It will create an error because the view includes the keyword "DISTINCT" which will not allow the database engine to trace back how many names from the base table were combined when creating the view. In summary, an updatable view must contain the SQL statement that allows the database engine to unambiguously trace the modification from the SQL statement back to a base table.

Review Question 1.26
When updating an updatable view, _______.
a. an error will occur.
b. the data in the view will be updated.

c. the data in the base table will be updated
d. nothing happens because the view has no data stored in it

Review Question 1.27
If you attempt to insert data into an updatable view, ______.
a. an error will occur.
b. the data is inserted in the view.
c. the data is inserted in the base table
d. nothing happens because the view has no data stored in it

Review Question 1.28
If a view contains data from more than one table, ______.
a. you cannot execute any update statement with the view.
b. you can execute an update statement as long as it affects data in one base table only
c. you can execute an update statement as long as it is correct
d. you can execute any update statement with the view

Review Question 1.29
A view is NOT updatable if it contains _______.
a. WHERE
b. SELECT
c. JOIN
d. MAX

Review Question 1.30
A view is NOT updatable if it contains ______.
a. SELECT
b. WHERE
c. Having
d. JOIN

Review Question 1.31
A view is NOT updatable if it contains ______.
a. DISTINCT
b. WHERE
c. BETWEEN
d. LEFT JOIN

Review Question 1.32
Why can't a view with aggregate functions, such as COUNT(), be used to update the base table?
a. Because aggregate functions are not supported by SQL
b. Because aggregate functions cannot be executed in a view
c. Because aggregate functions create ambiguity in the update process
d. Because aggregate functions make the view non-existent

Review Question 1.33
What happens if a view includes the keywords GROUP BY, HAVING, or DISTINCT in its SQL statement?
a. It becomes more updatable
b. It remains unchanged

c. It becomes non-updatable
d. It allows for easier base table updates

Review Question 1.34
What is the reason for the restriction on updating views that reference columns from multiple base tables?
a. To simplify database management
b. To promote the use of aggregate functions
c. To avoid ambiguity in update operations
d. To encourage the use of DISTINCT keyword

Review Question 1.35
What is the key requirement for an updatable view?
a. It should include the DISTINCT keyword
b. It should reference columns from multiple base tables
c. It should have complex SQL statements
d. It should allow the database engine to trace modifications back to a base table

1.5 Modifying and Deleting an Existing View

To modify an existing view, the ALTER VIEW command can be employed.

SQL Example 1.8

Let's modify the Customers2017 view created in SQL Example 1.7 to include Order ID, Customer Name, and Order Date.

SQL Example 1.8 Statement

```sql
ALTER VIEW Sales.Customers2017
AS
SELECT O.OrderId, C.CustomerName, O.OrderDate
FROM Sales.Customers AS C JOIN Sales.Orders AS O
ON C.CustomerId = O.CustomerId
WHERE YEAR(O.OrderDate) = 2017;
```

When the ALTER VIEW command is executed, the database engine checks whether the current view is in use by other database objects. If not, it drops the existing view and then creates a new view with the same name. The key advantage of ALTER VIEW over DROP and CREATE is that it maintains dependencies like permissions. With the latter approach, all relationships need to be reset.

SQL Example 1.9

Delete the view Customers2017 created in SQL Example 1.7 and modified in SQL Example 1.8.

SQL Example 1.9 Statement

```
IF OBJECT_ID('Sales.Customers2017') IS NOT NULL
DROP VIEW Sales.Customers2017;
```

Dropping a view is typically done when the underlying tables or views are altered, and the current view is no longer functional. It's important to note that dropping a view does not impact the base table.

Review Question 1.36
When the ALTER View command is issued, ______.
a. the view will be updated.
b. the view will be first dropped and then a new view with the same name will be created.
c. the view will be first dropped and then a new view with the same name will be created only if the view is not in use.
d. the base table will be updated.

Review Question 1.37
What is the difference between 1) ALTER VIEW and 2) DROP and then CREATE VIEW?
a. The former allows all objects that depend on the view to be unaffected.
b. The latter allows all objects that depend on the view to be unaffected.
c. The former just update the view without drop it.
d. The two are actually the same.

Review Question 1.38
How can you modify an existing view in SQL?
a. Use the DELETE command
b. Employ the ALTER VIEW command
c. Execute the CREATE VIEW command
d. Run the UPDATE statement

Review Question 1.39
When the ALTER VIEW command is executed, what does the database engine check for before modifying the view?
a. It checks if the view is in use by other database objects
b. It verifies if the view's name is correct
c. It checks for syntax errors in the view
d. It validates the view's primary key

Review Question 1.40
What is a key advantage of using ALTER VIEW over DROP and CREATE?
a. It is faster in execution
b. It can modify multiple views simultaneously
c. It maintains dependencies like permissions
d. It requires fewer SQL statements

Review Question 1.41
Why might one choose to delete a view in SQL?
a. To remove all related tables
b. To clear the entire database

c. When the view is no longer functional due to changes in underlying tables or views
d. To simplify the SQL code

Review Question 1.42
What impact does dropping a view have on the associated base table?
a. It deletes the base table
b. It updates the base table
c. It has no impact on the base table
d. It adds new data to the base table

1.6 Indexing

Imagine a tall skyscraper in a bustling city with multiple elevators. Each elevator serves a specific range of floors: one for floors 1-20, another for 21-40, and so on. This arrangement makes it more efficient for residents to reach their desired floor quickly.

Similarly, in the world of database management, indexes play a crucial role in optimizing data retrieval. When working with a large database table or view, using indexes can significantly reduce the time required for searching and accessing specific data.

When an index is created for a table or view, it essentially adds a new table that stores search criteria and corresponding row numbers (this is often referred to as a nonclustered index, which we'll discuss shortly). Let's consider a simplified example using a student table (the left table is the index table and the right table is the table to be indexed):

GPA	Row number
Less than 2.0	2
Between 2.0 and 3.0	3
Higher than 3.0	1, 4, 5

Student ID	Student Name	GPA
111	Michael Wilson	3.4
222	Larry Bergman	1.9
333	Phillip Young	2.6
444	Gregory Wagner	3.5
555	Alissa Smith	3.9

Indexes for tables or views come in two primary types: clustered and nonclustered.

In a nonclustered index, a separate table is used to store the index data and pointers to the actual table. As a result, you can have multiple indexes on one table.

On the other hand, a table or view with a clustered index organizes the table's rows based on the indexed column. For instance, if we create a clustered index on the GPA column in the Student table, the table will be physically sorted by each student's GPA, resulting in an arrangement like this:

Student ID	Student Name	GPA
222	Larry Bergman	1.9
333	Philip Young	2.6
111	Michael Wilson	3.4
444	Gregory Wagner	3.5
555	Alissa Smith	3.9

It's important to note that a table can only have one clustered index since you can't sort the same table in multiple ways simultaneously. Additionally, much like using a composite primary key, you can create a single index on multiple columns to optimize searches and data retrieval. Understanding the difference between clustered and nonclustered indexes is crucial for optimizing data retrieval in database management.

Review Question 1.43
One purpose of adding index to a table is _______.
a. searching records faster
b. making a table better organized
c. using less storage space
d. for security

Review Question 1.44
Adding a nonclustered index to a table will _______.
a. always make searches faster
b. never make searches slower
c. add a new table to the database
d. not hurt the performance of the database

Review Question 1.45
Which of the followings are index types used in SQL Server?
a. clustered and key indexed
b. clustered and composite
c. nonclustered and composite
d. clustered and nonclustered

Review Question 1.46
In the context of database management, what is the purpose of using indexes?
a. To store additional data
b. To organize tables and views
c. To reduce the time needed for data retrieval
d. To define primary keys

Review Question 1.47
What is the primary function of a clustered index in a database table or view?
a. It organizes the table's rows based on the indexed column.
b. It creates a separate table to store index data.
c. It defines primary keys for the table.
d. It adds new rows to the table.

Review Question 1.48
What type of index uses a separate table to store index data and pointers to the actual table?
a. Clustered index
b. Nonclustered index
c. Composite index
d. Primary index

Review Question 1.49
Why is it essential to understand the distinction between clustered and nonclustered indexes?
a. To define primary keys in a table
b. To create multiple indexes on a single table
c. To effectively manage database permissions
d. To optimize data retrieval in database management

Review Question 1.50
What is the purpose of creating a single index on multiple columns in a database table?
a. To simplify SQL queries
b. To sort the table in multiple ways simultaneously
c. To create a composite primary key
d. To optimize searches and data retrieval

Review Question 1.51
How does the analogy of elevators in a skyscraper relate to the concept of indexes in a database?
a. Elevators and indexes both define primary keys.
b. Elevators and indexes both add new data to a system.
c. Elevators efficiently transport residents to desired floors, similar to how indexes optimize data retrieval in a database.
d. Elevators and indexes both create separate tables for data storage.

1.7 Clustered Index: Choosing the Right Column(s)

When deciding which column(s) to include in a clustered index, two key considerations come into play: the types of queries frequently executed against the table or view and the structure of the column(s) itself.

Queries That Benefit from Clustered Index:

1. Queries Involving BETWEEN, "<," or ">" in the WHERE Clause: A table or view with a clustered index is pre-sorted based on the index. For instance, if a query seeks all students with a GPA greater than 3.0, as soon as the first student with a GPA of 3.0 is encountered, the database engine doesn't need to check the remaining rows. This significantly saves time, especially with larger result sets.

2. Queries with ORDER BY or GROUP BY Clauses: When the column(s) specified in the ORDER BY clause match the column(s) on which the index is built, the database engine can avoid sorting the result set, further enhancing query performance.

Preferred Characteristics for Clustered Index Candidates:

1. Columns with High Distinct Values: Columns that consistently contain distinct values, such as primary key columns, make excellent candidates for clustered indexes. In fact, by default, all primary keys are automatically clustered indexed in SQL Server.

2. Columns Frequently Accessed Sequentially: When a column is accessed sequentially, the database engine merely needs to locate the first and last records, reducing query time.

3. Columns Used for Sorting Result Sets: Since clustered indexed columns are already physically sorted, queries involving sorting the result set benefit from this built-in organization.

Columns to Avoid as Clustered Index Candidates:

1. Columns with Frequent Value Changes: Columns that undergo frequent value changes should be avoided as clustered index candidates. Altering values may necessitate reordering the entire table, which is particularly problematic for large, data-intensive tables.

2. Wide Keys: Wide keys, composed of multiple columns and/or large-size columns, can pose challenges. Nonclustered indexes often use clustered indexes as lookup keys, and wide keys can lead to significantly longer search times for nonclustered indexes.

In summary, a well-chosen clustered index can dramatically improve query performance. By selecting columns with the right characteristics and avoiding those prone to frequent changes, you can harness the full potential of clustered indexes for efficient data retrieval.

SQL Example 1.10

Create a clustered index on HireDate of HR.Employees table

SQL Example 1.10 Statement

```
CREATE CLUSTERED INDEX IX_Employees_HireDate
    ON HR.Employees (HireDate);
```

The result of the execution of the above statement is:

```
Msg 1902, Level 16, State 3, Line 158
Cannot create more than one clustered index on table 'HR.Employees'. Drop the existing clustered
index 'PK_Employees' before creating another.
```

The HR.Employees table has a primary key EmployeeId, which is automatically clustered indexed and every table can have only one clustered index. So if a clustered index has to be created on a non-primary key column, the primary key should be removed from the table.

SQL Example 1.11

Create a new table called UsedProducts with a product name and quantity. No primary key is set for the UsedProducts table. Then create a clustered index on product name column.

SQL Example 1.11 Statement

```
CREATE TABLE Sales.UsedProducts
(
    ProductName NVARCHAR(30) NOT NULL,
    Quantity int NULL
);
GO
CREATE CLUSTERED INDEX IX_UsedProducts_ProductName
    ON Sales.UsedProducts (ProductName);
```

Review Question 1.52
The table column(s) with the following characteristics are better candidates for clustered index:
a. A column that contains more similar values
b. A column that is often accessed sequentially
c. A column that is never used to sort the result set
d. A column that is rarely accessed sequentially

Review Question 1.53
The table column(s) with the following characteristics are better candidates for clustered index:
a. A column that contains more distinct values
b. A column that changes values frequently
c. A column that is rarely used to sort the result set
d. A column that is rarely accessed sequentially

Review Question 1.54

The table column(s) with the following characteristics are better candidates for clustered index:
a. A column that contains more similar values
b. A column that is often used to sort the result set
c. A wide key
d. A column that is rarely accessed sequentially

1.8 Nonclustered Index: Making the Right Selection

Just as with clustered indexes, the decision on which columns to include in a nonclustered index is influenced by two primary factors: the types of queries commonly executed and the attributes of the columns themselves.

Queries Benefitting from Nonclustered Index:

1. Queries with JOIN or GROUP BY Clauses: When two tables are joined, the database engine needs to compare matching rows from both tables, a process that can be time-consuming. Nonclustered indexes can significantly enhance the performance of such queries.
2. Queries Resulting in a Small Result Set: In contrast to clustered indexes, which excel when dealing with large result sets, nonclustered indexes are ideal for queries producing a limited number of records. For queries with a WHERE clause that matches only a few records from a vast table, implementing a nonclustered index on the columns involved in the WHERE clause is a wise choice.

Considerations for Nonclustered Index Candidates:

1. Frequently Used Query Columns: Nonclustered indexes are flexible in that they can cover all columns utilized in a query. This differs from clustered indexes, which require caution regarding "wide keys." Therefore, columns frequently used in queries are strong contenders for nonclustered indexes.
2. Columns with Abundant Distinct Values: It's essential to focus on columns with a substantial number of distinct values. For instance, a column containing first names alone may not exhibit as many distinct values as when combined with last names. Conversely, columns with very few distinct values, like gender, are unsuitable for nonclustered indexes.

In summary, nonclustered indexes can significantly improve query performance, particularly in scenarios involving JOIN or GROUP BY clauses and queries resulting in smaller result sets. By selecting columns that meet these criteria and avoiding those with few distinct values, you can optimize your database's performance with nonclustered indexes.

SQL Example 1.12

Create a nonclustered index on the first name and last name of the employees table.

SQL Example 1.12 Statement

```
CREATE NONCLUSTERED INDEX IX_Employees_Name
    ON HR.Employees(FirstName, LastName);
```

Review Question 1.55
Which of the following types of queries often benefit from nonclustered index?
a. Queries contain WHERE or ORDER BY clauses
b. Queries contain SELECT or INSERT clauses
c. Queries contain JOIN or GROUP BY clauses
d. Queries that return a large result set

Review Question 1.56
Which of the following types of queries often benefit from nonclustered index?
a. Queries contain WHERE or ORDER BY clauses
b. Queries contain SELECT or INSERT clauses
c. Queries contain SELECT or ORDER BY clauses
d. Queries that return a small result set

1.9 Understanding the B+ Tree Structure of Indexes

In SQL Server, both clustered and nonclustered indexes are stored using a data structure known as a B+ Tree. This structure is designed to provide balanced and efficient access to data, ensuring that the time taken to locate a record within the index remains consistent, regardless of the record's location. The term "tree" is derived from the shape of this data structure, which resembles an upside-down tree.

A B+ Tree is composed of nodes, and there are three main types:

Root Node: The root node is unique in that it has no parent. It serves as the starting point for all index searches.
Internal Node: Internal nodes have one parent and one or more children. They play a role in directing the search process as it moves towards the desired destination.
Leaf Node: Leaf nodes have no children and contain pointers to actual data records. These nodes are crucial for locating the final destination of a search.

Each node within the B+ Tree stores two essential pieces of data: a key and a pointer. During a search, a comparison is made between the search value and the keys stored in the nodes. The result of this comparison determines which branch the search will follow.

To illustrate this concept, let's consider an example with a table of students, where the search is based on student IDs. The B+ Tree may look like the following:

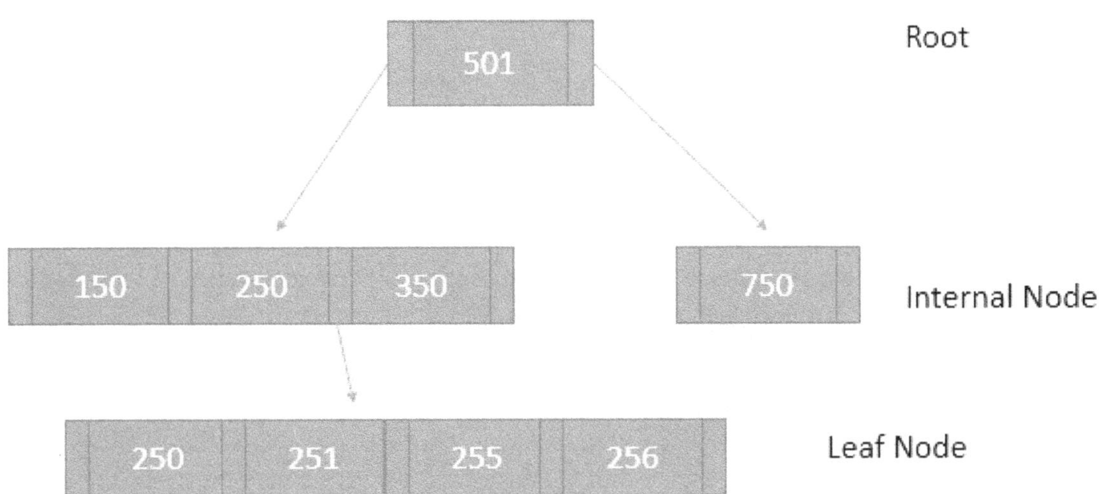

Suppose we are searching for student ID 255. The search begins at the root, where 255 is compared to the key 501. Since 255 is less than 501, the pointer directs us to the left branch. Next, we compare 255 to the internal node on the left branch, discovering that it falls between the values 250 and 350. The pointer now guides us to the leaf node, where we finally locate student ID 255.

Conversely, if we were searching for student ID 252, the index tree would return a "not found" result.

For a B+ Tree to function efficiently, it is imperative that all keys on both the internal and leaf nodes are sorted.

Review Question 1.57
The SQL Server stores both clustered and nonclustered indexes in ______ Tree format
a. A+
b. B+
c. C+
d. C++

Review Question 1.58
To make a B+ Tree work efficiently, all keys on the internal node and leaf node must be ______.
a. small
b. large
c. similar
d. sorted

1.10 Chapter Summary

This chapter has equipped you with essential knowledge about two critical aspects of database management: views and indexes. Here's a concise summary of what you've learned:

Views: You gained an understanding of what a view is and the advantages it offers in database management. Additionally, you learned how to create views and explored the types of views that can be employed to modify the base table.

Indexes: You delved into the concept of indexes and their role in enhancing database performance. You also acquired the skills needed to create indexes, and you explored the two primary types of indexes utilized in SQL Server: clustered indexes and nonclustered indexes.

By mastering these key topics, you are now well-prepared to optimize your database management and leverage views and indexes to their full potential.

1.11 Discussion

Discussion 1.1

Explain the benefits of using views in relational databases.

Discussion 1.2

When a new row is inserted into a view, will it update the base table automatically? Why or Why not?

Discussion 1.3

The index of a book is used to save the readers time to find a specific term in the book. Similarly, indexes can assist the database engine to save time in retrieving data. Would you recommend adding as many indexes to a table as possible? Why or why not?

Discussion 1.4

Compare and contrast the clustered index and nonclustered index in SQL Server.

Discussion 1.5

What data structure does SQL Server use? Briefly explain how it work.

1.12 SQL Exercises

Exercise 1.1

Create a view named 'EmployeeData' that encompasses all columns from the 'HR.Employees' table, excluding the 'HireDate' and 'ManagerId' columns. We recommend executing 'SELECT * FROM EmployeeData' to compare the results with the table below:

	EmployeeId	FirstName	LastName	BirthDate	HomeAddress	City	State	PostalCode	Phone
1	1	Alex	Hall	1990-02-03	85 Main Ln	New Canton	VA	23123	(434) 290-3322
2	2	Dianne	Hart	1978-12-03	209 Social Hall Blvd	New Canton	VA	23123	(434) 290-1122
3	3	Maria	Law	1988-07-13	258 Blinkys St	New Canton	VA	23123	(434) 531-5673
4	4	Alice	Law	1988-12-13	300 Vista Valley Blvd	Buckingham	VA	23123	(434) 531-1010
5	5	Black	Hart	1982-11-09	1 Old Fifteen St	Buckingham	VA	23123	(434) 531-1034
6	6	Christina	Robinson	1978-07-13	217 Chapel St	New Canton	VA	23123	NULL
7	7	Nicholas	Pinkston	1977-10-05	26 N James Madison Rd	Buckingham	VA	23123	NULL

Exercise 1.2

Create a view named 'Product1Customers' that includes all customer IDs and names of those who purchased Product ID 1. Running 'SELECT * FROM Product1Customers' will yield a table like the one shown below:

	CustomerId	CustomerName
1	1	Just Electronics
2	3	Beyond Electronics

Exercise 1.3

Create a view named 'Product1TotalUnitByCustomer' that comprises all customers who purchased Product 1. The view should include Customer ID, Customer Name, and the units of Product 1 they purchased. Running 'SELECT * FROM Product1TotalUnitByCustomer' will generate a table that resembles the one below:

	CustomerId	CustomerName	Total Unit
1	1	Just Electronics	2
2	3	Beyond Electronics	1

Exercise 1.4

Create a view named 'Customer1Orders' that encompasses all orders placed by Customer 1. Can you utilize this view to modify the Order Date for one of Customer 1's orders? Running 'SELECT * FROM Customer1Orders' will generate a table that resembles the one below:

	OrderId	CustomerId	EmployeeId	OrderDate
1	1	1	5	2017-01-03
2	2	1	3	2017-03-05
3	5	1	4	2017-05-03

Exercise 1.5

Create a view called Supplier2SaleDetails that will include all sales of Supplier 2's products, including the customer ID, data of sales, product ID, price, and quantity. Can you use this view to change the price and quantity in one statement? Can you use this view to change date of sales and quantity in one statement?

The SELECT * FROM Supplier2SalesDetails should return a table that looks like this:

	CustomerId	OrderDate	ProductId	Price	quantity
1	1	2017-03-05	6	189.99	5
2	2	2017-02-23	6	199.99	1
3	2	2017-02-23	8	69.99	2
4	4	2017-04-13	8	69.99	1
5	1	2017-05-03	6	199.99	3
6	7	2016-12-23	8	59.99	2

Exercise 1.6

Create a view called Supplier2OrderCount that includes all sales of all products by Supplier 2 with sales date/orderdate and total sales value of that date. Can you use this view to change the quantity of a certain sale?

The SELECT * FROM Supplier2OrderCount should return a table that looks like this:

	OrderDate	TotalSales
1	2016-12-23	119.98
2	2017-02-23	339.97
3	2017-03-05	949.95
4	2017-04-13	69.99
5	2017-05-03	599.97

Exercise 1.7

Create a view called Employees2017 that includes all employees who handled at least an order in the year 2017 with employee first name and last name. Can you use this view to update the employees' first name?

The SELECT * FROM Employees2017 should return a table that looks like this:

	FirstName	LastName
1	Alice	Law
2	Black	Hart
3	Christina	Robinson
4	Maria	Law

Exercise 1.8

Modify the view Employees2017 created in SQL Exercise 1.7. This time the view should include Order ID, first name, and last name.

The SELECT * FROM Employees2017 should return a table that looks like this:

	OrderId	FirstName	LastName
1	1	Black	Hart
2	2	Maria	Law
3	3	Black	Hart
4	4	Black	Hart
5	5	Alice	Law
6	6	Christina	Robinson

Exercise 1.9

Write SQL statement to delete the view Employees2017 created in SQL Exercise 1.7 and modified in SQL Exercise 1.8.

Exercise 1.10

Can you create a clustered index on ManagerId of HR.Employees table?

Exercise 1.11

Create a new table called TempEmployees with an employee name and date hired. No primary key is set for the TempEmployees table.

Then create a clustered index on employee name column.

Exercise 1.12

Create a nonclustered index on the customer name of the customers table.

1.13 Solutions to the Review Questions

1.1 C; 1.2 A; 1.3 C; 1.4 B; 1.5 B; 1.6 D; 1.7 C; 1.8 B; 1.9 A; 1.10 B; 1.11 B; 1.12 B; 1.13 C; 1.14 C; 1.15 B; 1.16 A; 1.17 D; 1.18 D; 1.19 C; 1.20 C; 1.21 D; 1.22 A; 1.23 B; 1.24 A; 1.25 D; 1.26 C; 1.27 C; 1.28 B; 1.29 D; 1.30 C; 1.31 A; 1.32 C; 1.33 C; 1.34 C; 1.35 D; 1.36 C; 1.37 A; 1.38 B; 1.39 A; 1.40 C; 1.41 C; 1.42 C; 1.43 A; 1.44 C; 1.45 D; 1.46 C; 1.47 A; 1.48 B; 1.49 D; 1.50 D; 1.51 C; 1.52 B; 1.53 A; 1.54 B; 1.55 C; 1.56 D; 1.57 B; 1.58 D;

CHAPTER 2: PROGRAMMING T-SQL

Chapter Learning Objectives

2.1 Differentiate between simple case expressions and searched case expressions in T-SQL.
2.2 Comprehension: Explain the concept of declaring, assigning, and using variables in T-SQL.
2.3 Application: Implement conditional flow control using T-SQL.
2.4 Application: Implement loops in T-SQL for iterative processes.
2.5 Analysis: Create and employ a cursor in T-SQL for row-level data manipulation.
2.6 Synthesis: Declare and utilize a table variable in T-SQL for temporary data storage and manipulation.

2.1 Introduction to T-SQL Programming

In our first database book, you've gained a foundational understanding of SQL, a language designed to be as close to English as possible, making it remarkably intuitive. SQL is primarily concerned with the "what" in your interaction with a database – what data you want to retrieve or manipulate. In contrast, if you're familiar with programming languages like C++ or Java, you might be wondering whether SQL offers mechanisms for conditional flow control or loops. The answer is a resounding yes. This chapter will introduce you to some of these essential programming elements within T-SQL.

Unlike conventional programming languages such as C++, where you focus on instructing the computer on "how" to perform a task, SQL concentrates on defining "what" you want the computer to do. For example, in SQL, you'd instruct the system to retrieve all students with a GPA of 3.5 or higher and specify that you're interested in their first names, last names, and declared majors. However, you won't explicitly tell the computer how to gather this information. Consequently, it's important to understand that SQL does not guarantee the order in which data will be presented in the result dataset. We'll delve deeper into this aspect towards the end of this book.

In contrast, in languages like C++, you would provide explicit instructions on "how" to identify students with a GPA of 3.5 or higher by implementing loops and conditional statements. The distinction lies in SQL's declarative nature, which focuses on specifying your desired outcome, leaving the database system to handle the "how" behind the scenes. This unique feature sets SQL apart and makes it a powerful language for working with data.

Review Question 2.1
SQL focuses on ______ while C++ centers on ______.
a. when, how
b. how, when
c. how, what
d. what, how

Review Question 2.2
In SQL, assuming a database keep the same state, if you run the same SQL SELECT statement many times, you will see ________ .
a. the same result dataset with the same record sequence
b. the same result dataset with no guaranteed record sequence
c. different result dataset from time to time
d. different result dataset with the same record sequence

Review Question 2.3
Which aspect of programming languages like C++ or Java differs significantly from SQL?
a. The focus on instructing the computer on "how" to perform a task
b. The declarative nature that specifies the desired outcome
c. The use of conditional statements in SQL
d. The similarity to English language in SQL

Review Question 2.4
What is the primary focus of SQL in database interactions?
a. Specifying the desired outcome
b. Instructing the computer on "how" to perform tasks
c. Loop implementation
d. Handling conditional statements

Review Question 2.5
In SQL, when you request data, such as all students with a GPA of 3.5 or higher, what aspect differs from traditional programming languages?
a. SQL explicitly tells the computer how to gather the data.
b. SQL does not guarantee the order in which data will be presented in the result dataset even with the ORDER BY clause.
c. SQL uses a declarative approach.
d. SQL involves loop and conditional statement implementation.

Review Question 2.6
How does SQL differ from traditional programming languages in terms of handling conditional flow control and loops?
a. SQL offers mechanisms for both conditional flow control and loops.
b. SQL is incapable of handling conditional flow control or loops.
c. SQL exclusively focuses on loops.
d. SQL exclusively focuses on conditional flow control.

Review Question 2.7
What is the key advantage of SQL's declarative nature?
a. It ensures the order of data presentation in the result dataset.
b. It allows for explicit instructions on "how" to gather data.
c. It simplifies the use of conditional statements.
d. It specifies the desired outcome, leaving the system to handle the "how."

Review Question 2.8
How does SQL approach specifying the desired outcome compared to traditional programming languages like C++?
a. SQL explicitly specifies "how" to perform tasks.
b. SQL guarantees the order of data presentation.
c. SQL employs loops and conditional statements.
d. SQL specifies "what" is needed, leaving the "how" to the system.

2.2 Case Expressions

A Case Expression in T-SQL allows you to return a value based on one or more conditional tests. Although it is not a traditional programming construct, its logical similarity to flow control makes it an important topic to cover in this chapter. Case Expressions can be utilized wherever an expression is allowed in SQL, including in SELECT, GROUP BY, HAVING, and ORDER BY clauses.

2.2.1 Simple Case Expressions

There are two primary types of Case Expressions: simple case expressions and searched case expressions. The simple case expression involves an input expression that is compared against a set of values. It returns a value based on the match found. For instance, in our LifeStyle LLC database example, the input expression could be the customer's country. If it matches "USA," the expression returns "Domestic"; otherwise, it returns "International."

The syntax for a simple case expression is as follows:

```
CASE inputExpression
    WHEN conditionValue1 THEN returnValue1
```

```
    WHEN conditionValue2 THEN returnValue2
    ....
    ELSE returnValueN
END
```

While the ELSE clause is optional, it is advisable to use it as a safety net to handle unexpected or invalid results. If no match is found in the conditions, the expression will return NULL.

SQL Example 2.1

Display customer names and their countries with "Domestic" for USA customers and "International" for customers from all other countries.

SQL Example 2.1 Analysis

Use the familiar SELECT statement to select customerName and Country from the Sales.Customers table. Use the CASE expression to convert the country name into "Domestic" or "International".

SQL Example 2.1 Statement

```
SELECT CustomerName, Country =
    CASE Country
        WHEN 'USA' THEN 'Domestic'
        ELSE 'International'
    END
FROM Sales.Customers;
```

SQL Example 2.1 Output

	CustomerName	Country
1	Just Electronics	Domestic
2	Beyond Electronics	Domestic
3	Beyond Electronics	Domestic
4	E Fun	Domestic
5	Overstock E	Domestic
6	E Fun	International
7	Electronics4U	International
8	Cheap Electronics	International

SQL Example 2.2

Display the results in a single column for Product name, alongside a new column labeled "Made In USA." If a product is manufactured by a supplier based in the USA, designate the column as "Yes." Otherwise, indicate it as "No."

SQL Example 2.2 Analysis

This example is not much different from the last one. Whether a product is made in USA depends on the supplier country. So, we need product name from Products table and the supplier country from the supplier table. A table JOIN is necessary.

SQL Example 2.2 Statement

```sql
SELECT P.ProductName, "Made In USA" =
    CASE Country
        WHEN 'USA' THEN 'YES'
        ELSE 'NO'
    END
FROM Purchasing.Products AS P JOIN Purchasing.Suppliers AS S
ON P.supplierid = S.SupplierId;
```

SQL Example 2.2 Output

	ProductName	Made In USA
1	65-Inch 4K Ultra HD Smart TV	NO
2	60-Inch 4K Ultra HD Smart LED TV	NO
3	3200 Lumens LED Home Theater Projector	NO
4	Wireless Color Photo Printer	NO
5	6Wireless Compact Laser Printer	YES
6	Color Laser Printer	YES
7	10" 16GB Android Tablet	NO
8	GPS Android Tablet PC	YES
9	20.2 MP Digital Camera	NO

2.2.2 Searched Case Expressions

The simple case expression, as demonstrated in SQL Examples 2.1 and 2.2, can only be employed for comparing the input expression with condition values for equality. If you need to perform other types of comparisons, you should utilize a searched case expression.

The searched case expression doesn't directly employ the input expression. Instead, it transforms the condition value into a Boolean expression, incorporating the input expression within it. For instance, when comparing the country to 'USA', you can simply use "WHEN Country == 'USA' THEN 'Domestic.'"

The syntax for the searched case expression is as follows:

```
CASE
    WHEN booleanExpression1 THEN returnValue1
    WHEN booleanExpression21 THEN returnValue2
    ….
    ELSE returnValueN
END
```

Once again, the ELSE clause is optional, but I recommend using it because it serves as a helpful way to handle unexpected or erroneous results.

If booleanExpression1 evaluates to true, returnValue1 is returned. If booleanExpression2 is true, returnValue2 is returned. In the absence of a match, the expression returns NULL.

SQL Example 2.3

Display customer names and their countries with "Domestic" for USA customers and "International" for customers from all other countries.

SQL Example 2.3 Analysis

You may notice that this is identical to SQL Example 2.1. This time, we will use a searched case expression to address the issue.

SQL Example 2.3 Statement

```
SELECT CustomerName, Country =
    CASE
        WHEN Country ='USA' THEN 'Domestic'
        ELSE 'International'
    END
FROM Sales.Customers;
```

SQL Example 2.3 Output

	CustomerName	Country
1	Just Electronics	Domestic
2	Beyond Electronics	Domestic
3	Beyond Electronics	Domestic
4	E Fun	Domestic
5	Overstock E	Domestic
6	E Fun	International
7	Electronics4U	International
8	Cheap Electronics	International

SQL Example 2.4

An employee can be categorized by the date they were hired. I understand that using the employee's tenure in the company would make more sense, but it could be challenging for readers to compare the solution because it depends on when they run the example. So, we'll categorize employees based on their hire date. If an employee was hired before January 1, 2013, they are categorized as "Experienced." If an employee was hired on or after January 1, 2013 but before January 1, 2015, they are categorized as "Trained." If an employee was hired on or after January 1, 2015, they are categorized as "Novice." The result should display the employee's full name and their respective category.

SQL Example 2.4 Analysis

The employee's Hire Date will serve as the input expression. We will establish conditions for three categories: before January 1, 2013; between January 1, 2013 and January 1, 2015; and after January 1, 2015. The corresponding return values for these categories will be "Experienced," "Trained," and "Novice." Since this involves comparisons that are not strictly equality-based, we will utilize a searched case expression to handle this scenario.

SQL Example 2.4 Statement

```
SELECT FirstName + ' ' + LastName AS "Employee Name", Category =
    CASE
        WHEN HireDate < '20130101' THEN 'Experienced'
        WHEN HireDate >= '20130101' AND HireDate < '20150101' THEN 'Trained'
        WHEN HireDate >= '20150101' THEN 'Novice'
    END
FROM HR.Employees;
```

SQL Example 2.4 Output

	Employee Name	Category
1	Alex Hall	Novice
2	Dianne Hart	Experienced
3	Maria Law	Experienced
4	Alice Law	Experienced
5	Black Hart	Novice
6	Christina Robinson	Trained
7	Nicholas Pinkston	Trained

SQL Example 2.5

Show the full name and job position of each employee. When an employee does not have a manager, their position is CEO. If an employee has a ManagerId of 1, they are classified as a manager, while all other employees are categorized as workers.

SQL Example 2.5 Analysis

An employee's job position is determined by their manager's ID. While this may seem suitable for a simple case expression, it's important to note that you can't directly compare a value with Null. Therefore, you should utilize a searched case expression in this scenario.

SQL Example 2.5 Statement

```sql
SELECT FirstName + ' ' + LastName AS "Employee Name", Position =
    CASE
        WHEN ManagerId IS Null THEN 'CEO'
        WHEN ManagerId = 1 THEN 'Manager'
        ELSE 'Worker'
    END
FROM HR.Employees;
```

SQL Example 2.5 Output

	Employee Name	Position
1	Alex Hall	CEO
2	Dianne Hart	Manager
3	Maria Law	Manager
4	Alice Law	Manager
5	Black Hart	Worker
6	Christina Robinson	Worker
7	Nicholas Pinkston	Worker

Review Question 2.9
T-SQL case expression can be used to return a value based on one or more ______.
a. cases
b. case expressions
c. conditional tests
d. if statements

Review Question 2.10
There are two types of case expressions, ______.
a. simple and complicated
b. simple and searched
c. complicated and searched
d. direct and indirect

Review Question 2.11
The ______ case expression has an input expression that is compared against a set of values. It returns the value based on what value is matched.
a. simple

b. complicated
c. searched
d. null

Review Question 2.12
The _______ case expression does not directly use the input expression. Instead, it changes the condition value to Boolean expression so that the input expression can be part of it
a. simple
b. complicated
c. searched
d. null

Review Question 2.13
What does a Case Expression in T-SQL allow you to do?
a. Define a new data type
b. Create a new database
c. Return a value based on conditional tests
d. Sort data in ascending order

Review Question 2.14
Where can Case Expressions be used in SQL?
a. Only in the SELECT clause
b. Only in the WHERE clause
c. In SELECT, GROUP BY, HAVING, and ORDER BY clauses
d. In the FROM clause

Review Question 2.15
What are the two primary types of Case Expressions?
a. Complex and simple case expressions
b. Simple and compound case expressions
c. Simple and advanced case expressions
d. Simple and searched case expressions

Review Question 2.16
When should you use a searched case expression?
a. When you need to compare input expressions for equality
b. When you want to return NULL values
c. When performing complex mathematical operations
d. When you need to perform other types of comparisons beyond equality

Review Question 2.17
What is the purpose of the ELSE clause in a case expression?
a. To define a new variable
b. To specify the input expression
c. To handle unexpected or invalid results
d. To create a new table

Review Question 2.18
In a searched case expression, how is the input expression incorporated?
a. The input expression is ignored

b. The input expression becomes the ELSE value
c. The input expression is used as a condition value
d. The input expression is transformed into a Boolean expression

Review Question 2.19
What does a searched case expression return if no conditions are met?
a. NULL
b. The input expression
c. The first condition value
d. The last condition value

2.3 Variables

In computer programming languages, such as JavaScript, a variable serves as a named space in computer memory used to store a value. When a variable is declared, memory space is allocated with the given name. For instance, when you declare var x, you're creating a variable named x in memory. You can then assign a value to this variable, like x = 5. Later in the program, you can refer to the variable by its name to access the stored value. For example, the statement var y = x * x squares the value of 5 and stores the result in another variable named y.

In T-SQL, local variable names always begin with the "@" symbol, followed by letters, numbers, or certain special characters (@, $, #, _), with some restrictions. The variable name cannot be a T-SQL reserved keyword, and it cannot contain embedded spaces or other special characters.

Local variables are only accessible within the scope of a batch or a stored procedure. A batch is a group of SQL statements executed together. In our first database book, we used the concept of a batch by including the keyword "GO" between statements. This was necessary because certain statements cannot be combined into a single batch. SQL Example 2.9 demonstrates that a variable is out of scope after "GO." More about stored procedures will be covered in Chapter 5.

In contrast, global variables in T-SQL are denoted by names starting with "@@" and are widely utilized by SQL Server.

SQL Example 2.6

Declare a variable called @Company with the initialized value of "LifeStyle LLC". Declare another variable called @Employee and assign a value of "Black Hart" later. Finally display the employee data with a

SELECT statement

SQL Example 2.6 Analysis

Use the DECLARE keyword to declare a variable. When declaring a variable, it must be accompanied by the appropriate data type (as discussed in Chapter 8 of my first book). An initial value can be assigned when declaring a variable. It is also possible to assign a value to a variable at a later point using the SET keyword.

SQL Example 2.6 Statement

```
DECLARE @Company CHAR(9) = 'LifeStyle';
DECLARE @Employee VARCHAR(20);
SET @Employee = 'Black Hart';
SELECT @Company AS Company, @Employee AS Employee;
```

SQL Example 2.6 Output

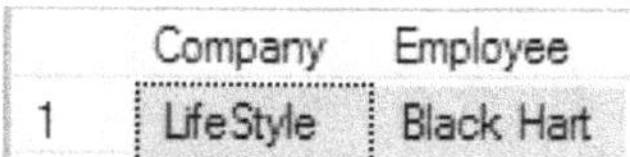

SQL Example 2.7

Declare a variable named @Company with an initial value of 'LifeStyle LLC'. Declare another variable named @Employee and assign it the name of the employee with ID 5 from the HR.Employees table. Finally, display the employee data using a SELECT statement.

SQL Example 2.7 Analysis

This example is nearly identical to SQL Example 2.6. The distinction lies in the fact that the value for the @employee variable is derived from a database table. Since @employee is a scalar variable, it's essential to ensure that the SELECT subquery returns only a single scalar value.

SQL Example 2.7 Statement

```
DECLARE @Company CHAR(9) = 'LifeStyle';
DECLARE @Employee VARCHAR(20);
SET @Employee = (SELECT FirstName + ' ' + LastName
                 FROM HR.Employees
                 WHERE EmployeeId = 5)
SELECT @Company AS Company, @Employee AS Employee;
```

SQL Example 2.7 Output

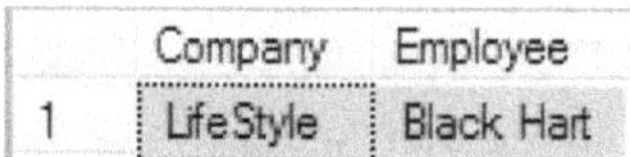

SQL Example 2.8

Declare a variable called @Company with the initialized value 'LifeStyle LLC,' and declare two more variables, @Employee and @BirthDate. Assign their corresponding values from the HR.Employees table. Finally, display the employee data with a SELECT statement.

SQL Example 2.8 Analysis

This example is similar to SQL Example 2.7. Just add one more variable, @BirthDate, and assign the data from the HR.Employees table.

SQL Example 2.8 Statement

```
DECLARE @Company CHAR(9) = 'LifeStyle';
DECLARE @Employee VARCHAR(20), @BirthDate Date;
SET @Employee = (SELECT FirstName + ' ' + LastName
                 FROM HR.Employees
                 WHERE EmployeeId = 5)
SET @BirthDate = (SELECT BirthDate
                  FROM HR.Employees
                  WHERE EmployeeId =5)
SELECT @Company AS Company, @Employee AS Employee, @BirthDate AS "Date of Birth";
```

SQL Example 2.8 Output

	Company	Employee	Date of Birth
1	LifeStyle	Black Hart	1982-11-09

Use SELECT Instead of SET:

In SQL Example 2.8, SET is required for every value retrieved from the database, which can lead to lengthy code when multiple values need to be assigned. An alternative approach is to use the SELECT statement. It's important to note that using SELECT to assign values to variables in SQL is nonstandard.

Here's an example:

```
DECLARE @Company CHAR(9) = 'LifeStyle';
DECLARE @Employee VARCHAR(20), @BirthDate Date;
SELECT @Employee =  FirstName + ' ' + LastName,
       @BirthDate = BirthDate
                FROM HR.Employees
                WHERE EmployeeId =5
SELECT @Company AS Company, @Employee AS Employee, @BirthDate AS "Date of Birth";
```

What happens if the SELECT subquery retrieves more than one record? If you remove the WHERE clause in the above example, the SELECT approach will return the last value (it's impossible to guarantee which record will be the last one retrieved), while the SET approach will result in the following error:

```
Msg 512, Level 16, State 1, Line 61
Subquery returned more than 1 value. This is not permitted when the subquery follows =, !=, <,
<= , >, >= or when the subquery is used as an expression.
```

Subquery returned more than 1 value. This is not permitted when the subquery follows =, !=, <, <= , >, >= or when the subquery is used as an expression.

For better error handling and to catch runtime errors more easily, we recommend using SET whenever possible over SELECT, especially when dealing with scenarios where multiple records can be returned.

SQL Example 2.9

Declare a variable, @CustomerId, and assign the value 7. Next, display the customer's name and email, followed by their order history, which includes order ID, order date, and the total value (quantity × price) of each order.

SQL Example 2.9 Analysis

The problem can be solved without using variables. Variables are helpful when a program becomes more complex, as they allow values to be used in multiple statements.

SQL Example 2.9 Statement

```
DECLARE @CustomerId INT;
SET @CustomerId = 7;
SELECT CustomerName, Email
FROM Sales.Customers
WHERE CustomerId = @CustomerId;
SELECT O.OrderId, O.OrderDate, SUM(OD.Price*OD.Quantity) "Order Total"
FROM Sales.Orders AS O JOIN Sales.OrderDetails AS OD
ON O.OrderId = OD.OrderId
WHERE O.CustomerId = @CustomerId
GROUP BY O.OrderId, O.OrderDate;
```

SQL Example 2.9 Output

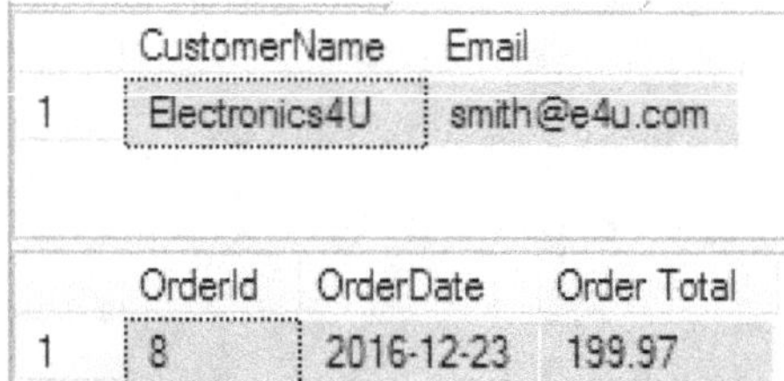

	CustomerName	Email
1	Electronics4U	smith@e4u.com

	OrderId	OrderDate	Order Total
1	8	2016-12-23	199.97

If you add a 'GO' keyword between the two SELECT statements, the variable @CustomerId will go out of scope, and the second SELECT statement won't recognize @CustomerId, resulting in the following error:

```
(1 row(s) affected)

Msg 137, Level 15, State 2, Line 88
Must declare the scalar variable "@CustomerId".
```

Review Question 2.20
In T-SQL, a local variable name always begins with ______.
a. $
b. #
c. @
d. _

Review Question 2.21
In T-SQL variable names, the subsequent characters after the first character can be ______.
a. letters or numbers, or space
b. @ or <>
c. $, #, or _
d. all of above

Review Question 2.22
A batch in T-SQL is a group of SQL statements that are executed together and different batches in a file can be separated by _______.
a. parentheses
b. square brackets
c. BATCH
d. GO

Review Question 2.23
A global variable name starts with ______ and is extensively used by SQL Server.
a. $$
b. ##
c. @@
d. _ _

Review Question 2.24
In Transact-SQL, you can use one SET to assign _______ or one SELECT to assign _______ .
a. one value to one variable, one value to many variables
b. one value to many variables, one value to one variable
c. one value to one variable, many values to many matching variables
d. many values to many matching variables, one value to one variable

Review Question 2.25
In Transact-SQL, what happens if there are more than one record retrieved from the SELECT subquery and assigned them to one variable?
a. A run time error message will return if you use SET
b. A tun time error message will return if you use SELECT
c. There are no error messages if you use SET

d. There are no error messages if you use either SET or SELECT

Review Question 2.26
In Transact-SQL, if you assign more than one values retrieved from a SELECT subquery to a variable, ____.
a. A run time error message will return
b. The first record value will be assigned
c. The average of all values will be assigned
d. The last record value will be assigned

Review Question 2.27
We suggest the use of SET wherever possible because programmers can _______.
a. get higher pay with more bugs
b. catch run time errors more easily than logical errors
c. get higher pay with more lines of code
d. enjoy the challenge of solving run time errors

Review Question 2.28
What does a variable do in computer programming languages like JavaScript?
a. Stores tables of data
b. Reserves memory space for storing values
c. Performs complex calculations
d. Manages network connections

Review Question 2.29
In T-SQL, what prefix is used for local variable names?
a. $ (dollar sign)
b. @@ (double at sign)
c. # (number sign)
d. @ (at sign)

Review Question 2.30
Where are local variables accessible in T-SQL?
a. Across multiple stored procedures
b. Within a single batch or stored procedure
c. In global scope
d. Only in the DECLARE statement

Review Question 2.31
What is the purpose of the "GO" keyword in SQL statements?
a. It specifies the location of variables
b. It combines multiple SQL statements into a single batch
c. It indicates the beginning of a T-SQL program
d. It separates batches of SQL statements

Review Question 2.32
How should you declare a variable with an initial value in T-SQL?
a. Using the DECLARE keyword and the data type
b. Using the @@ prefix followed by the variable name
c. By not declaring it, but assigning a value directly
d. Using the SET keyword

Review Question 2.33
When using the SELECT statement to assign values to variables in T-SQL, what happens if the subquery retrieves more than one record?
a. It returns the first record
b. It raises an error
c. It returns the last record
d. It returns all records as an array

2.4 Conditional Flow Control

In computer programming, conditional statements play a pivotal role in shaping the flow and logic of your code. Just as languages like Java employ the versatile IF statement for decision-making and branching, Transact-SQL (T-SQL) also boasts its own implementation of the IF statement, offering database developers a crucial tool to control program flow and make data-driven decisions. The inclusion of conditional constructs, such as the IF statement, makes T-SQL a potent language for not only retrieving and manipulating data but also for implementing complex business rules, automated processes, and conditional operations within the database server.

The IF statement in T-SQL empowers developers to make decisions within their database scripts. With this feature, you can define conditions that, when met, trigger specific actions or set the course for different code paths. These conditions can involve various data comparisons, results of queries, or even user input, offering flexibility and adaptability to your database operations.

T-SQL's IF statement is not just a simple "yes" or "no" gate; it can handle complex logic, allowing for the execution of multiple statements or blocks of code depending on the evaluation of a condition. This flexibility makes it an essential tool in scenarios like data validation, error handling, and even dynamic query construction, where the database needs to respond intelligently to changing conditions.

SQL Example 2.10
If there are more than 5 orders placed in 2017, display "Congratulations to LifeStyle LLC". Otherwise, display "Try harder next year."

SQL Example 2.10 Analysis
The PRINT command can be used to directly output the message. However, our preference is to store the message in a variable called @Message and then display it.

SQL Example 2.10 Statement

```
DECLARE @Message VARCHAR(100);
IF (SELECT COUNT(*) FROM Sales.Orders WHERE YEAR(OrderDate) = 2017) > 5
    SET @Message = 'Congratulations to LifeStyle LLC';
ELSE
    SET @Message = 'Try harder next year.';
SELECT @Message AS Feedback;
```

SQL Example 2.10 Output

	Feedback
1	Congratulations to LifeStyle LLC

SQL Example 2.11

If there are more than 5 orders placed in 2017, display the message "Congratulations to LifeStyle LLC".

Then find out exactly how many orders are placed in 2017 and what their total value is.

Otherwise display "Try harder next year."

SQL Example 2.11 Analysis

The distinction between SQL Example 2.10 and SQL Example 2.11 lies in the condition that if more than five orders were placed in 2017, multiple statements need to be executed. To achieve this, all these statements should be enclosed within a BEGIN...END block.

SQL Example 2.11 Statement

```
DECLARE @Message VARCHAR(100), @NumberOfOrders INT, @TotalSales Numeric(7, 2);
IF (SELECT COUNT(*) FROM Sales.Orders WHERE YEAR(OrderDate) = 2017) > 5
BEGIN
    SET @Message = 'Congratulations to LifeStyle LLC';
    SET @NumberOfOrders = (SELECT COUNT(*)
        FROM Sales.Orders
        WHERE YEAR(OrderDate)= 2017);
    SET @TotalSales = (SELECT SUM(Price*Quantity)
    FROM Sales.Orders AS O
    JOIN Sales.OrderDetails AS OD
    ON O.OrderId = OD.OrderId
    WHERE YEAR(O.OrderDate) = 2017);
END
ELSE
    SET @Message = 'Try harder next year.';
SELECT @Message AS Feedback,
        @NumberOfOrders AS "Number of Orders",
        @TotalSales as "Total Sales";
```

SQL Example 2.11 Output

	Feedback	Number of Orders	Total Sales
1	Congratulations to LifeStyle LLC	6	12049.63

Review Question 2.34
In T-SQL, if a condition is true, a block of statements can be executed. In that case, the block of statements should be inside ______.
a. (and)
b. [and]
c. { and }
d. BEGIN and END

Review Question 2.35
In T-SQL, which of the following correctly assign a value to a variable?
a. @x = 5.
b. x = 5,
c. SET @x = 5
d. SET x = 5.

Review Question 2.36
What is the primary role of conditional statements in computer programming?
a. Controlling program flow and making data-driven decisions.
b. Managing database operations efficiently.
c. Handling complex logic in SQL.
d. Ensuring data integrity in T-SQL.

Review Question 2.37
What is the primary purpose of T-SQL's IF statement?
a. To manage database server operations.
b. To validate data in databases.
c. To execute multiple statements based on a condition.
d. To implement complex business rules in Java.

Review Question 2.38
What kind of conditions can be used with T-SQL's IF statement?
a. Complex data structures.
b. User interface design.
c. Data comparisons, query results, and user input.
d. Automated processes.

Review Question 2.39
How does the flexibility of T-SQL's IF statement benefit database operations?
a. It enforces strict data security.
b. It allows for dynamic query construction.
c. It guarantees error-free coding.
d. It simplifies data retrieval.

2.5 Flow Control with WHILE Loop

In the vast domain of Transact-SQL (T-SQL), we encounter a multitude of tools and constructs that empower us to work with data, manipulate databases, and implement complex logic. Among these essential constructs, the WHILE loop stands out as a dynamic and versatile tool that brings a sense of repetition and iteration to T-SQL. Just as in traditional computer programming languages, T-SQL's WHILE loop can be used to execute a block of statements repeatedly as long as a specified condition holds true.

The WHILE loop is a fundamental component of flow control in T-SQL, offering the means to create iterative processes within your scripts. Whether you need to perform a series of database operations on a set of records, calculate cumulative values, or simulate recursive behavior, the WHILE loop can prove indispensable. It enables the execution of a block of statements repeatedly until a condition evaluates to false, providing the foundation for dynamic, data-driven decision-making within the world of T-SQL.

Syntax and Structure

In T-SQL, the structure of a WHILE loop is concise and intuitive. It begins with the WHILE keyword, followed by a condition that determines whether the loop should continue iterating. The block of statements to be executed is enclosed within the BEGIN...END structure. The loop is terminated with the END keyword. Let's take a look at the basic syntax:

```
WHILE [condition]
BEGIN
    -- Statements to be executed
END
```

Here, the [condition] represents the logical expression that decides whether the loop should continue. As long as this condition remains true, the statements within the loop will be executed repeatedly.

The applications of the WHILE loop in T-SQL are diverse and encompass a wide range of scenarios. Some common use cases include:

Iterating Through Data: You can use a WHILE loop to process rows in a database table, making it useful for tasks like data cleansing, validation, or calculation.

Cumulative Calculations: The loop is handy for cumulative calculations, such as running totals, averages, or aggregating values over a set of rows.

Recursive Logic: It enables the implementation of recursive algorithms, which are particularly useful in hierarchical data structures like organizational charts or product hierarchies.

Simulating Control Flow: The WHILE loop can simulate control structures that are not directly available in T-SQL, adding conditional branching and dynamic decision-making capabilities to your scripts.

While the WHILE loop is a powerful construct, it should be used judiciously. Poorly designed loops can lead to performance issues or even infinite loops if the termination condition is not met. To avoid potential pitfalls, it's essential to carefully plan and test your WHILE loops, ensuring that they execute efficiently and effectively. In addition, always consider alternative constructs like SET-based operations when they are more appropriate for your specific task.

SQL Example 2.12

The total sales for LifeStyle LLC amount to $13,249.59. The management is determined to increase the sales price incrementally in one percent steps to reach a total sales target of $15,000.00. How much should they increase the price by?

SQL Example 2.12 Analysis

You can employ a loop to iteratively update and increase the unit price for all items in the Sales.OrderDetails table by one percent at a time until the total value reaches $15,000. The end result will display the percentage increase required to achieve the $15,000 total value.

SQL Example 2.12 Statement

```sql
DECLARE @Percentage INT = 0;
WHILE (SELECT SUM(Price*Quantity) FROM Sales.OrderDetails) < 15000
BEGIN
    UPDATE Sales.OrderDetails
        SET Price = Price *(1+ @Percentage/100.0)
    SET @Percentage = @Percentage + 1;
END
SELECT 'Sale price must be increased by ' +
    CAST(@Percentage-1 AS VARCHAR) +
    ' percent to reach $15,000.00' AS Result;
```

SQL Example 2.12 Output

	Result
1	Sale price must be increased by 5 percent to reach $15,000.00

SQL Example 2.13

This scenario is similar to SQL Example 2.12, with one crucial difference: once the price of the most expensive item reaches $1,700.00, further price increases will be halted. The goal is to determine the percentage of increase required to achieve a total sales value of $15,000.00 for LifeStyle LLC, all while ensuring that the costliest item remains under $1,700.00. This analysis involves incremental one-percent price increases.

SQL Example 2.13 Analysis

A WHILE loop remains essential to increment the price until the total sales reach the desired $15,000. However, a critical condition must be observed: the loop should terminate as soon as the price of the most expensive product reaches or surpasses $1,700. In such cases, the total sales might fall short of the $15,000 target. To address this situation, we introduce the usage of an IF statement.

Within each iteration of the loop, an examination is made of the price of the most expensive product. If it has reached $1,700 or more, the loop is immediately terminated using the BREAK statement. Conversely, if the condition is not met, the CONTINUE statement is issued, allowing the loop to proceed to the next iteration. It's important to note that, in this specific example, we do not require an 'else' block, but it is included to demonstrate the use of the CONTINUE statement for clarity.

SQL Example 2.13 Statement

```
DECLARE @Percentage INT = 0;
WHILE (SELECT SUM(Price*Quantity) FROM Sales.OrderDetails) < 15000
BEGIN
    UPDATE Sales.OrderDetails
        SET Price = Price *(1+ @Percentage/100.0)
    SET @Percentage = @Percentage + 1;
    IF(SELECT MAX(Price) FROM Sales.OrderDetails) >= 1700
        BREAK
    ELSE
        CONTINUE
END
SELECT 'Sale price can be increased by ' +
    CAST(@Percentage-1 AS VARCHAR) +
    ' percent for highest price reaches 1700 or total sales reaches $15,000.00' AS Result;
```

SQL Example 2.13 Output

	Result
1	Sale price can be increased by 4 percent for highest price reaches 1700 or total sales reaches $15,000.00

Review Question 2.40

In T-SQL, to repeat a block of statements, you can use ______.
a. for loop

b. while loop
c. until loop
d. do … while loop.

Review Question 2.41
What is the fundamental purpose of the WHILE loop in T-SQL?
a. To create static database queries.
b. To replace SET-based operations.
c. To execute a block of statements repeatedly based on a condition.
d. To handle recursive logic in T-SQL.

Review Question 2.42
Which keyword is used to terminate a WHILE loop in T-SQL?
a. EXIT
b. STOP
c. END
d. TERMINATE

Review Question 2.43
In T-SQL, what is the role of the [condition] in a WHILE loop?
a. It specifies the number of iterations.
b. It determines whether the loop should continue iterating.
c. It defines the loop's name.
d. It sets the loop's initial value.

Review Question 2.44
When might a WHILE loop in T-SQL be used for cumulative calculations?
a. To create static database queries.
b. To manage data validation.
c. To handle conditional branching.
d. To calculate running totals or averages.

Review Question 2.45
What is one of the common applications of a WHILE loop in T-SQL with respect to data processing?

a. Aggregating data for complex queries.
b. Replacing SET-based operations.
c. Simulating infinite loops.
d. Processing rows in a database table for tasks like data cleansing or validation.

Review Question 2.46
What is a key consideration when using a WHILE loop in T-SQL to avoid potential issues?
a. Using the EXIT statement for loop termination.
b. Replacing the loop with SET-based operations.
c. Careful planning and testing to ensure efficient execution.
d. Avoiding all recursive algorithms.

2.6 Cursors

A cursor is a T-SQL object that facilitates the storage and retrieval of a result set from a SELECT statement, providing control over the sequence of the data.

SQL primarily operates on sets of data, with a SELECT statement returning a set of rows known as a result set. However, there are scenarios where processing data on a row-by-row basis is necessary, and this is where cursors come into play.

The rationale for using a cursor in T-SQL includes:

Row-Level Processing: Cursors allow you to work with individual rows within a result set. This is useful when you need to apply different operations or business logic to each row, such as calculations, updates, or validations that cannot be easily accomplished with set-based operations. Additionally, cursors provide a way to iterate through data in a specific order. If you need to access rows in a predetermined sequence, such as processing data in a hierarchical structure or in a specific order based on certain criteria, a cursor can be the right choice.

Complex Logic: In situations where the processing logic is intricate and involves multiple steps or conditions, cursors can simplify the coding process. They allow you to handle complex, conditional operations on individual rows more easily than attempting to write complex set-based queries.

Data Cleanup and Transformation: When dealing with data integration or data migration tasks, cursors can be beneficial for cleaning, transforming, and reformatting data on a row-by-row basis.

Updating table data: Cursors are commonly used to update or modify data in a table by iterating through the rows. This provides more control than just executing an UPDATE statement.

Temporarily storing result set: A cursor stores the result set from a query temporarily in memory so you can work with the rows at your own pace. The results are available beyond the execution cycle of the query.

While cursors have their uses, it's important to note that they should be used judiciously and with caution. They tend to be less efficient than set-based operations and can lead to performance issues, especially when dealing with large datasets. Before opting for a cursor, consider whether the same task can be accomplished through set-based operations, which are generally more efficient and better aligned with the relational nature of SQL databases. Cursors should be a choice of last resort when no other feasible alternatives exist. Additionall, cursors can result in complex, hard to understand code causing maintaenance issues. Fianally, overusing cursors can signal poor database design.

To create and use a cursor, follow these five steps:

1. Declaration: Declare a cursor using the DECLARE statement, similar to how you declare a variable. This declaration often includes a SELECT statement that specifies the result set upon which the cursor is based.
2. Opening the Cursor: Open the cursor for use. This step allows you to begin iterating through the rows in the result set.
3. Processing: Perform any necessary processing on the fetched values. This is where you can manipulate individual rows as required.
4. Closing the Cursor: After using the cursor, it's important to close it to free up resources and ensure proper cleanup.
5. Deallocation: Remove the cursor by issuing the DEALLOCATE command. This step is essential for releasing any resources associated with the cursor.

SQL Example 2.14

Create a cursor called TaxCursor that includes customer state, order ID, unit price, and quantity of each product in the order. Then, use TaxCursor to add a 7% tax to California customers. Finally, display the grand total for all customers with tax included.

SQL Example 2.14 Analysis

Follow the five steps in this section to declare, open, fetch, process, close, and deallocate the cursor, and ensure you have the necessary variables to hold the fetched values for processing.

SQL Example 2.14 Statement

```sql
DECLARE @CustomerState VARCHAR(20), @OrderId INT, @UnitPrice MONEY, @Quantity INT, @LineTotal
MONEY, @TaxRate INT, @GrandTotal MONEY;
SET @TaxRate = 7;
SET @GrandTotal = 0;
DECLARE TaxCursor CURSOR FOR
SELECT C.[State], O.OrderId, OD.Price, OD.quantity
FROM Sales.Customers AS C JOIN Sales.Orders AS O
ON C.CustomerId = O.CustomerId
JOIN Sales.OrderDetails AS OD
ON O.OrderId = OD.OrderId
ORDER BY OrderId, ProductId;
OPEN TaxCursor;
FETCH NEXT FROM TaxCursor INTO @CustomerState, @OrderId, @UnitPrice, @Quantity;
WHILE @@FETCH_STATUS = 0
BEGIN
    SET @LineTotal = SUM(@UnitPrice*@Quantity);
    IF @CustomerState = 'CA'
        SET @LineTotal = @LineTotal*(1+@TaxRate/100.0);
    SET @GrandTotal = @GrandTotal + @LineTotal;

    FETCH NEXT FROM TaxCursor INTO @CustomerState, @OrderId, @UnitPrice, @Quantity;
END
CLOSE TaxCursor;
DEALLOCATE TaxCursor;
SELECT CAST(@GrandTotal AS NUMERIC(10, 2)) AS "Grand Total with CA Tax";
```

SQL Example 2.14 Output

	Grand Total with CA Tax
1	13319.59

Review Question 2.47
A _____ is a T-SQL object that stores the result set from a SELECT statement, allowing for the programming.
a. table
b. view
c. index
d. cursor

Review Question 2.48
There are five steps involved to create and use a cursor: declare, open, process, close, and _____ the cursor.
a. reopen
b. exit
c. quit
d. deallocate

Review Question 2.49
What is a cursor in T-SQL primarily used for?
a. Storing temporary variables
b. Performing set-based operations
c. Working with individual rows in a result set
d. Defining database structure

Review Question 2.50
When is it suitable to use a cursor in T-SQL?
a. For all data processing tasks
b. When dealing with set-based operations
c. When processing data on a row-by-row basis is necessary
d. Only for complex logic

Review Question 2.51
Which of the following is a valid rationale for using cursors in T-SQL?
a. To achieve maximum performance
b. For simplicity and ease of coding
c. To work with complex, conditional operations on individual rows
d. To avoid row-level processing

Review Question 2.52
What is one common task for which cursors are often used in T-SQL?
a. Retrieving data from the database
b. Deleting all rows in a table
c. Updating or modifying data in a table
d. Running complex analytical queries

Review Question 2.53
What does it mean to "declare" a cursor in T-SQL?
a. To define the structure of a database
b. To specify the result set upon which the cursor is based
c. To remove the cursor from memory
d. To open the cursor for use

Review Question 2.54
What is the purpose of "closing" a cursor in T-SQL?
a. To remove the cursor from memory
b. To free up system resources
c. To specify the result set for the cursor
d. To execute a complex query

Review Question 2.55
Which of the following is a potential disadvantage of using cursors in T-SQL?
a. Improved query performance
b. Complex and hard-to-understand code
c. Efficient data processing
d. Enhanced database design

Review Question 2.56
When should cursors be chosen in T-SQL?
a. As the first option for any data processing task
b. As a last resort when no other feasible alternatives exist
c. For all set-based operations
d. When dealing with small datasets

Review Question 2.57
What is the final step in using a cursor in T-SQL?
a. Opening the cursor
b. Processing the fetched values
c. Dealing with the result set
d. Deallocating the cursor

2.7 Table Variables

Much like other variables, a table variable allows you to store and manipulate data within your T-SQL batch. However, what sets table variables apart is their ability to hold an entire table's worth of data. This makes them a versatile tool for managing and manipulating data within a batch, without the need for a permanent physical table in your database.

Defining a table variable is straightforward. You can declare a table variable using the DECLARE keyword, followed by the variable name and the table data type. Table variables use a data type called "table," which is followed by the structure of the table, specifying its columns, data types, and constraints.

```sql
DECLARE @MyTableVariable TABLE
(
    Column1 DataType,
    Column2 DataType,
    -- Additional columns can be defined here
);
```

In the above example, @MyTableVariable is declared as a table variable that can hold data with the specified column structure. Table variables are only visible within the current batch. A batch in T-SQL can be a single query, a stored procedure, a trigger, or a batch of commands submitted to the database engine. This means that the table variable's scope is limited to the specific batch in which it is declared. It cannot be referenced or accessed from outside of that batch.

Table variables offer several advantages in T-SQL:

Temporary Storage: They provide a temporary storage mechanism for storing result sets or intermediate data within a T-SQL batch without the need to create a permanent table in the database.

Isolation: As they are only visible within the current batch, table variables do not conflict with similarly named table variables in other batches or stored procedures. This isolation makes them ideal for encapsulating data.

Performance: Table variables are stored in memory, which can lead to improved performance for smaller datasets as compared to physical tables. This is especially valuable for temporary data storage.

Reduced Locking: Since table variables are typically used for short-term data manipulation, they tend to result in fewer locking conflicts and resource contention compared to temporary or physical tables.

Despite their many benefits, table variables do have some limitations:

Limited Indexing: Table variables do not support the creation of indexes. Therefore, operations that require indexing for optimization may not perform as well with table variables as they would with physical tables.

Statistics: The query optimizer may not have access to statistics on table variables, which can affect query optimization and execution plans.

No Constraints: Unlike permanent tables, table variables do not support the use of constraints, such as primary keys, unique constraints, or foreign key relationships.

No Logging: Changes made to table variables are not logged, which may be a concern for applications requiring transactional consistency and logging.

SQL Example 2.15

Calculate the total quantity for each order by every customer and then display the cumulative total for each customer. For instance, if Customer 1 has a first order of 10 units, a second order of 20 units, and a third order of 30 units, Customer 1's running total would be 10 units after the first order, 30 units after the second order, and 60 units after the third order.

To accomplish this, create a table variable to store all the data, and then present all the data from this table variable.

SQL Example 2.15 Analysis

First, declare a table variable named @CustomerOrder with four columns: CustomerId, OrderId, Quantity, and CumulativeQuantity, where the primary key is CustomerId and OrderId.

Second, declare five variables: @CustomerId, @OrderId, @Quantity, @CumulativeQuantity, and @PreviousCustomerId. The first four will store values to be inserted into the corresponding columns of the @CustomerOrder table established in the first step. The @PreviousCustomerId will hold the previous customer's ID. This variable helps identify when a new customer's data begins.

Third, declare a cursor named CumulativeQuantityCursor containing customer ID, order ID, and total quantity, in that order.

Fourth, fetch the first row from the cursor and assign the data to @CustomerId, @OrderId, and @Quantity. Set @PreviousCustomerId to the value of @CustomerId and @CumulativeQuantity to 0.

Fifth, begin looping through each row in the cursor. If the customer ID remains the same, add @Quantity to @CumulativeQuantity and insert the cursor's values into the table variable @CustomerOrder. Fetch another row and continue the loop.

If the customer ID is different, reset @PreviousCustomerId to the new customer ID and reset @CumulativeQuantity to 0. Continue the loop until the next customer or the cursor reaches its end.

Sixth, close the cursor.

Seventh, deallocate the cursor.

Finally, display the contents of the table variable.

SQL Example 2.15 Statement

```sql
DECLARE @CustomerOrder AS TABLE
(
    CustomerId   INT,
    OrderId      INT,
    Quantity INT,
    CumulativeQuantity    INT,
    PRIMARY KEY (CustomerId, OrderId)
);
```

```
DECLARE @CustomerId INT, @PreviousCustomerId INT, @OrderId INT, @Quantity INT,
@CumulativeQuantity INT;
DECLARE CumulativeQuantityCursor CURSOR FOR
SELECT C.CustomerId, O.OrderId, SUM(OD.quantity)
FROM Sales.Customers AS C JOIN Sales.Orders AS O
ON C.CustomerId = O.CustomerId
JOIN Sales.OrderDetails AS OD
ON O.OrderId = OD.OrderId
GROUP BY C.CustomerId, O.OrderId
ORDER BY CustomerId, OrderId;
OPEN CumulativeQuantityCursor;
FETCH NEXT FROM CumulativeQuantityCursor INTO @CustomerId, @OrderId, @Quantity;
SET @PreviousCustomerId = @CustomerId;
SET @CumulativeQuantity = 0;
WHILE @@FETCH_STATUS = 0
BEGIN
    IF @CustomerId <> @PreviousCustomerId
    BEGIN
        SET @PreviousCustomerId = @CustomerId;
        SET @CumulativeQuantity = 0;
    END
    SET @CumulativeQuantity = @CumulativeQuantity + @Quantity;
    INSERT INTO @CustomerOrder (CustomerId, OrderId, Quantity, CumulativeQuantity)
        VALUES (@CustomerId, @OrderId, @Quantity, @CumulativeQuantity);
    FETCH NEXT FROM CumulativeQuantityCursor INTO @CustomerId, @OrderId, @Quantity;
END
CLOSE CumulativeQuantityCursor;
DEALLOCATE CumulativeQuantityCursor;
SELECT CustomerId, OrderId, Quantity, CumulativeQuantity
FROM @CustomerOrder
ORDER BY CustomerId, OrderId;
```

SQL Example 2.15 Output

	CustomerId	OrderId	Quantity	CumulativeQuantity
1	1	1	3	3
2	1	2	13	16
3	1	5	9	25
4	2	3	8	8
5	3	6	1	1
6	4	4	3	3
7	5	7	1	1
8	7	8	3	3

Review Question 2.58

A(n) _______ variable can hold values of a whole table.

a. table

b. view

c. index

d. database

2.8 Chapter Summary

In this chapter, you were introduced to the case expression, a valuable tool for returning values based on input. Case expressions come in handy when you need to display different values derived from the original data. You also delved into the programming aspect of T-SQL, where you learned how to utilize variables to store values for future use. Additionally, you explored the power of IF statements for controlling the flow of your code and WHILE loops for executing a statement or a block of statements repeatedly.

Lastly, you gained insights into cursors. Cursors provide the capability to read the result set within the cursor and perform operations on the data it contains.

2.9 Discussion

Discussion 2.1

There are two types of case expression in T-SQL. Compare and contrast these two types. Use an example to show the similarity and differences. When would you use each type?

Discussion 2.3

What is a batch in T-SQL? Give an example and explain why it is an important concept.

Discussion 2.4

In T-SQL, you can use either SELECT or SET to assign values to variables. What's the difference? Would you recommend one over the other? Why?

2.10 SQL Exercises

Exercise 2.1

Display employee names and the cities they live in with "In town" for "New Canton" residents and "Nearby" for employees in any other cities.

	Employee Name	Resident
1	Alex Hall	In Town
2	Dianne Hart	In Town
3	Maria Law	In Town
4	Alice Law	Nearby
5	Black Hart	Nearby
6	Christina Robinson	In Town
7	Nicholas Pinkston	Nearby

Exercise 2.2

Use simple case expressions for this exercise. Display product name and a column called "High Volume". If a product is sold five or more units in an order, mark the column as "Yes". Otherwise, mark the column as "No". Display one row every time a product is sold. As a result, the same product may be high volume sometimes and low volume other times.

	ProductName	High Volume
1	65-Inch 4K Ultra HD Smart TV	No
2	3200 Lumens LED Home Theater Projector	No
3	65-Inch 4K Ultra HD Smart TV	No
4	60-Inch 4K Ultra HD Smart LED TV	No
5	Wireless Color Photo Printer	Yes
6	Color Laser Printer	Yes
7	3200 Lumens LED Home Theater Projector	No
8	Color Laser Printer	No
9	10" 16GB Android Tablet	No
10	GPS Android Tablet PC	No
11	20.2 MP Digital Camera	No
12	Wireless Color Photo Printer	No
13	GPS Android Tablet PC	No
14	3200 Lumens LED Home Theater Projector	Yes
15	Color Laser Printer	No
16	65-Inch 4K Ultra HD Smart TV	No
17	60-Inch 4K Ultra HD Smart LED TV	No
18	10" 16GB Android Tablet	No
19	GPS Android Tablet PC	No

Exercise 2.3

Use searched case expression to work on the same problem as Exercise 2.2 above.

Exercise 2.4

A product that is delivered on or before October 10, 2016 is called "Obsolete inventory" due to the short product life cycle of the industry. Display product names and whether a product is obsolete or not.

	DeliveryId	ProductName	Inventory
1	1	65-Inch 4K Ultra HD Smart TV	Obsolete
2	2	65-Inch 4K Ultra HD Smart TV	Current
3	3	60-Inch 4K Ultra HD Smart LED TV	Obsolete
4	4	3200 Lumens LED Home Theater Projector	Obsolete
5	5	Wireless Color Photo Printer	Obsolete
6	6	6Wireless Compact Laser Printer	Obsolete
7	7	Color Laser Printer	Obsolete
8	8	10" 16GB Android Tablet	Current
9	9	10" 16GB Android Tablet	Current

Exercise 2.5

Display customer name and its type. If a customer spends $1000 or more, the customer type is VIP. If a customer spends $500 or more, but less than $1000, the customer type is Valued. If a customer spends less than $500, but more than zero, the customer type is Normal. If a customer has not purchased anything, the customer type is New.

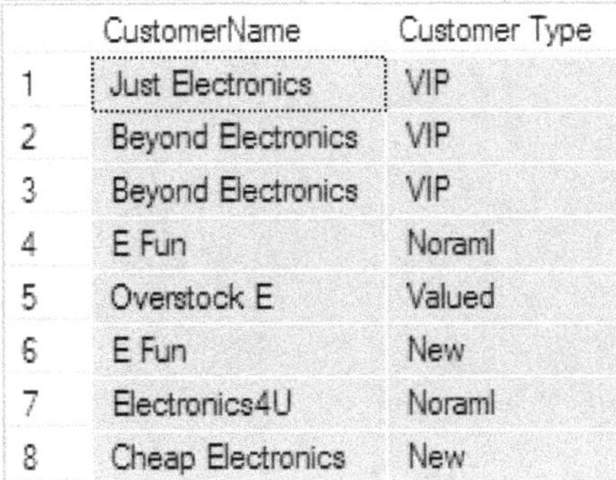

Exercise 2.6

Declare a variable called @Company with the initialized value of "Overstock E". Declare another variable called @Contact and assign a value of "Daniel Yellow" in a separate statement. Finally display the customer data with a SELECT statement.

Exercise 2.7

Declare a variable called @Company with the initialized value of "Overstock E". Declare another variable called @Contact and assign a value of the name of the customer ID 5 contact from the Sales.Customers table in a separate statement. Finally display the company data with a SELECT statement.

Exercise 2.8

Declare three variables called @Company, @Contact, and @Email. On separate statements, assign corresponding values from Sales.Customers for customer ID 5 in two different ways (SET and SELECT). What happens if you do not limit to customer ID 5?

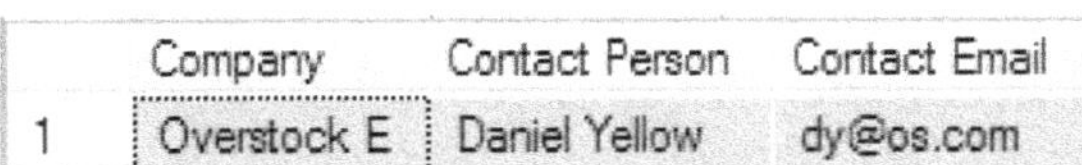

Exercise 2.9

Declare a variable called @SupplierId and assign the value of 4. Then display the supplier name and address of that supplier. Followed by the supplier's delivery history with supplier name, product name, and total value (Quantity×Price) of the product from the supplier.

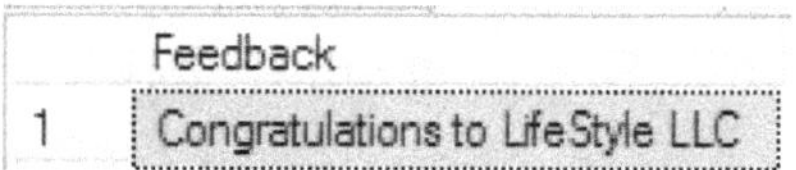

	SupplierName	Address
1	Samsong	1 Electronics Road Yeongtong Suwon 30174 South Korea

	SupplierName	ProductName	Delivery Total
1	Samsong	65-Inch 4K Ultra HD Smart TV	8199.93
2	Samsong	60-Inch 4K Ultra HD Smart LED TV	11999.90
3	Samsong	10" 16GB Android Tablet	2219.70

Exercise 2.10

If there is more than $10,000.00 revenue (Total of Quantity X Price from the OrderDetails table) in 2017, display "Congratualtions to LifeStyle LLC". Otherwise, display "Try harder next year."

	Feedback
1	Congratulations to LifeStyle LLC

Exercise 2.11

If there is more than $10,000.00 revenue (Total of Quantity × Price from the OrderDetails table) in 2017, display "Congratualtions to LifeStyle LLC". Then find out exactly how many orders were placed in 2017 and what is their total value.

Otherwise display "Try harder next year.". Then include how many orders were placed in 2017 and their total value. Check to see if the code still works if a few large orders are removed.

	Feedback	Total Revenue	Number of Orders
1	Congratulations to LifeStyle LLC	12049.63	6

Exercise 2.12

The total product delivered from suppliers is valued at $31668.83. The management wants to know how much percent to decrease all prices in order for the total inventory cost to go down to $30000.00 or less (Price must be decreased one percent at a time).

	Result
1	Price must be decreased by 3 percent to reach $30,000.00

Exercise 2.13

Same as Exercise 2.12, but once the lowest priced product reaches $65.00, the price decrease stops. What percent of decrease is needed to bring the total inventory costs down to $30,000.00 or less (Price must be decreased one percent at a time)?

	Result
1	Sale price can be decreased by 2 percent for lowest price reaches $69 or total inventory reaches $30,000.00

Exercise 2.14

Create a cursor called ImportTariffCursor that includes supplier country, delivery Id, Product Id, unit delivery price, and quantity of each product in the delivery. Then use the ImportTariffCursor to add 15% tax to all foreign suppliers. Finally, display the grand total with import tariff included.

	Grand Total with Tariff
1	35466.71

Exercise 2.15

Display the running total for each supplier by delivery. For example, if supplier 1 has first delivery of 10 units, second delivery of 20 units, and third delivery of 30 units, then supplier 1 has the running total of 10 units after the first delivery, 30 units after the second delivery, and 60 units after the third delivery. Create a table to hold all the data and finally select all data from this table variable.

	SupplierId	DeliveryId	Quantity	CumulativeQuantity
1	2	6	15	15
2	2	7	25	40
3	3	4	10	10
4	4	1	2	2
5	4	2	5	7
6	4	3	10	17
7	4	8	12	29
8	4	9	18	47
9	5	5	20	20

2.11 Solutions to the Review Questions

2.1 D; 2.2 B; 2.3 A; 2.4 A; 2.5 C; 2.6 A; 2.7 D; 2.8 D; 2.9 C; 2.10 B; 2.11 A; 2.12 C; 2.13 C; 2.14 C; 2.15 D; 2.16 D; 2.17 C; 2.18 D; 2.19 A; 2.20 C; 2.21 C; 2.22 D; 2.23 C; 2.24 C; 2.25 A; 2.26 D; 2.27 B; 2.28 B; 2.29 D; 2.30 B; 2.31 D; 2.32 A; 2.33 C; 2.34 D; 2.35 C; 2.36 A; 2.37 C; 2.38 C; 2.39 B; 2.40 B; 2.41 C; 2.42 C; 2.43 B; 2.44 D; 2.45 D; 2.46 C; 2.47 D; 2.48 D; 2.49 C; 2.50 C; 2.51 C; 2.52 C; 2.53 B; 2.54 B; 2.55 B; 2.56 B; 2.57 D; 2.58 A;

CHAPTER 3: CTE AND SUBQUERY

Chapter Learning Objectives

3.1 Apply common table expressions to solve specific data retrieval challenges.
3.2 Utilize subqueries effectively to retrieve or manipulate data.
3.3 Implement correlated subqueries to address complex SQL problems.

3.1 Introduction to Common Table Expression (CTE)

The length of an SQL statement can impact its readability. As SQL statements grow longer, they become more challenging to comprehend. However, breaking down lengthy SQL statements into multiple smaller ones can significantly enhance their clarity. This approach divides a complex problem into manageable steps, with each step resulting in a dataset that's closer to the specific issue at hand. In SQL, a Common Table Expression (CTE) is a powerful tool to achieve this.

Let's consider an example. Suppose you need to determine how much each customer spent on purchases from LifeStyle LLC. Without using a CTE, you can solve this problem in one step, as shown here:

```sql
SELECT C.CustomerName, SUM(OD.Price * OD.Quantity) AS "Total Order Value"
FROM Sales.Customers AS C JOIN Sales.Orders AS O
ON C.CustomerId = O.CustomerId
JOIN Sales.OrderDetails AS OD
ON O.OrderId = OD.OrderId
GROUP BY C.CustomerId, C.CustomerName;
```

However, with the use of a CTE, you can break the problem into two more digestible steps. The first step involves gathering the required data from three tables: the Customers table for customer information, the

Orders table for order details, and the OrderDetails table for individual order values. In this step, you assemble all necessary data into a CTE, which acts as an intermediary dataset.

The second step is focused on extracting the total purchase value of each customer from the CTE. Think of the CTE as a large virtual table containing all the essential data. To retrieve the relevant data, you simply use an aggregate function like SUM(Price * Quantity), as illustrated below:

```sql
WITH CustomerOrder (CustomerId, CustomerName, Price, Quantity) AS
(
    SELECT C.CustomerId, C.CustomerName, OD.Price, OD.Quantity
    FROM Sales.Customers AS C JOIN Sales.Orders AS O
    ON C.CustomerId = O.CustomerId
    JOIN Sales.OrderDetails AS OD
    ON O.OrderId = OD.OrderId
)
SELECT CustomerName, SUM(Price * Quantity) AS "Total Order Value"
FROM CustomerOrder
GROUP BY CustomerId, CustomerName;
```

Both approaches yield the same output:

	CustomerName	Total Order Value
1	Just Electronics	7949.75
2	Beyond Electronics	2329.92
3	Beyond Electronics	1499.99
4	E Fun	269.97
5	Overstock E	999.99
6	Electronics4U	199.97

The syntax for using a CTE is as follows:

```sql
WITH CTE_Name (Column1NewName, Column2NewName, …) AS
(
    SELECT Column1, Column2, …
    FROM TableName [JOIN if needed]
    [any clause you normally used]
)
SELECT …
FROM CTE_Name
[any clause you would like];
```

In essence, a Common Table Expression serves as a virtual table that temporarily holds a result set, allowing further processing within the same SQL statement.

The advantages of using CTEs include:

Improved Readability: CTEs make SQL statements more readable, acting as intermediary steps for tackling complex problems.

Ease of Testing: With CTEs, you can test individual parts of the SQL statement independently, facilitating debugging and development.

Support for Recursion: CTEs enable recursion, which allows a query to call itself, a topic we'll explore in the next section.

SQL Example 3.1

Display number of orders handled by each employee for each year.

SQL Example 3.1 Analysis

First, create a CTE to store employee ID, order ID, and the year in which the order was processed. Then, from the CTE, select employee ID, year, and the count of orders for each year.

SQL Example 3.1 Statement

```
WITH EmployeeSales (EmployeeId, EmployeName, OrderId, OrderYear) AS
(
    SELECT E.EmployeeId, E.FirstName + ' ' + LastName, O.OrderId, YEAR(O.OrderDate)
    FROM HR.Employees AS E JOIN Sales.Orders AS O
    ON E.EmployeeId = O.EmployeeId
)
SELECT EmployeeId, EmployeName, COUNT(OrderId) AS "Number of Orders", OrderYear
FROM EmployeeSales
GROUP BY EmployeeId, EmployeName, OrderYear
ORDER BY OrderYear;
```

SQL Example 3.1 Output

	EmployeeId	EmployeName	Number of Orders	OrderYear
1	2	Dianne Hart	1	2016
2	7	Nicholas Pinkston	1	2016
3	3	Maria Law	1	2017
4	4	Alice Law	1	2017
5	5	Black Hart	3	2017
6	6	Christina Robinson	1	2017

SQL Example 3.2

Display number of orders LifeStyle LLC received every year.

SQL Example 3.2 Analysis

This is a simple problem. You may try the following and see an error message:

```
SELECT YEAR(OrderDate) AS OrderYear, COUNT(OrderId) AS "Number of Orders"
FROM Sales.Orders
GROUP BY OrderYear;
```

Error Message:

```
Msg 207, Level 16, State 1, Line 37
Invalid column name 'OrderYear'.
```

The reason for this is that the OrderYear is not assigned as YEAR(OrderDate) before using GROUP BY.

With the CTE approach, first create a CTE to store OrderYear and OrderId. Then, from the CTE, count the OrderId and apply a GROUP BY operation on the OrderYear.

SQL Example 3.2 Statement

```
WITH OrderByYear (OrderId, OrderYear) AS
(
    SELECT OrderId, YEAR(OrderDate)
    FROM Sales.Orders
)
SELECT OrderYear, COUNT(OrderId) AS "Number of Orders"
FROM OrderByYear
GROUP BY OrderYear;
```

SQL Example 3.2 Output

	OrderYear	Number of Orders
1	2016	2
2	2017	6

Review Question 3.1
In T-SQL, CTE stands for ______.
a. Computer Tasks Expression
b. Compute Table Expression
c. Common Tasks Expression
d. Common Table Expression

Review Question 3.2
By making smaller steps for a complex problem of T-SQL, each step will result in a data set that is closer to the problem at hand. A(n) ___ is an expression in SQL to retrieve such data set
a. While loop
b. if statement
c. Common Table Expression
d. Case Expression

Review Question 3.3
Common Table Expression is a ______ table that can temporarily hold result set for further processing in the same SQL statement.
a. large
b. virtual
c. middle
d. transit

Review Question 3.4
Which of the following is a benefit of CTE?
a. shorter code
b. faster execution
c. more readable
d. more secure

Review Question 3.5
Which of the following is a benefit of CTE?
a. easier to test
b. shorter code
c. faster execution
d. more secure

Review Question 3.6
Which of the following is a benefit of CTE?
a. shorter code
b. possible recursions
c. faster execution
d. more secure

Review Question 3.7
Common Table Expression is a virtual table that is _______.
a. anonymous
b. anonymous and must be used immediately
c. named and can be used to save dataset
d. named and can be used like a table for further data handling

Review Question 3.8
What is the primary role of a Common Table Expression (CTE) in SQL?
a. To improve SQL statement performance
b. To simplify SQL syntax
c. To temporarily hold a result set for further processing
d. To enforce data integrity rules

Review Question 3.9
How does a CTE improve SQL statement readability?
a. By reducing the number of tables in the database
b. By making the SQL statement shorter
c. By acting as an intermediary step for complex problems
d. By eliminating the need for JOIN clauses

Review Question 3.10
What does "Ease of Testing" refer to in the context of using CTEs?
a. The simplicity of writing SQL queries
b. The ability to test SQL statements for syntax errors
c. The ability to test individual parts of an SQL statement independently
d. The ease of database administration

Review Question 3.11
What feature of CTEs allows a query to call itself?
a. Recursion
b. Grouping
c. Joining
d. Aggregation

Review Question 3.12
Why does the SQL query result in an "Invalid column name 'OrderYear'" error message?
```
SELECT YEAR(OrderDate) AS OrderYear, COUNT(OrderId) AS "Number of Orders"
FROM Sales.Orders
GROUP BY OrderYear;
```
a. Because the GROUP BY clause is missing.
b. Because the ORDER BY clause is missing.
c. Because the column name 'OrderYear' is not valid in the SELECT clause.
d. Because 'OrderYear' needs to be assigned as 'YEAR(OrderDate)' before using GROUP BY.

3.2 JOIN CTE with Regular Tables

Once a Common Table Expression (CTE) is created, it can be seamlessly integrated into a SQL statement, effectively behaving like a conventional table. This means you can join a CTE with regular tables to retrieve more complex data.

SQL Example 3.3

Display each customer's total order value with 10% sales tax.

SQL Example 3.3 Analysis

In this example, we aim to display each customer's total order value with a 10% sales tax. We achieve this by utilizing a CTE to add a 10% sales tax to each line of an order in the OrderDetails table. Then, we join the CTE with the Customers table to retrieve customer ID, name, and the total order value, including tax.

SQL Example 3.3 Statement

```
WITH CustomerOrder (OrderId, PlusTax) AS
(
    SELECT OrderId, CAST (Price*Quantity*1.1 AS NUMERIC(10, 2))
    FROM Sales.OrderDetails
)
SELECT C.CustomerId, C.CustomerName, SUM(PlusTax) AS "Total with Tax"
FROM Sales.Customers AS C JOIN Sales.Orders AS O
ON C.CustomerId = O.CustomerId
JOIN CustomerOrder AS CO
ON O.OrderId = CO.OrderId
```

```
GROUP BY C.CustomerId, C.CustomerName;
```

SQL Example 3.3 Output

	CustomerId	CustomerName	Total with Tax
1	1	Just Electronics	8744.73
2	2	Beyond Electronics	2562.92
3	3	Beyond Electronics	1649.99
4	4	E Fun	296.97
5	5	Overstock E	1099.99
6	7	Electronics4U	219.97

SQL Example 3.4

Display all customer's ID, name, and if they placed an order during 2016, show 2016. If not, show null.

SQL Example 3.4 Analysis

In this scenario, we want to display all customer IDs and names, and for those who placed an order during 2016, show the year 2016. For customers who did not place an order in 2016, we should display NULL. Achieving this without CTE can be challenging. The CTE approach involves first selecting only the orders placed in 2016 into a CTE. Then, the Customers table is left-joined with this CTE to produce the desired result set.

Without using CTE, this can be difficult. Suppose you use the following SQL statement:

```
SELECT C.CustomerId, C.CustomerName, YEAR(O.OrderDate) AS "Order Year"
FROM Sales.Customers AS C LEFT JOIN Sales.Orders AS O
ON C.CustomerId = O.CustomerId
WHERE Year(OrderDate) = 2016
```

It will result in the following result set:

	CustomerId	CustomerName	Order Year
1	5	Overstock E	2016
2	7	Electronics4U	2016

Those customers who did not place an order during 2016 are supposed to show NULL for Order Year. With using CTE, first, only those orders placed in 2016 will be in CTE. Next, the customers table is left joined with this CTE. The correct result set will be found.

SQL Example 3.4 Statement

```
WITH Orders2016 (OrderId, CustomerId, OrderYear) AS
(
    SELECT OrderId, CustomerId, YEAR(OrderDate)
    FROM Sales.Orders
    WHERE YEAR(OrderDate) = 2016
```

```
)
SELECT C.CustomerId, C.CustomerName, O.OrderYear
FROM Sales.Customers AS C LEFT JOIN Orders2016 AS O
ON C.CustomerId = o.CustomerId
ORDER BY OrderYear DESC;
```

SQL Example 3.4 Output

	CustomerId	CustomerName	OrderYear
1	5	Overstock E	2016
2	7	Electronics4U	2016
3	8	Cheap Electronics	NULL
4	6	E Fun	NULL
5	1	Just Electronics	NULL
6	2	Beyond Electronics	NULL
7	3	Beyond Electronics	NULL
8	4	E Fun	NULL

Review Question 3.13
Once a CTE is created, it can be treated as a _______ within the statement.
a. special table
b. normal table
c. special view
b. normal view

Review Question 3.14
A CTE table can _______ to retrieve more complex data.
a. join a regular table
b. not join a regular table
c. only join other CTE
d. cannot join a table where it retries the data

Review Question 3.15
Using the LifeStyleDB of the book, suppose you want to display all customer's ID, name, and if they placed an order during 2016, show 2016. If not, show null. What is wrong with the following SQL statement?
```
SELECT C.CustomerId, C.CustomerName, YEAR(O.OrderDate) AS "Order Year"
FROM Sales.Customers AS C JOIN Sales.Orders AS O
ON C.CustomerId = O.CustomerId
WHERE Year(OrderDate) = 2016
```
a. LEFT JOIN should be used instead of INNER JOIN
b. RIGHT JOIN should be used instead of INNER JOIN
c. Use outer join to keep all customers who did not place an order in 2016
d. Use a CTE for 2016 orders first, and then the customers table is left joined with this CTE

3.3 Using Multiple CTEs

In T-SQL, you have the flexibility to declare and utilize multiple Common Table Expressions (CTEs) within a single statement. To include multiple CTEs, simply separate their declarations with commas. Furthermore, a single CTE can be referenced multiple times within a statement, eliminating the need to duplicate code. This feature enhances code organization and readability, particularly when dealing with complex queries involving several CTEs.

SQL Example 3.5

Display a list of employees hired on January 1, 2013, or later, along with the customers they assisted.

SQL Example 3.5 Analysis

Solve the problem using multiple CTEs. The first CTE should include the IDs and names of all employees hired on or after January 1, 2013. The second CTE should encompass the names and contact information of all customers found in the Orders table. To obtain the desired result, combine these two CTEs with a join operation.

SQL Example 3.5 Statement

```
WITH NoviceEmployee (EmployeeId, EmployeeName) AS
(
    SELECT EmployeeId, FirstName + ' ' + LastName
    FROM HR.Employees
    WHERE HireDate >= '20130101'
),
ActiveCustomer (CustomerName, Contact, EmployeeId) AS
(
    SELECT CustomerName, Contact, EmployeeId
    FROM Sales.Customers AS C JOIN Sales.Orders AS O
    ON C.CustomerId = O.CustomerId
)
SELECT EmployeeName, CustomerName, Contact AS "Customer Contact"
FROM NoviceEmployee AS NE JOIN ActiveCustomer AS AC
ON NE.EmployeeId = AC.EmployeeId;
```

SQL Example 3.5 Output

	EmployeeName	CustomerName	Customer Contact
1	Black Hart	Just Electronics	John White
2	Black Hart	Beyond Electronics	Scott Green
3	Black Hart	E Fun	Ben Gold
4	Christina Robinson	Beyond Electronics	Alice Black
5	Nicholas Pinkston	Overstock E	Daniel Yellow

SQL Example 3.6

Display the count of customers for each year and indicate the increase or decrease compared to the previous year.

SQL Example 3.6 Analysis

Start by creating a Common Table Expression (CTE) that holds the year and the corresponding number of customers for each year. Then, incorporate this CTE twice within a JOIN statement. This join operation combines the customer count for the current year minus the count from the previous year. To achieve this, we use the condition of comparing the Year value in one instance of the CTE with the Year value in another instance increased by one. This comparison brings together the customer counts for the current and previous years, effectively fulfilling our objective.

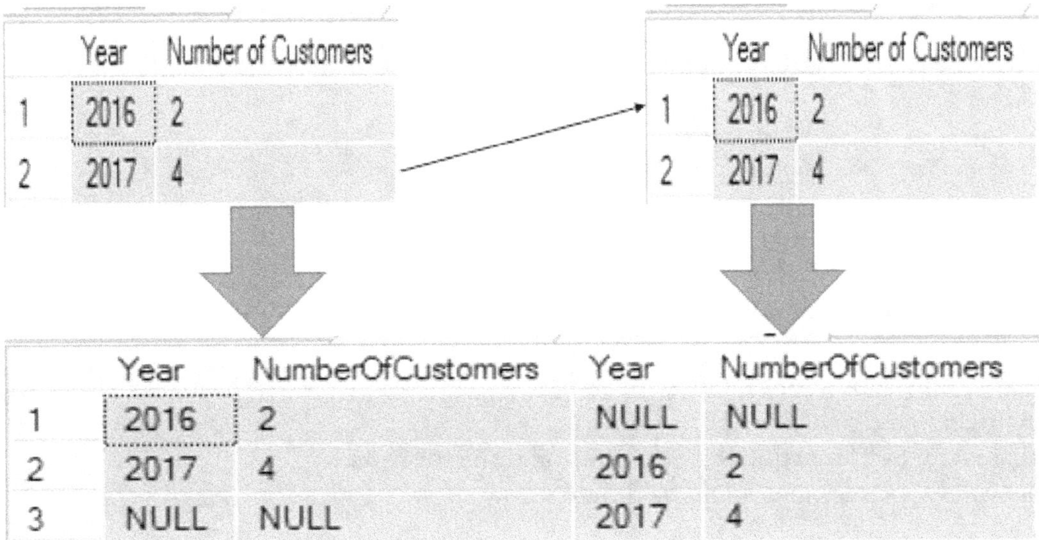

SQL Example 3.6 Statement

```sql
WITH CustomerByYear ([Year], NumberOfCustomers) AS
(
    SELECT YEAR(OrderDate), COUNT(DISTINCT CustomerId)
    FROM Sales.Orders
    GROUP BY YEAR(OrderDate)
)
SELECT ThisYearCustomer.[Year], ThisYearCustomer.NumberOfCustomers,
    ThisYearCustomer.NumberOfCustomers -LastYearCustomer.NumberOfCustomers AS "Increase/Decrease
from last year"
FROM CustomerByYear AS ThisYearCustomer
JOIN CustomerByYear AS LastYearCustomer
ON ThisYearCustomer.[Year] = LastYearCustomer.[Year] + 1;
```

SQL Example 3.6 Output

	Year	NumberOfCustomers	Increase/Decrease from last year
1	2017	4	2

Review Question 3.16
How many CTEs can be declared and used in one T-SQL statement?
a. one
b. two
c. three
d. many

Review Question 3.17
One CTE can be referenced multiple times so that _______.
a. there is no need to duplicate code
b. consistent result can be generated
c. it works with object-oriented programs
d. there is no need to create multiple CTE in a statement

Review Question 3.18
Several CTEs can be created in one SQL statement with _______ in between them.
a. line break
b. comma
c. period
d. &

Review Question 3.19
If you need to perform a mathematical operation on values from two different rows of the same toable, you
_______.
a. cannot do it because SQL only allows for same row operation
b. just do it like they are in the same row
c. cannot do it unless there is an SQL function that performs on different rows.
d. can self join the table with ON clause indicating the different rows.

3.4 Recursive Common Table Expressions (CTEs)

A recursive Common Table Expression, often referred to as a recursive CTE, is a powerful feature in T-SQL that allows a CTE to reference itself. It initiates with an initial CTE and then, based on the data within the initial CTE, retrieves a subset of that data. This process continues recursively until no more rows are returned.

Syntax for Recursive CTE:

```
WITH CTE_Name (Column1NewName, Column2NewName, …) AS
(
    Anchor member
    UNION ALL
    Recursive member
)
SELECT …
```

```
FROM CTE_Name
[any optional clauses];
```

Let's illustrate this with an example:

```
WITH RecursiveCTEExample AS
(
    SELECT   SQRT(256) AS n
    UNION ALL
    SELECT SQRT(n)
    FROM RecursiveCTEExample
    WHERE n >= 2
)
SELECT n
FROM RecursiveCTEExample;
```

In this example, the recursive CTE is named RecursiveCTEExample. The anchor member is represented by the initial SQL statement: SELECT SQRT(256) AS n. The recursive member, on the other hand, is the subsequent SQL statement: SELECT SQRT(n) FROM RecursiveCTEExample WHERE n >= 2.

The initial row will contain the initial value, which is the square root of 256, equal to 16. This value is then used in the recursive statement, where the square root of 16 is computed, resulting in a value of 4. The second row holds the value 4, the third row has 2, and the fourth row contains 1.4142…, which is less than 2, indicating the end of the recursion. As a result, no fifth row is generated. The output of this query will be a sequence of values representing the results of these calculations.

	n
1	16
2	4
3	2
4	1.4142135623731

Recursive CTEs are invaluable for managing hierarchical structures, such as a chain of managers in an organizational hierarchy. They can also be applied to scenarios like university course prerequisites, where you need to discover all the prerequisite courses for a given course.

By default, SQL Server restricts the number of times the recursive member can be invoked to 100. However, you can modify this limit by adding the OPTION (MAXRECURSION n) clause at the end of your query, where 'n' is an integer value that can range from 1 to 32767, allowing for greater control over the recursion depth.

SQL Example 3.7

Display all supervisors and subordinators of employee ID 1.

SQL Example 3.7 Analysis

The use of a recursive CTE is well-suited to this scenario. The anchor member is defined as follows:

```sql
SELECT EmployeeId, ManagerId, FirstName, LastName
FROM HR.Employees
WHERE EmployeeId = 1
```

The recursive member is a SELECT statement that involves a JOIN operation between the CTE and the HR.Employees table, with the condition that the CTE's employee ID must match the HR.Employee's manager ID. This results in a subset containing all subordinates or supervisors of the employees already present in the CTE. This process continues until there are no more subordinates or supervisors to include. The recursive member is formulated as follows:

```sql
SELECT E.EmployeeId, E.ManagerId, E.FirstName, E.LastName
FROM Subordinators AS S JOIN HR.Employees AS E
ON E.ManagerId = S.EmployeeId
```

This recursive CTE structure effectively allows for the retrieval of hierarchical relationships within an organization.

SQL Example 3.7 Statement

```sql
WITH Subordinators (EmployeeId, ManagerId, FirstName, LastName) AS
(
    SELECT EmployeeId, ManagerId, FirstName, LastName
    FROM HR.Employees
    WHERE EmployeeId = 1
    UNION ALL
    SELECT E.EmployeeId, E.ManagerId, E.FirstName, E.LastName
    FROM Subordinators AS S JOIN HR.Employees AS E
    ON E.ManagerId = S.EmployeeId
)
SELECT EmployeeId, ManagerId, FirstName, LastName
FROM Subordinators;
```

SQL Example 3.7 Output

	EmployeeId	ManagerId	FirstName	LastName
1	1	NULL	Alex	Hall
2	2	1	Dianne	Hart
3	3	1	Maria	Law
4	4	1	Alice	Law
5	7	3	Nicholas	Pinkston
6	5	2	Black	Hart
7	6	2	Christina	Robinson

Review Question 3.20
What does this describe? "It starts with an initial CTE. Then based on the initial CTE, it will retrieve a subset of that CTE. This will repeat by itself until no rows are returned."
a. group CTEs
b. group by CTEs
c. recursive CTEs
d. CTE loop

Review Question 3.21
A ______ CTE is a CTE that references itself.
a. group
b. SELF
c. recursive
d. loop

Review Question 3.22
The ______ CTE is good for organizational structure such as a chain of managers.
a. group
b. SELF
c. recursive
d. loop

Review Question 3.23
How many rows will be in the output of the following code?
```
WITH RecursiveCTEExample AS
(
    SELECT   SQRT(256) AS n
    UNION ALL
    SELECT SQRT(n)
    FROM RecursiveCTEExample
    WHERE n >= 2
)
SELECT n
FROM RecursiveCTEExample;
```
a. 1
b. 3
c. 4
d. 5

Review Question 3.24
In the following statement, what is `RecursiveCTEExample`?
```
WITH RecursiveCTEExample AS
(
    SELECT   SQRT(256) AS n
    UNION ALL
    SELECT SQRT(n)
    FROM RecursiveCTEExample
    WHERE n >= 2
)
SELECT n
FROM RecursiveCTEExample;
```
a. Indicating this is just an example
b. Indicting this is just an example and won't use data from LifeStyleDB
c. Common Table Expression name

d. Common Table Expression example

Review Question 3.25
In the following statement, what is `SELECT SQRT(256) AS n`?

```
WITH RecursiveCTEExample AS
(
    SELECT  SQRT(256) AS n
    UNION ALL
    SELECT SQRT(n)
    FROM RecursiveCTEExample
    WHERE n >= 2
)
SELECT n
FROM RecursiveCTEExample;
```

a. Anchor member
b. UNION member
c. Recursive member
d. Common Table Expression member

Review Question 3.26
In the following statement, what is `SELECT SQRT(n) FROM RecursiveCTEExample WHERE n >= 2`?

```
WITH RecursiveCTEExample AS
(
    SELECT  SQRT(256) AS n
    UNION ALL
    SELECT SQRT(n)
    FROM RecursiveCTEExample
    WHERE n >= 2
)
SELECT n
FROM RecursiveCTEExample;
```

a. Anchor member
b. UNION member
c. Recursive member
d. Common Table Expression member

3.5 Utilizing Subqueries in the WHERE Clause

In our first textbook, we introduced the concept of subqueries. In this chapter, we will delve deeper into the use of subqueries. A subquery is essentially a query that can be embedded within another query. The first query, often referred to as the inner query, is nested within the second query, known as the outer query. The database management system (DBMS) executes the inner query prior to processing the outer query.

To illustrate, consider the task of retrieving all products from domestic suppliers for LifeStyle LLC. To accomplish this, we can employ a subquery to first select all domestic supplier IDs from the suppliers table (the inner query). Subsequently, we use an outer query to identify all products provided by those domestic suppliers. This is achieved by utilizing a WHERE clause with the IN keyword.

SQL Example 3.8

Display all products provided by LifeStyle LLC's domestic suppliers.

SQL Example 3.8 Analysis

Employ a subquery to extract the supplier IDs of domestic suppliers. Utilize the IN keyword to filter the products offered by these suppliers. Additionally, it's worth noting that the NOT IN keyword can be employed in a similar manner, as demonstrated in this example. Incidentally, it's important to mention that this problem can also be resolved using an INNER JOIN.

SQL Example 3.8 Statement

```
SELECT ProductId, ProductName
FROM Purchasing.Products
WHERE supplierid IN
    (SELECT supplierid
    FROM Purchasing.Suppliers
    WHERE Country = 'USA');
```

SQL Example 3.8 Output

	ProductId	ProductName
1	5	6Wireless Compact Laser Printer
2	6	Color Laser Printer
3	8	GPS Android Tablet PC

SQL Example 3.9

Display all products with above average sales prices. Show product ID.

SQL Example 3.9 Analysis

Utilize an inner query to calculate the average sales price from the Sales.OrderDetails table. In the outer query, employ a WHERE clause to retain all products within the Sales.OrderDetails table with prices exceeding the calculated average. When working with subqueries involving comparison operators (e.g., $>$, $=$, $<$, $!=$), ensure that the inner query yields a single value. Failure to do so may result in an error.

SQL Example 3.9 Statement

```
SELECT DISTINCT ProductId
FROM Sales.OrderDetails
WHERE Price >
    (SELECT AVG(Price)
    FROM Sales.OrderDetails);
```

SQL Example 3.9 Output

	ProductId
1	1
2	2
3	9

SQL Example 3.10

Each product supplied by a supplier is associated with a price. Furthermore, every supplier has their own highest priced product. To accomplish this, showcase all products that have been supplied and are priced higher than the highest priced product of any supplier.

SQL Example 3.10 Analysis

Employ an inner query to determine the highest price for each product supplied by a supplier. To achieve this, a JOIN operation between the Products and Deliveries tables is necessary, enabling the usage of a GROUP BY statement on the supplier ID. In the outer query's WHERE clause, employ the ANY keyword to retain prices that surpass the highest price associated with any supplier. Additionally, it's worth noting that the keywords SOME and ALL can be applied in a similar fashion for comparable operations.

SQL Example 3.10 Statement

```sql
SELECT ProductId, Price
FROM Purchasing.Deliveries
WHERE Price > ANY
    (
        SELECT MAX(Price)
        FROM Purchasing.Deliveries AS D
            JOIN Purchasing.Products AS P
            ON D.ProductId = P.ProductId
        GROUP BY P.SupplierId
    );
```

SQL Example 3.10 Output

	ProductId	Price
1	1	1099.99
2	1	1199.99
3	2	1199.99
4	3	129.99
5	5	139.99
6	6	169.99

SQL Example 3.11

Display all products that are made in Japan (a product is made in Japan if the supplier's country is Japan). Show product IDs and product names.

SQL Example 3.11 Analysis

This example illustrates the usage of the EXISTS keyword. When the inner query successfully identifies all suppliers located in Japan, the outer query proceeds to display all products supplied by these identified suppliers. The connection between the two queries is established through the condition WHERE P.SupplierId = S.SupplierId in the inner query. A product is displayed by the outer query if the inner query evaluates to true. It's important to note that the inner query doesn't produce a specific dataset. The NOT EXISTS keyword can be employed in a similar manner to achieve a negative condition.

SQL Example 3.11 Statement

```
SELECT ProductId, ProductName
FROM Purchasing.Products AS P
WHERE EXISTS
    (
        SELECT *
        FROM Purchasing.Suppliers AS S
        WHERE P.supplierid = S.SupplierId
            AND Country = 'Japan'
    );
```

SQL Example 3.11 Output

	ProductId	ProductName
1	4	Wireless Color Photo Printer
2	9	20.2 MP Digital Camera

SQL Example 3.12

Display all customer IDs, names, and contacts that were served by employees with first names that start with letter B.

SQL Example 3.12 Analysis

This example further illustrates the application of the EXISTS keyword. In this case, the outer query is designed to exhibit customer ID, name, and contract information from the customers table when the inner query exists or evaluates to true. The inner query, in turn, is responsible for identifying all employees whose first names commence with the letter "B." Notably, the connection between the customers and employees tables is facilitated through their association with the Orders table, and thus, the inner query involves a

JOIN operation between the Orders and Employees tables.

SQL Example 3.12 Statement

```
SELECT CustomerId, CustomerName, Contact
FROM Sales.Customers AS C
WHERE EXISTS
     (SELECT * FROM Sales.Orders AS O
          JOIN HR.Employees AS E
          ON O.EmployeeId = E.EmployeeId
          WHERE C.CustomerId = O.CustomerId
              AND E.FirstName LIKE 'B%');
```

SQL Example 3.12 Output

	CustomerId	CustomerName	Contact
1	1	Just Electronics	John White
2	2	Beyond Electronics	Scott Green
3	4	E Fun	Ben Gold

Review Question 3.27
A query can be used in another query. The former is often called ______ query and the latter query is often called the ______ query.
a. inner, outer
b. outer, inner
c. first, second
d. second, first

Review Question 3.28
For a subquery that uses comparison operator (e.g. >, =, <, !=), make sure the inner query returns ______. Otherwise, an error will occur.
a. a single value
b. exactly two values
c. more than two values
d. the data type that matches the outer query

Review Question 3.29
A ______ is a query that can be embedded within another query.
a. embed
b. subquery
c. within query
d. wrapped query

Review Question 3.30
The database management system (DBMS) executes ______.
a. the inner query or outer query based on the sequence it appears in the code
b. the inner query and outer query simultaneously
c. the inner query before the outer query
d. the inner query after the outer query

Review Question 3.31
Consider the task of retrieving all products from domestic suppliers for LifeStyle LLC. To accomplish this, we can employ a subquery to first select all domestic supplier IDs from the suppliers table (the _______). Subsequently, we use an _______ to identify all products provided by those domestic suppliers.
a. inner query, outer query
b. inner query, inner query
c. outer query, inner query
d. outer query, outer query

Review Question 3.32
In the following statement:
```
SELECT ProductId, ProductName
FROM Purchasing.Products AS P
WHERE EXISTS
    (
        SELECT *
        FROM Purchasing.Suppliers AS S
        WHERE P.supplierid = S.SupplierId
            AND Country = 'Japan'
    );
```
How are the connection between the two queries is established?
a. SELECT ProductId, ProductName
b. FROM Purchasing.Products AS P
c. WHERE EXISTS
d. WHERE P.SupplierId = S.SupplierId

Review Question 3.33
What will the following clause, `WHERE FirstName LIKE 'B%'` do?
a. The person whose first name likes B.
b. The person whose first name looks like B.
c. The first name contains letter B.
d. The first name begins with letter B.

3.6 Utilizing Subqueries in the SELECT Clause

Subqueries can be employed in a variety of contexts where an expression is required. This includes their use in the SELECT clause, where a column expression is typically utilized. Here are some contexts where using subqueries in the SELECT clause can be particularly valuable:

1. *Calculations and Aggregations*: Subqueries can be used to calculate or aggregate values from related tables and include these results in the result set. For instance, you can calculate the total sales for each customer by summing up individual sales from a linked Sales table.

2. *Data Transformation*: Subqueries enable you to transform data to meet specific reporting needs. You can, for example, convert codes or IDs into meaningful descriptions by looking up related reference tables.

3. *Conditional Display*: Subqueries in the SELECT clause can control whether a specific column is displayed based on certain conditions. This allows you to dynamically include or exclude columns based on the outcome of the subquery.

4. *Ranking and Sorting*: Subqueries can assist in ranking or sorting rows based on criteria that may involve aggregations or comparisons. For instance, you can rank products within each category based on their sales performance.

5. *Derived Columns*: Subqueries are helpful when you need to derive additional columns in your result set. These derived columns might represent calculated values, percentages, or other meaningful insights from the data.

However, it's vital to remember that when utilizing subqueries in the SELECT clause, the inner query should always return a scalar (single) value for each row generated by the outer query. This ensures the subquery's output aligns with the expectations of the SELECT clause and enhances the overall quality of the result set.

SQL Example 3.13

Display order ID 2 details, including total quantity in the order.

SQL Example 3.13 Analysis

Add a column in the SELECT clause that shows the total quantity in the order.

SQL Example 3.13 Statement

```sql
SELECT OrderId, ProductId, Quantity,
    (SELECT SUM(Quantity)
        from Sales.OrderDetails
        WHERE OrderId = 2)
    AS "Total Quantity"
FROM Sales.OrderDetails
WHERE OrderId = 2;
```

SQL Example 3.13 Output

	OrderId	ProductId	Quantity	Total Quantity
1	2	1	1	13
2	2	2	1	13
3	2	4	6	13
4	2	6	5	13

Review Question 3.34
A subquery can be used in a SELECT clause where a column expression is expected. Just make sure the inner query returns a ______ for each row that is returned by the outer query.
a. a single value
b. exactly two values
c. more than two values
d. the same value

Review Question 3.35
In the SELECT clause, subqueries can be effectively used for which of the following purposes?
a. Sorting rows based on multiple criteria
b. Calculating and aggregating values from related tables
c. Dynamically renaming column headers
d. Deleting rows that meet specific conditions

Review Question 3.36
Subqueries can assist in data transformation within the SELECT clause. What is one example of data transformation using subqueries?
a. Deleting unnecessary rows
b. Reordering columns
c. Converting codes or IDs into meaningful descriptions
d. Merging multiple tables into one

Review Question 3.37
How can subqueries in the SELECT clause impact the display of columns in the result set?
a. They can dynamically include or exclude columns based on specific conditions.
b. They can reorder the columns in the result set.
c. They can apply formatting to numeric columns.
d. They can concatenate text values in a single column.

Review Question 3.38
In what scenario might you use subqueries to rank or sort rows in the SELECT clause?
a. When you need to delete rows that meet specific criteria
b. When you want to join multiple tables together
c. When you need to calculate average values
d. When you want to rank products based on specific criteria

Review Question 3.39
Derived columns in the SELECT clause refer to:
a. Columns that are automatically generated by the DBMS
b. Columns that are imported from external sources
c. Additional columns created using subqueries to represent calculated values or insights
d. Columns that are flagged as primary keys in a table

Review Question 3.40
What is a crucial requirement when using subqueries in the SELECT clause?
a. The inner query should return multiple values for each row generated by the outer query.
b. The inner query should return a table with multiple columns.
c. The inner query should return a scalar (single) value for each row generated by the outer query.
d. The inner query should return a boolean value indicating a match.

3.7 Utilizing Subqueries in UPDATE, DELETE, and INSERT

In T-SQL, subqueries prove to be invaluable not only in SELECT statements but also in various other SQL operations, including UPDATE, DELETE, and INSERT statements. Let's explore the utilization of subqueries in these contexts.

An UPDATE statement is frequently used to modify existing records in a table. It typically includes a WHERE clause to specify which rows should be updated. Here, subqueries come into play as they can be employed within the WHERE clause of an UPDATE statement. For instance, you may use a subquery to determine the records that need to be updated based on certain conditions, making the UPDATE operation more precise and targeted.

DELETE statements are used to remove records from a table. Just as with UPDATE statements, subqueries can be integrated into the WHERE clause of a DELETE statement. This enables you to specify the records for deletion based on specific criteria. Whether you want to remove related data or eliminate obsolete records, subqueries can refine the process.

INSERT statements are utilized to add new records into a table. While subqueries are not directly used within INSERT statements as they are in UPDATE and DELETE statements, they can be an essential part of the data that you're inserting. You can use a subquery to retrieve data from other tables and insert it into the target table, enriching the newly added records with information from elsewhere in the database.

SQL Example 3.14

Customer ID 1 placed an order on May 3, 2017, which includes six units of Product ID 3 at the price of $149.99. The correct quantity should be sixteen units of Product ID 3. Provide an SQL statement to update the record.

SQL Example 3.14 Analysis

Utilize a subquery to retrieve the Order ID associated with the customer, and then apply the outer query to update the OrderDetails table. Be sure to reset the database to its original data before proceeding with other examples.

SQL Example 3.14 Statement

```
UPDATE Sales.OrderDetails
```

```
SET Quantity = 16
WHERE ProductId = 3
    AND Price = 149.99
    AND OrderId =
        (SELECT OrderId
        FROM Sales.Orders
        WHERE CustomerId = 1
        AND OrderDate = '20170503');
```

SQL Example 3.14 Output

```
(1 row(s) affected)
```

You can check the record being updated by issuing:

```
SELECT * FROM Sales.OrderDetails;
```

Review Question 3.41
You are least likely to find a subquery in which of the following clause?
a. SELECT
b. FROM
c. WHERE
d. ORDER BY

Review Question 3.42
Subqueries in T-SQL are primarily used in which types of SQL operations?
a. SELECT, UPDATE, INSERT, and DELETE statements
b. SELECT statements only
c. INSERT and DELETE statements
d. INSERT and UPDATE statements

Review Question 3.43
In the context of an UPDATE statement, where are subqueries typically utilized?
a. In the SET clause
b. In the FROM clause
c. In the WHERE clause
d. In the VALUES clause

Review Question 3.44
When using subqueries in DELETE statements, what is their primary function?
a. To define the columns to be deleted
b. To specify the ORDER BY clause
c. To determine the records to be deleted based on specific criteria
d. To create new records to replace the deleted ones

Review Question 3.45
How are subqueries incorporated into INSERT statements?
a. Subqueries replace the WHERE clause in INSERT statements.
b. Subqueries are used directly in the INSERT INTO clause.
c. Subqueries cannot be used in INSERT statements.
d. Subqueries are employed to retrieve data for insertion from other tables.

Review Question 3.46
How are subqueries incorporated into INSERT statements?
a. Subqueries replace the VALUES clause in INSERT statements.
b. Subqueries are used directly in the INSERT INTO clause.
c. Subqueries cannot be used in INSERT statements.
d. Subqueries are employed to replace the WHERE clause in INSERT statements.

Review Question 3.47
Which of the following SQL operations do not directly utilize subqueries?
a. DELETE statements
b. CREATE statements
c. SELECT statements
d. UPDATE statements

Review Question 3.48
What is the primary advantage of using subqueries in SQL operations like UPDATE and DELETE statements?
a. They simplify the SQL syntax.
b. They can eliminate the need for WHERE clauses.
c. They make the operations more precise and targeted.
d. They enable the modification of table structures.

3.8 Correlated Subquery

A correlated subquery is a powerful concept where a subquery refers to the attributes or values of the outer query. In other words, it is a subquery that is executed for each row processed by the outer query. This provides a dynamic and interrelated way to retrieve data from the database.

Imagine you have a database with customers and their orders. Each customer may have multiple orders, and each order has a specific value. You want to determine what percentage each order contributes to the total value of each customer's orders. This is a typical scenario where correlated subqueries can be applied effectively.

In this case, you need to find each customer's total order value and then relate it to the value of each individual order. The key aspect is that the customer ID changes as you iterate through each customer in the outer query. With correlated subqueries, you can dynamically calculate percentages for each order without specifying individual customer IDs or values in the subquery. This illustrates the power and flexibility of correlated subqueries in T-SQL. Please note that while correlated subqueries can be powerful, they can also be slow and should be used judiciously.

SQL Example 3.15

Display the customer ID, order ID, order date, order total, and the percentage of the order total in relation to the customer's overall total.

SQL Example 3.15 Analysis

The inner query calculates the total for each customer. For instance, the following statement retrieves the total order value for Customer ID 1:

```
SELECT SUM(Price * Quantity) FROM Sales.OrderDetails AS OD JOIN Sales.Orders AS O ON OD.OrderId
= O.OrderId WHERE O.CustomerId = 1;
```

By replacing the "1" in the above statement with the customer ID from the outer query, the customer's total can dynamically change to another customer's total as the outer query's customer ID changes.

Since both the inner and outer queries involve joining three tables, it presents an ideal scenario for using a Common Table Expression (CTE) that effectively joins all three tables (Customers, Orders, and OrderDetails).

SQL Example 3.15 Statement

```
WITH CustomerOrder (CustomerId, OrderId, OrderDate, OrderTotal) AS
(
    SELECT O.CustomerId, O.OrderId, O.OrderDate, SUM(Price * Quantity)
    FROM Sales.Orders AS O JOIN Sales.OrderDetails AS OD
    ON O.OrderId = OD.OrderId
    GROUP BY O.CustomerId, O.OrderId, O.OrderDate
)
SELECT CO1.CustomerId, CO1.OrderId, CO1.OrderDate, CO1.OrderTotal,
    CAST(100.0 * OrderTotal/
    (SELECT SUM(CO2.OrderTotal)
    FROM CustomerOrder AS CO2
    WHERE CO2.CustomerId = CO1.CustomerId)
    AS NUMERIC(5, 2))
    AS Percentage
FROM CustomerOrder AS CO1
ORDER BY CO1.CustomerId, CO1.OrderId;
```

SQL Example 3.15 Output

	CustomerId	OrderId	OrderDate	OrderTotal	Percentage
1	1	1	2017-01-03	1799.97	22.64
2	1	2	2017-03-05	4649.87	58.49
3	1	5	2017-05-03	1499.91	18.87
4	2	3	2017-02-23	2329.92	100.00
5	3	6	2017-05-08	1499.99	100.00
6	4	4	2017-04-13	269.97	100.00
7	5	7	2016-11-08	999.99	100.00
8	7	8	2016-12-23	199.97	100.00

Review Question 3.49

A(n) _______ subquery is a subquery that refers to the attributes of the outer query.
a. correlated
b. inner
c. update
d. insert

Review Question 3.50
What is a correlated subquery in T-SQL?
a. A subquery that is unrelated to the outer query
b. A subquery that is executed once for all rows in the outer query
c. A subquery that refers to the attributes or values of the outer query and is executed for each row processed by the outer query
d. A subquery used exclusively in SELECT statements

Review Question 3.51
In what context can correlated subqueries be effectively applied (best used for)?
a. Determining decimal place for values in a dataset
b. Retrieving data from unrelated tables
c. Calculating the percentage of each order relative to the total value of each customer's orders
d. Filtering rows based on simple criteria

Review Question 3.52
What is the primary benefit of using correlated subqueries in the book example?
a. They simplify the SQL syntax.
b. They eliminate the need for the outer query.
c. They allow you to specify individual customer IDs and values in the subquery.
d. They provide a dynamic and context-aware way to calculate percentages.

Review Question 3.53
In the context of LifeStyleDB, when using correlated subqueries to calculate percentages for each order, what is the key aspect to consider?
a. The number of columns in the subquery
b. The use of subqueries in DELETE statements
c. The dynamic change in the customer ID as the outer query iterates through customers
d. The total number of orders in the database

Review Question 3.54
What aspect of correlated subqueries makes them a versatile and powerful tool in T-SQL?
a. Their ability to simplify SQL syntax
b. Their elimination of the need for an outer query
c. Their capability to reference the attributes or values of the outer query
d. Their exclusive use in SELECT statements

Review Question 3.55
Which of the following statements best describes an important consideration when working with correlated subqueries in T-SQL?
a. Correlated subqueries are always faster than non-correlated subqueries.
b. Correlated subqueries are typically used to replace the need for an outer query.
c. Correlated subqueries can be powerful but may introduce performance challenges and should be used judiciously.

d. Correlated subqueries are primarily used in UPDATE statements.

3.9 Chapter Summary

In this chapter, you were introduced to Common Table Expressions (CTE), a valuable tool for addressing more complex problems. CTE enables you to temporarily store a result set for further use and enhances the clarity of your SQL statements. Additionally, you delved into Recursive CTE, a potent technique that empowers SQL statements to retrieve interrelated data effectively.

You also explored subqueries, which are instrumental in crafting easily comprehensible SQL statements. Subqueries can be integrated into SELECT, WHERE, UPDATE, INSERT, DELETE, and even the FROM clause, much like CTE. Furthermore, you were introduced to the concept of correlated subqueries, a powerful technique that establishes a relationship between inner and outer queries, providing a dynamic and context-aware approach to data retrieval.

3.10 Discussion

Discussion 3.1

If you do not know anything about CTE, you can still solve several of the problems in this chapter that use CTE. Do you really need to learn CTE? Answer the question by explaining what CTE is and your opinions on the benefits of using it.

Discussion 3.2

Recursive CTE is a CTE that refers to itself. Many beginners have difficulties understanding this topic. Explain in your own words how recursive CTE works with an example.

Discussion 3.3

Subqueries are queries in other queries. In this chapter we only nest a subquery once. In fact, T-SQL allows multiple levels of nesting. Explain how subqueries work and whether we should use multiple level of nesting.

Discussion 3.4

Correlated subquery is a subquery that refers to the attributes of the outer query. Many beginners have difficulties understanding this topic. Explain in your own words how correlated subquery works with an example.

3.11 SQL Exercises

Exercise 3.1

Use CTE to display number of orders placed by each customer for each year.

	CustomerId	CustomerName	Number of Orders	OrderYear
1	5	Overstock E	1	2016
2	7	Electronics4U	1	2016
3	1	Just Electronics	3	2017
4	2	Beyond Electronics	1	2017
5	3	Beyond Electronics	1	2017
6	4	E Fun	1	2017

Exercise 3.2

Display number of employees involved in customer orders each year.

	OrderYear	Number of Employees
1	2016	2
2	2017	4

Exercise 3.3

Display each customer's total order value (Price * Quantity). If the customer is from the state of CA, add 10% sales tax.

	CustomerId	CustomerName	Total with Tax
1	1	Just Electronics	7949.75
2	2	Beyond Electronics	2329.92
3	3	Beyond Electronics	1499.99
4	4	E Fun	269.97
5	5	Overstock E	1099.99
6	7	Electronics4U	199.97

Exercise 3.4

Display all employee's ID, name, and if he or she handled an order during 2017, show 2017. If not, show null.

	EmployeeId	EmployeeName	OrderYear
1	3	Maria Law	2017
2	4	Alice Law	2017
3	5	Black Hart	2017
4	6	Christina Robinson	2017
5	1	Alex Hall	NULL
6	2	Dianne Hart	NULL
7	7	Nicholas Pinkston	NULL

Exercise 3.5

List all employees who were born on January 1, 1980 or earlier and the customers they helped in 2016. If an employee did not handle any order in 2016 show null.

	EmployeeName	CustomerName	Customer Contact
1	Dianne Hart	Electronics4U	Grace Smith
2	Christina Robinson	NULL	NULL
3	Nicholas Pinkston	Overstock E	Daniel Yellow

Exercise 3.6

Show total sales value for each year and the increase or decrease from the previous year.

	Year	SalesVlue	Increase/Decrease from last year
1	2017	12049.63	10849.67

Exercise 3.7

Display all supervisors and subordinators of employee ID 2.

	EmployeeId	ManagerId	FirstName	LastName
1	2	1	Dianne	Hart
2	5	2	Black	Hart
3	6	2	Christina	Robinson

Exercise 3.8

Use subqueries only to display all products purchased by a customer whose state abbreviation's second letter is 'A' (e.g. CA, MA).

	ProductId	ProductName
1	1	65-Inch 4K Ultra HD Smart TV
2	2	60-Inch 4K Ultra HD Smart LED TV
3	4	Wireless Color Photo Printer
4	8	GPS Android Tablet PC

Exercise 3.9

Display all products with above average delivery price. Show product ID.

	ProductId
1	1
2	2

Exercise 3.10

Each product in an order has a price. Each order has a highest priced product. Display all products that are more expensive than any other order's highest priced product.

	OrderId	ProductId	Price
1	1	1	1499.99
2	1	3	149.99
3	2	1	1499.99
4	2	2	1599.99
5	2	4	99.99
6	2	6	189.99
7	3	3	159.99
8	3	6	199.99
9	3	7	109.99
10	3	9	1449.99
11	4	4	99.99
12	5	3	149.99
13	5	6	199.99
14	6	1	1499.99
15	7	2	999.99

Exercise 3.11

Use EXISTS keyword, display all customers that purchased before January 1, 2017.

	CustomerId	CustomerName
1	5	Overstock E
2	7	Electronics4U

Exercise 3.12

Use EXISTS keyword, display all products that have been sold to foreign customers. Show product IDs and names.

	ProductId	ProductName
1	7	10" 16GB Android Tablet
2	8	GPS Android Tablet PC

Exercise 3.13

Display all orders with order ID, total quantity in each order, and average quantity in all orders.

	OrderId	Quantity in Order	Total Quantity
1	1	3	41
2	2	13	41
3	3	8	41
4	4	3	41
5	5	9	41
6	6	1	41
7	7	1	41
8	8	3	41

Exercise 3.14

Employee ID 2 helped Customer ID 7 on December 23, 2016, which includes one unit of Product ID 7 at the price of 79.99. It should be 2 units of product ID 3 at the price of 78.99. Write an SQL statement to update the record.

You may need to reset the database afterwards so that you have the same data to match the examples for the remaining examples of the book.

Exercise 3.15

Display supplier ID, supplier name, delivery ID, delivery date, delivery total, and percent of the delivery total out of the supplier's total.

	SupplierId	DeliveryId	DeliveryDate	DeliveryTotal	Percentage
1	2	6	2016-10-07	2099.85	33.07
2	2	7	2016-10-10	4249.75	66.93
3	3	4	2016-10-05	1299.90	100.00
4	4	1	2016-10-01	2199.98	9.81
5	4	2	2016-11-01	5999.95	26.76
6	4	3	2016-10-02	11999.90	53.52
7	4	8	2016-10-11	959.88	4.28
8	4	9	2016-10-12	1259.82	5.62
9	5	5	2016-10-07	1599.80	100.00

3.12 Solutions to the Review Questions

3.1 D; 3.2 C; 3.3 B; 3.4 C; 3.5 A; 3.6 B; 3.7 D; 3.8 C; 3.9 C; 3.10 C; 3.11 A; 3.12 D; 3.13 B; 3.14 A; 3.15 D;

3.16 D; 3.17 A; 3.18 B; 3.19 D; 3.20 C; 3.21 C; 3.22 C; 3.23 C; 3.24 C; 3.25 A; 3.26 C; 3.27 A; 3.28 A; 3.29 B;

3.30 C; 3.31 A; 3.32 D; 3.33 D; 3.34 A; 3.35 B; 3.36 C; 3.37 A; 3.38 D; 3.39 C; 3.40 C; 3.41 D; 3.42 A; 3.43 C; 3.44 C; 3.45 D; 3.46 A; 3.47 B; 3.48 C; 3.49 A; 3.50 C; 3.51 C; 3.52 D; 3.53 C; 3.54 C; 3.55 C;

CHAPTER 4: WINDOW FUNCTIONS AND RANKING

Chapter Learning Objectives

4.1 Describe the distinctions between aggregate functions and window functions in T-SQL.
4.2 Summarize the applications of window-partition, window-order by, and window-framing.
4.3 Execute the functions RANK(), DENSE_RANK(), ROW_NUMBER(), and NTILE().
4.4 Employ offset window functions to perform advanced data analysis and exploration in T-SQL.
4.5 Construct a comparative analysis differentiating CUBE() and ROLLUP() for summarizing data in SQL.

4.1 Window Functions

Consider a table called FamilyIncome, which contains data about various families and their individual incomes. It may look something like this:

Family	Person	Income
1	1	100k
1	2	90k
2	1	80k

To determine the total income for each family, you can use the following SQL statement:

```
SELECT Family, SUM(Income)
FROM FamilyIncome
GROUP BY Family;
```

The result set of the above statement will be as follows:

Family	Income
1	190k
2	80k

But what if you need to display both individual incomes and family income in the same SELECT statement?

With the knowledge you've acquired so far, achieving this in a single query is not possible. In other words, you cannot use a single SELECT statement to simultaneously show individual incomes and the family's total income, as demonstrated below:

Family	Person	Income	Running total
1	1	100k	100k
1	2	90k	190k
2	1	80k	80k

The solution to this problem lies in the use of window functions.

A window function in T-SQL is a function that returns a scalar value for a set of rows and includes it in a new column. Consequently, it enables the display of both individual rows and summary values in the output. Window functions provide more detailed information than aggregate functions combined with a GROUP BY clause. This set of rows collectively forms what is known as a "window." In the example of family income mentioned earlier, each family represents a window. In the limited dataset, the first window comprises the first two rows, while the second window consists of the third row.

To specify the set of rows for window functions, the OVER() function is employed. For instance, consider the following statement:

```
SELECT Family, Person, SUM(Income) OVER()
FROM FamilyIncome;
```

This statement yields the following result set:

Family	Person	Income
1	1	270k
1	2	270k
2	1	270k

A basic OVER() includes all the underlying rows. To restrict the subset of rows to each family, you can use the window-partition clause (PARTITION BY). Take the following statement as an example:

```
SELECT Family, Person, SUM(Income) OVER(PARTITION BY Family)
FROM FamilyIncome;
```

This statement produces the following result set:

Family	Person	Income
1	1	190k
1	2	190k
2	1	80k

The OVER() function can also include a window-order by clause (ORDER BY), which specifies the order in which rows are considered when calculating aggregates. Adding a window-order by clause to the previous example results in the following statement:

```
SELECT Family, Person, SUM(Income) OVER(PARTITION BY Family ORDER BY Person)
FROM FamilyIncome;
```

The result set for this statement is as follows:

Family	Person	Income
1	1	100k
1	2	190k
2	1	80k

In the aboe statement, the PARTITION BY divides the result set into partitions or groups based on the specified column(s). Window functions that include PARTITION BY perform their calculations independently within each partition. On the other hand, the ORDER BY specifies the order in which rows are processed within the window frame of each partition.

It defines how the rows are logically arranged before the window function's calculations are performed. Window functions, therefore, offer a dynamic way to retrieve data, providing valuable insights and flexibility when working with complex datasets.

SQL Example 4.1

Show the employee's monthly sales values for the year 2017, and provide a cumulative total for each employee. Present the employee ID, the respective month, the sales value for that month, and the ongoing cumulative total for the employee.

SQL Example 4.1 Analysis

The required data will be sourced from two tables: the 'orders' table and the 'orderdetails' table. To facilitate this, you can employ a Common Table Expression (CTE) to consolidate all the necessary information. Next, utilize the outer SELECT statement with the OVER() function to calculate the running total.

SQL Example 4.1 Statement

```
WITH EmployeeSales(EmployeeId, OrderMonth, MonthlyTotal) AS
(
    SELECT O.EmployeeId, MONTH(O.OrderDate), SUM(OD.Price * OD.Quantity)
    FROM Sales.Orders AS O JOIN Sales.OrderDetails AS OD
    ON O.OrderId = OD.Orderid
    WHERE YEAR(O.OrderDate) = 2017
```

```
    GROUP BY O.EmployeeId, MONTH(O.OrderDate)
)
SELECT EmployeeId, OrderMonth, MonthlyTotal,
    SUM(MonthlyTotal) OVER (PARTITION BY EmployeeId
        ORDER BY OrderMonth)
        AS "Employee Running Total"
FROM EmployeeSales;
```

SQL Example 4.1 Output

	EmployeeId	OrderMonth	MonthlyTotal	Employee Running Total
1	3	3	4649.87	4649.87
2	4	5	1499.91	1499.91
3	5	1	1799.97	1799.97
4	5	2	2329.92	4129.89
5	5	4	269.97	4399.86
6	6	5	1499.99	1499.99

SQL Example 4.2

Display the total quantity sold after each order is placed, showing the Order ID and quantity running total.

SQL Example 4.2 Analysis

First, use a CTE to select the order ID and the total order quantity. Then, employ the OVER() function along with the ORDER BY clause to calculate the running total for each order.

SQL Example 4.2 Statement

```
WITH OrderCount (OrderId, TotalQuantity) AS
(
    SELECT OrderId, SUM(Quantity)
    FROM Sales.OrderDetails
    GROUP BY OrderId
)
SELECT OrderId, SUM(TotalQuantity) OVER (ORDER BY OrderId) AS "Running Total Quantity"
FROM OrderCount
```

SQL Example 4.2 Output

	OrderId	Running Total Quantity
1	1	3
2	2	16
3	3	24
4	4	27
5	5	36
6	6	37
7	7	38
8	8	41

Review Question 4.1
What is the issue with the following SQL stateemnt assuming all tables and column names are correct?
SELECT Family, SUM(Income)
FROM FamilyIncome
GROUP BY Family;
a. It will not execute
b. It should remove GROUP BY to make it work
c. It hides the details of the group member
d. It won't show correct answer for single member family

Review Question 4.2
A(n) _______ function is a T-SQL function that will return a scalar value over a set of rows in a new column.
a. aggregate
b. summary
c. window
d. group

Review Question 4.3
Window function returns a scalar value over a set of rows. These set of rows are collectively called a(n) ____.
a. window
b. over() function
c. range() function
d. aggregate function

Review Question 4.4
The window functions provide more details than an aggregate function with _______ clause/function.
a. WINDOW
b. WINDOWS
c. GROUP BY
d. OVER

Review Question 4.5
The window functions in Trasnsact-SQL are called using the ________ clause.
a. WINDOW
b. WINDOWS
c. GROUP BY
d. OVER

Review Question 4.6
In a window function, a(n) _______ function can be used to specify the set of rows.
a. RECORDS()
b. SET()
c. OVER()
d. NUMBER()

Review Question 4.7
Which clause is often used together with OVER() function to limit the subset of the rows?
a. SUBSET BY
b. PARTITION BY
c. ORDER BY

d. GROUP BY

Review Question 4.8
The OVER() function can include a window _______ clause which will specify which rows to visit when the aggregates are calculated.
a. SUBSET BY
b. PARTITION BY
c. ORDER BY
d. GROUP BY

Review Question 4.9
Given a table named FamilyIncome with Family, Person, and Income columns, what is the purpose of the SQL statement SELECT Family, SUM(Income) FROM FamilyIncome GROUP BY Family;?
a. Display individual incomes.
b. Calculate the total income for each family.
c. Combine family and person data.
d. Show running totals for each family.

Review Question 4.10
Why is it not possible to use a single SELECT statement to show both individual incomes and the family's total income?
a. Lack of SQL knowledge.
b. Limitations of the GROUP BY clause.
c. SQL syntax restrictions.
d. Incompatibility of aggregate and window functions.

Review Question 4.11
What is the purpose of a window function in T-SQL?
a. Perform calculations for each row within a specific window or set of rows.
b. Calculate the total income for each family.
c. Group rows based on a specified column.
d. Sort rows in a result set.

Review Question 4.12
In the context of family income data of the book, what does a "window" represent?
a. A group of tables.
b. A specific SQL query.
c. A set of rows.
d. A database schema.

Review Question 4.13
What function is used to specify the set of rows for window functions in T-SQL?
a. PARTITION BY
b. GROUP BY
c. SORT BY
d. OVER BY

Review Question 4.14
Given a table with Family, Person, and Income columns, what does the SQL statement SELECT Family, Person, SUM(Income) OVER(PARTITION BY Family) do?

a. Calculate the total income for each family.
b. Calculate the total income for each person.
c. Group data by person.
d. Display individual incomes.

Review Question 4.15
What does the ORDER BY clause in a window function determine?
a. The total number of rows in the result set.
b. The logical order of rows within the window frame.
c. The number of partitions in the result set.
d. The SQL query's execution order.

Review Question 4.16
When using the OVER() function, what does a basic OVER() include?
a. All rows in the result set.
b. Only rows that meet specific conditions.
c. A subset of rows based on the ORDER BY clause.
d. Partitions determined by the PARTITION BY clause.

Review Question 4.17
What is the role of the PARTITION BY clause in a window function?
a. It specifies the order of rows.
b. It defines the logical grouping of rows.
c. It restricts the subset of rows to each family.
d. It combines data from multiple tables.

Review Question 4.18
What flexibility do window functions offer when working with complex datasets?
a. The ability to combine data from different tables.
b. The power to replace aggregate functions.
c. A dynamic way to retrieve data, offering valuable insights.
d. A mechanism for creating complex queries.

4.2 Ranking Window Functions

In T-SQL, there are four essential ranking window functions: RANK(), DENSE_RANK(), ROW_NUMBER(), and NTILE(). These functions allow you to perform ranking operations on result sets based on specific criteria.

RANK() is one of these functions, and it is used to assign a ranking to rows in the result set. To determine the ranking, you use the OVER() function in conjunction with the ORDER BY clause, specifying which column to rank by. When there is a tie, meaning multiple rows have the same value and deserve the same rank, the RANK() function will assign the same ranking to those tied rows. However, it will skip the ranking number after the tie, resulting in rankings like 1, 2, 3, 3, 5.

DENSE_RANK() is another ranking window function, closely resembling RANK(). The key distinction is that DENSE_RANK() will not skip ranking values when there are ties. For the example in the RANK() above, the ranking would appear as 1, 2, 3, 3, 4 rather than 1, 2, 3, 3, 5 like in RANK().

ROW_NUMBER() is the third ranking window function, and it differs from RANK() and DENSE_RANK. It assigns a unique incremental sequential integer to each row in the result set without considering ties. To ensure its functionality, you must use an ORDER BY clause. It's essential to note that if the ORDER BY clause does not return a unique set, the results produced by ROW_NUMBER() may be non-deterministic. In other words, the same SQL statement may yield different results under such circumstances.

The fourth T-SQL ranking window function, NTILE(), shares some similarities with ROW_NUMBER (e.g. non-deterministic). It assigns an incremental sequential integer to each block of rows, and each block typically contains an equal number of rows, except for the last block, which may have fewer rows. These blocks are often referred to as "tiles." You have control over the number of tiles, but the database management system (DBMS) determines the size of each tile.

Notably, ROW_NUMBER() is a specific case of NTILE() in which the number of tiles is equal to the number of rows in the result set, ensuring that each row receives a unique integer.

SQL Example 4.3

Rank quantity of products in each order from high to low.

SQL Example 4.3 Analysis

First use a CTE to select the order ID and total quantity in each order. Then use RANK() OVER (ORDER BY) to rank. Just note that we want the larger quantity to have a higher ranking. So, we should use DESC in the ORDER BY clause.

SQL Example 4.3 Statement

```sql
WITH OrderCount (OrderId, TotalQuantity) AS
(
    SELECT OrderId, SUM(Quantity)
    FROM Sales.OrderDetails
    GROUP BY OrderId
)
SELECT OrderId, TotalQuantity, RANK() OVER (ORDER BY TotalQuantity DESC) AS Rank
FROM OrderCount;
```

SQL Example 4.3 Output

	OrderId	TotalQuantity	Rank
1	2	13	1
2	5	9	2
3	3	8	3
4	4	3	4
5	1	3	4
6	8	3	4
7	6	1	7
8	7	1	7

SQL Example 4.4

In the same context as demonstrated in SQL Example 4.3, rank the quantity of products in each order from high to low, but this time, employ DENSE_RANK().

SQL Example 4.4 Analysis

The SQL statement is almost the same as that in SQL Example 4.3. Just replace RANK() with DENSE_RANK().

SQL Example 4.4 Statement

```
WITH OrderCount (OrderId, TotalQuantity) AS
(
    SELECT OrderId, SUM(Quantity)
    FROM Sales.OrderDetails
    GROUP BY OrderId
)
SELECT OrderId, TotalQuantity, DENSE_RANK()
    OVER (ORDER BY TotalQuantity DESC) AS "Quantity Dense Rank"
FROM OrderCount;
```

SQL Example 4.4 Output

	OrderId	TotalQuantity	Quantity Dense Rank
1	2	13	1
2	5	9	2
3	3	8	3
4	4	3	4
5	1	3	4
6	8	3	4
7	6	1	5
8	7	1	5

SQL Example 4.5

In a scenario identical to SQL Example 4.3, rank the quantity of products in each order from lowest to highest by assigning a row number to each row in the result set.

SQL Example 4.5 Analysis

The SQL statement is almost the same as in SQL Example 4.3 and 4.4 (No DESC this time). Just replace RANK() or DENSE_RANK() with ROW_NUMBER()

SQL Example 4.5 Statement

```
WITH OrderCount (OrderId, TotalQuantity) AS
(
    SELECT OrderId, SUM(Quantity)
    FROM Sales.OrderDetails
    GROUP BY OrderId
)
SELECT OrderId, TotalQuantity, ROW_NUMBER()
    OVER (ORDER BY TotalQuantity) AS "Row number"
FROM OrderCount;
```

SQL Example 4.5 Output

	OrderId	TotalQuantity	Row number
1	6	1	1
2	7	1	2
3	8	3	3
4	1	3	4
5	4	3	5
6	3	8	6
7	5	9	7
8	2	13	8

SQL Example 4.6

In a scenario similar to SQL Example 4.5, rank the quantity of products in each order from lowest to highest by assigning a tile number in the result set. Divide the entire result set into three tiles.

SQL Example 4.6 Analysis

The SQL statement is almost the same as SQL Example 4.3 and 4.4. Just replace ROW_NUMBER() with NTILE(3).

SQL Example 4.6 Statement

```
WITH OrderCount (OrderId, TotalQuantity) AS
(
    SELECT OrderId, SUM(Quantity)
    FROM Sales.OrderDetails
    GROUP BY OrderId
)
SELECT OrderId, TotalQuantity, NTILE(3)
    OVER (ORDER BY TotalQuantity) AS "Tile number"
FROM OrderCount;
```

SQL Example 4.6 Output

	OrderId	TotalQuantity	Tile number
1	6	1	1
2	7	1	1
3	8	3	1
4	1	3	2
5	4	3	2
6	3	8	2
7	5	9	3
8	2	13	3

SQL Example 4.7

Use the four ranking window functions in the same SQL statement to see the differences among the four functions. Rank order quantities in the Sales.OrderDetails table. Make the whole result set into 3 tiles.

SQL Example 4.7 Analysis

Add all four functions using commas to separate. In the statement below, the DESC keyword is removed for easy of comparison.

SQL Example 4.7 Statement

```
WITH OrderCount (OrderId, TotalQuantity) AS
(
    SELECT OrderId, SUM(Quantity)
    FROM Sales.OrderDetails
    GROUP BY OrderId
)
SELECT OrderId, TotalQuantity,
    RANK() OVER (ORDER BY TotalQuantity) AS "Quantity Rank",
    DENSE_RANK() OVER (ORDER BY TotalQuantity) AS "Quantity Dense Rank",
    ROW_NUMBER() OVER (ORDER BY TotalQuantity) AS "Row number",
    NTILE(3) OVER (ORDER BY TotalQuantity) AS "Tile number"
FROM OrderCount;
```

SQL Example 4.7 Output

	OrderId	TotalQuantity	Quantity Rank	Quantity Dense Rank	Row number	Tile number
1	6	1	1	1	1	1
2	7	1	1	1	2	1
3	8	3	3	2	3	1
4	1	3	3	2	4	2
5	4	3	3	2	5	2
6	3	8	6	3	6	2
7	5	9	7	4	7	3
8	2	13	8	5	8	3

Review Question 4.19
When there is a tie, the ______ function will return the same ranking. It will skip the ranking number after the tie. For example, a ranking may look like 1, 2, 3, 3, 5.
a. RANK()
b. DENSE_RANK()
c. ROW_NUMBER()
d. NTILE()

Review Question 4.20
The ______ function will return the distinct ranking values below the current row. For example, a ranking may look like 1, 2, 3, 3, 4.
a. RANK()
b. DENSE_RANK()
c. ROW_NUMBER()
d. NTILE()

Review Question 4.21
The ______ function assigns an incremental sequential integer to each row of the result set no matter if there is a tie. For example, a ranking may look like 1, 2, 3, 4, 5.
a. RANK()
b. DENSE_RANK()
c. ROW_NUMBER()
d. NTILE()

Review Question 4.22
Which of the following is a nondeterministic function?
a. RANK()
b. DENSE_RANK()
c. ROW_NUMBER()
d. DESC()

Review Question 4.23
Which of the following is a nondeterministic function?
a. RANK()
b. DENSE_RANK()
c. SIZE()
d. NTILE()

Review Question 4.24
The _______ function assigns an incremental sequential integer to each block of rows. Each block of rows has the same number of rows in it except for the last block, which may have fewer rows than the other blocks.
a. RANK()
b. DENSE_RANK()
c. ROW_NUMBER()
d. NTILE()

Review Question 4.25
Which T-SQL ranking window function assigns the same ranking value to tied rows and skips the ranking number after the tie?
a. RANK()
b. DENSE_RANK()
c. ROW_NUMBER()
d. NTILE()

Review Question 4.26
How does DENSE_RANK() differ from RANK() in handling tied rows?
a. DENSE_RANK() assigns the same ranking value to tied rows and skips the ranking number after the tie.
b. DENSE_RANK() will not skip ranking values when there are ties.
c. DENSE_RANK() doesn't handle tied rows.
d. DENSE_RANK() always returns 1 as the ranking value.

Review Question 4.27
Which ranking window function assigns an incremental sequential integer to each row without considering ties?
a. RANK()
b. DENSE_RANK()
c. ROW_NUMBER()
d. NTILE()

Review Question 4.28
When might the results produced by ROW_NUMBER() become non-deterministic?
a. When there are no tied rows in the result set.
b. When the ORDER BY clause returns a unique set of rows.
c. When the ORDER BY clause returns tied rows.
d. When the ORDER BY clause is not used with ROW_NUMBER().

Review Question 4.29
What is the main purpose of the NTILE() ranking window function?
a. Assigning a unique integer to each row in the result set.
b. Sorting rows in descending order.
c. Dividing rows into blocks and assigning sequential integers to those blocks.
d. Assigning the same ranking value to all rows.

Review Question 4.30
Which ranking window function ensures that each row receives a unique integer, and it is a specific case of NTILE()?
a. RANK()

b. DENSE_RANK()
c. ROW_NUMBER()
d. NTILE()

4.3 Offset Window Functions

Offset window functions in T-SQL enable you to pinpoint and retrieve rows relative to the current row. T-SQL offers four primary offset window functions: FIRST_VALUE(), LAST_VALUE(), LAG(), and LEAD.

FIRST_VALUE() returns the first row within the defined window frame. Conversely, LAST_VALUE() retrieves the last row in the window frame.

The LAG() function lets you fetch a designated number of rows preceding the current row, while the LEAD() function does the same for rows following the current row. In cases where you don't specify the number of rows, it defaults to 1.

SQL Example 4.8

Display the total quantity of products in each order, along with the customer ID, order ID, order date, and total quantity in each order. Include details for the first order and the most recent order of the customer, with the order sequence determined by the order date.

SQL Example 4.8 Analysis

Utilize a Common Table Expression (CTE) to retrieve the customer ID, order ID, order date, and total quantity in the order. Subsequently, incorporate the FIRST_VALUE() and LAST_VALUE() functions within the outer SELECT statement.

SQL Example 4.8 Statement

```sql
WITH OrderCount (CustomerId, OrderId, OrderDate, TotalQuantity) AS
(
    SELECT O.CustomerId, O.OrderId, O.OrderDate, SUM(OD.Quantity)
    FROM Sales.Orders AS O JOIN Sales.OrderDetails AS OD
    ON O.OrderId = OD.OrderId
    GROUP BY O.CustomerId, O.OrderId, O.OrderDate
)
SELECT CustomerId, OrderId, OrderDate, TotalQuantity,
    FIRST_VALUE(TotalQuantity)
        OVER(PARTITION BY CustomerId ORDER BY OrderDate, OrderId)
        AS "First Order Quantity",
    LAST_VALUE(TotalQuantity)
```

```
    OVER(PARTITION BY CustomerId ORDER BY OrderDate, OrderId
    ROWS BETWEEN CURRENT ROW AND UNBOUNDED FOLLOWING)
    AS "Most Recent Order Quantity"
FROM OrderCount;
```

SQL Example 4.8 Output

	CustomerId	OrderId	OrderDate	TotalQuantity	First Order Quantity	Most Recent Order Quantity
1	1	5	2017-05-03	9	3	9
2	1	2	2017-03-05	13	3	9
3	1	1	2017-01-03	3	3	9
4	2	3	2017-02-23	8	8	8
5	3	6	2017-05-08	1	1	1
6	4	4	2017-04-13	3	3	3
7	5	7	2016-11-08	1	1	1
8	7	8	2016-12-23	3	3	3

SQL Example 4.9

Display the total quantity of products in each order and include customer ID, order ID, order date, and total quantity in each order, the previous order, and the next order for the customer. The order sequence is determined by the order date.

SQL Example 4.9 Analysis

The only differences between examples 4.8 and 4.9 are the different functions used. This time we use LAG(TotalQuantity) for previous order quantity and LEAD(TotalQuantity) for next order quantity.

SQL Example 4.9 Statement

```
WITH OrderCount (CustomerId, OrderId, OrderDate, TotalQuantity) AS
(
    SELECT O.CustomerId, O.OrderId, O.OrderDate, SUM(OD.Quantity)
    FROM Sales.Orders AS O JOIN Sales.OrderDetails AS OD
    ON O.OrderId = OD.OrderId
    GROUP BY O.CustomerId, O.OrderId, O.OrderDate
)
SELECT CustomerId, OrderId, OrderDate, TotalQuantity,
    LAG(TotalQuantity)
        OVER(PARTITION BY CustomerId ORDER BY OrderDate, OrderId)
        AS "Previous Order Quantity",
    LEAD(TotalQuantity)
        OVER(PARTITION BY CustomerId ORDER BY OrderDate, OrderId)
        AS "Next Order Quantity"
FROM OrderCount;
```

SQL Example 4.9 Output

	CustomerId	OrderId	OrderDate	TotalQuantity	Previous Order Quantity	Next Order Quantity
1	1	1	2017-01-03	3	NULL	13
2	1	2	2017-03-05	13	3	9
3	1	5	2017-05-03	9	13	NULL
4	2	3	2017-02-23	8	NULL	NULL
5	3	6	2017-05-08	1	NULL	NULL
6	4	4	2017-04-13	3	NULL	NULL
7	5	7	2016-11-08	1	NULL	NULL
8	7	8	2016-12-23	3	NULL	NULL

SQL Example 4.10

Display the total quantity of products in each order. Show customer ID, order ID, order date, and the total quantity in each order, along with the total quantity of the order before the previous order. The order sequence is determined by the order date.

SQL Example 4.10 Analysis

Similar to Example 4.9, but introduce a second argument into the LAG() function to specify the number of rows (in this case, 2) before the current row.

SQL Example 4.10 Statement

```sql
WITH OrderCount (CustomerId, OrderId, OrderDate, TotalQuantity) AS
(
    SELECT O.CustomerId, O.OrderId, O.OrderDate, SUM(OD.Quantity)
    FROM Sales.Orders AS O JOIN Sales.OrderDetails AS OD
    ON O.OrderId = OD.OrderId
    GROUP BY O.CustomerId, O.OrderId, O.OrderDate
)
SELECT CustomerId, OrderId, OrderDate, TotalQuantity,
    LAG(TotalQuantity, 2)
        OVER(PARTITION BY CustomerId ORDER BY OrderDate, OrderId)
        AS " 2 Previous Order Quantity"
FROM OrderCount;
```

SQL Example 4.10 Output

	CustomerId	OrderId	OrderDate	TotalQuantity	2 Previous Order Quantity
1	1	1	2017-01-03	3	NULL
2	1	2	2017-03-05	13	NULL
3	1	5	2017-05-03	9	3
4	2	3	2017-02-23	8	NULL
5	3	6	2017-05-08	1	NULL
6	4	4	2017-04-13	3	NULL
7	5	7	2016-11-08	1	NULL
8	7	8	2016-12-23	3	NULL

Review Question 4.31
A(n) ______ window function allows you to specify which row (relative to the current row) you want to retrieve.
a. set
b. onset
c. offset
d. selectset

Review Question 4.32
Which of the following is not an offset window function?
a. FIRST_VALUE()
b. LARGEST_VALUE()
c. LAG()
d. LEAD().

Review Question 4.33
The ______ function will return the first row in the specified window frame.
a. FIRST_VALUE()
b. LARGEST_VALUE()
c. LAG()
d. LEAD().

Review Question 4.34
The ______ function returns the specified number of rows before/above the current row. The default number of rows is ______.
a. LAG(), 0
b. LEAD(), 0
c. LAG(), 1
d. LEAD(), 1

Review Question 4.35
The ______ function returns the specified number of rows after/below the current row. The default number of rows is ______.
a. LAG(), 0
b. LEAD(), 0
c. LAG(), 1
d. LEAD(), 1

Review Question 4.36
Which of the following is not one of the primary offset window functions in T-SQL?
a. FIRST_VALUE()
b. LAST_VALUE()
c. LAG()
d. ROW_NUMBER()

Review Question 4.37
What does the FIRST_VALUE() function return?
a. The first row in the result set.
b. The first row within the defined window frame.
c. The last row in the result set.

d. The last row within the defined window frame.

Review Question 4.38
What does the LAST_VALUE() function retrieve?
a. The first row within the defined window frame.
b. The last row in the result set.
c. The last row within the defined window frame.
d. The second-to-last row in the result set.

Review Question 4.39
When using the LAG() function, what does it allow you to do?
a. Fetch the row following the current row.
b. Fetch the row preceding the current row.
c. Sort rows in ascending order.
d. Skip a specific number of rows in the result set.

Review Question 4.40
In the absence of specifying the number of rows, what does the LAG() function default to?
a. 0
b. 1
c. 2
d. It requires specifying the number of rows.

Review Question 4.41
Which offset window function would you use to retrieve rows following the current row?
a. FIRST_VALUE()
b. LAST_VALUE()
c. LAG()
d. LEAD()

Review Question 4.42
What does the LAG() in the following statement do?
```
SELECT CustomerId, OrderId, OrderDate, TotalQuantity,
    LAG(TotalQuantity, 2) OVER(PARTITION BY CustomerId ORDER BY OrderDate, OrderId)
FROM OrderCount;
```
a. Disaply the TotalQuantity of 2 rows above.
b. Display the TotalQuantity of 2 orders.
c. Display the TotalQuantity with the sum of 2 orders.
d. Display the TotalQuantity with the sum of the previous 2 orders.

4.4 ROWS Clause for Framing

In SQL Example 4.8, we introduced the concept of "Offset Window Functions" and employed the ROWS clause when we needed to determine the relative position of a calculation within the window frame. In this example, the OVER() function is employed as follows:

```
OVER(PARTITION BY CustomerId ORDER BY OrderDate, OrderId
ROWS BETWEEN CURRENT ROW AND UNBOUNDED FOLLOWING)
```

The OVER() function contains three key clauses. You have already become familiar with the window-partition clause and the window-order by clause in previous sections of this chapter. However, in the above OVER() function, a new clause called the window-rows clause is introduced. This clause serves to further refine the window within the partition and essentially acts as a partition within another partition. The syntax for this clause is as follows:

```
ROWS BETWEEN <start of frame> AND <end of frame>
```

By carefully selecting the start and end of the frame using the ROWS clause, you can tailor your window functions to suit various analytical tasks. The allowable values for the start and end of the frame are described below:

Possible Value	Meaning
UNBOUNDED PRECEDING	Start at the beginning of the current partition
<n> PRECEDING	Start n rows before the current row
CURRENT ROW	Start or End at current row
<n> FOLLOWING	End n rows after the current row
UNBOUNDED FOLLOWING	End at the end of the current partition

Table 4.1 Window-ROWS clause values

The window-rows clause, as illustrated in the example, allows you to define a specific frame of rows within the partition over which your window function operates. This can be particularly useful when you want to perform calculations that involve a subset of rows relative to the current row. Here are some scenarios where you might use the ROWS clause:

Running Totals: You can use the ROWS clause to compute running totals for values within a partition. For instance, you may want to calculate the cumulative sum of sales values for each customer within their respective order dates.

Ranking and Percentiles: When ranking or determining percentiles within a partition, the ROWS clause enables you to specify the range of rows you want to consider. This is valuable when you need to identify, for example, the top-performing products within a given category.

Moving Averages: Calculating moving averages over a specific number of preceding or following rows can provide insights into trends. The ROWS clause allows you to establish the moving window for this purpose.

Understanding when and how to use the ROWS clause will significantly enhance your ability to perform advanced analytical operations with T-SQL's window functions.

SQL Example 4.11

Display the average quantity for three consecutive orders per year, including the Order ID, the year of the order, the total quantity in each order, and the average quantity of three consecutive orders.

SQL Example 4.11 Analysis

Use the ROWS clause with the following code:

```
ROWS BETWEEN 1 PRECEDING AND 1 FOLLOWING.
```

SQL Example 4.11 Statement

```
WITH AverageOrderQuantity (OrderId, OrderYear, TotalQuantity) AS
(
    SELECT O.OrderId, YEAR(O.OrderDate), SUM(OD.Quantity)
    FROM Sales.Orders AS O JOIN Sales.OrderDetails AS OD
    ON O.OrderId = OD.OrderId
    GROUP BY O.OrderId, YEAR(O.OrderDate)
)
SELECT OrderId, OrderYear, TotalQuantity,
    AVG(TotalQuantity) OVER (
    PARTITION BY OrderYear
    ORDER BY OrderId
    ROWS BETWEEN 1 PRECEDING AND 1 FOLLOWING)
    AS Quantity3OrderAverage
FROM AverageOrderQuantity;
```

SQL Example 4.11 Output

	OrderId	OrderYear	TotalQuantity	Quantity3OrderAverage
1	7	2016	1	2
2	8	2016	3	2
3	1	2017	3	8
4	2	2017	13	8
5	3	2017	8	8
6	4	2017	3	6
7	5	2017	9	4
8	6	2017	1	5

Review Question 4.43
There are three clauses inside the OVER() function. They are window-partition clause, window-order by clause, and ______ clause. This clause further limits the window inside the partition. It works like a partition inside another partition.
a. PARTITION BY
b. OVER()
c. ORDER BY
d. WINDOWS-ROWS

Review Question 4.44
The syntax for windows-rows clause is:
ROWS BETWEEN <start of frame> AND <end of frame>

Which of the following is NOT a possible value for start and end of frame?
a. UNBOUNDED PRECEDING
b. <n> PRECEDING
c. THIS ROW
d. <n> FOLLOWING

Review Question 4.45
What is the primary purpose of the ROWS clause in SQL?
```
OVER(PARTITION BY CustomerId ORDER BY OrderDate, OrderId
ROWS BETWEEN CURRENT ROW AND UNBOUNDED FOLLOWING)
```
a. To partition the data by CustomerId
b. To order the data by OrderDate and OrderId
c. To determine the relative position of a calculation within the window frame
d. To select specific columns in the result set

Review Question 4.46
In the given example of this book, what is the syntax of the window-rows clause?
a. BETWEEN <start of frame> TO <end of frame>
b. BETWEEN <start of frame> - <end of frame>
c. BETWEEN <start of frame> AND <end of frame>
d. BETWEEN <start of frame> + <end of frame>

Review Question 4.47
What does the UNBOUNDED PRECEDING value in the ROWS clause mean?
a. Start at the end of the current partition
b. Start at the beginning of the current partition
c. Start at the current row
d. Start n rows before the current row

Review Question 4.48
When might you use the ROWS clause to compute running totals?
a. When you need to calculate averages
b. When you want to determine the relative position of a row
c. When you want to compute the cumulative sum of values within a partition
d. When you want to identify the top-performing products

Review Question 4.49
What is the ROWS clause useful for when ranking or determining percentiles?
a. Determining the relative position of the current row
b. Specifying the range of rows to consider
c. Ordering the rows within a partition
d. Starting at the end of the current partition

Review Question 4.50
In which scenarios can the ROWS clause be employed to calculate moving averages?
a. To determine the top-performing products
b. To start at the current row
c. To compute running totals
d. To calculate over a specific number of preceding or following rows

Review Question 4.51
What is the main benefit of carefully selecting the start and end of the frame using the ROWS clause?
a. It simplifies the SQL query
b. It increases the number of rows in the result set
c. It customizes the window function for various analytical tasks
d. It reduces the number of available window functions

Review Question 4.52
How can understanding the ROWS clause enhance your ability to work with T-SQL's window functions?
a. It reduces the need for window functions
b. It eliminates the need for partitioning
c. It simplifies the SQL syntax
d. It significantly enhances your ability to perform advanced analytical operations

4.5 CUBE and ROLLUP Subclauses

In T-SQL, both the CUBE and ROLLUP subclauses can be effectively employed in conjunction with the GROUP BY clause to enhance your data summarization and reporting capabilities.

The CUBE subclause creates multidimensional result sets, including grand totals and all possible combinations of selected column values. It's useful for exploring multiple data dimensions simultaneously. For instance, it can help analyze total sales across product categories and regional subtotals.

In contrast, the ROLLUP subclause generates a structured hierarchy, featuring grand totals and subtotals at different levels. This is valuable for drill-down data analysis, such as examining total sales, yearly subtotals, quarterly breakdowns, and monthly figures in a sales dataset. Your choice between CUBE and ROLLUP depends on your specific reporting or analysis needs—multidimensional exploration (CUBE) or structured drill-down analysis (ROLLUP).

Here are some key concepts to keep in mind when working with these subclauses:
Multidimensional Analysis: CUBE and ROLLUP enable multidimensional analysis of data. This is essential when dealing with datasets where multiple factors or attributes need to be simultaneously considered in summary reports. The CUBE operation calculates all possible combinations of aggregations, allowing efficient analysis across multiple dimensions. On the other hand, the ROLLUP operation creates subtotals at any level of aggregation needed, from the most detailed up to a grand total. It's similar to CUBE, but it doesn't calculate all possible combinations of subtotals.
Drill-Down Reporting: ROLLUP, in particular, is useful for creating drill-down reports. This hierarchical view

helps users analyze data at different levels of detail or granularity.

Business Intelligence: In the context of business intelligence and data warehousing, CUBE and ROLLUP are often used to build comprehensive data cubes, facilitating complex analyses and data visualization.

By mastering the use of these subclauses, you can elevate your SQL skills and provide more insightful data summaries to support decision-making processes.

SQL Example 4.12

Display the total quantity of products each customer placed. Add the grand total for LifeStyle LLC.

SQL Example 4.12 Analysis

Use the CUBE sub clause with GROUP BY to obtain the grand total.

SQL Example 4.12 Statement

```
WITH OrderCount (CustomerId, OrderId, TotalQuantity) AS
(
    SELECT O.CustomerId, O.Orderid, SUM(OD.Quantity)
    FROM Sales.Orders AS O JOIN Sales.OrderDetails AS OD
    ON O.OrderId = OD.OrderId
    GROUP BY O.CustomerId, O.OrderId
)
SELECT CustomerId, SUM(TotalQuantity) AS "Total Quantity"
FROM OrderCount
GROUP BY CUBE(CustomerId);
```

SQL Example 4.12 Output

	CustomerId	Total Quantity
1	1	25
2	2	8
3	3	1
4	4	3
5	5	1
6	7	3
7	NULL	41

SQL Example 4.13

Same as SQL Example 4.12. This time, change the Null in the last row of the result set to "Total".

SQL Example 4.13 Analysis

Utilize the CASE expression introduced in Chapter 2. To prevent any confusion arising from NULL values in the CustomerId column and those generated by the CUBE() function, it is advisable to employ the GROUPING() function. The GROUPING() function accepts a column name and returns 0 if the value is a member of the column (as exemplified by the value 3 in our example). Otherwise, it returns 1 (as demonstrated by NULL in our example). Furthermore, the ISNULL() function can be employed. ISNULL(checkExpression, replacementValue) assesses the checkExpression to determine if it is NULL. If it is, the checkExpression will be substituted with the replacementValue.

SQL Example 4.13 Statement

```sql
WITH OrderCount (CustomerId, OrderId, TotalQuantity) AS
(
    SELECT O.CustomerId, O.Orderid, SUM(OD.Quantity)
    FROM Sales.Orders AS O JOIN Sales.OrderDetails AS OD
    ON O.OrderId = OD.OrderId
    GROUP BY O.CustomerId, O.OrderId
)
SELECT CASE WHEN (GROUPING(CustomerId) = 1) THEN 'Total'
            ELSE ISNULL(CAST(CustomerId AS VARCHAR), 'UNKNOWN')
        END AS CustomerId, SUM(TotalQuantity) AS "Total Quantity"
FROM OrderCount
GROUP BY CUBE(CustomerId);
```

SQL Example 4.13 Output

	CustomerId	Total Quantity
1	1	25
2	2	8
3	3	1
4	4	3
5	5	1
6	7	3
7	Total	41

SQL Example 4.14

Display the total quantity of each order. Add a sub total for each customer and the grand total for LifeStyle.

SQL Example 4.14 Analysis

Same as Example 4.12. Use the ROLLUP sub clause with the ORDER BY clause.

SQL Example 4.14 Statement

```sql
WITH OrderCount (CustomerId, OrderId, TotalQuantity) AS
(
    SELECT O.CustomerId, O.Orderid, SUM(OD.Quantity)
```

```
    FROM Sales.Orders AS O JOIN Sales.OrderDetails AS OD
    ON O.OrderId = OD.OrderId
    GROUP BY O.CustomerId, O.OrderId
)
SELECT CustomerId, OrderId, SUM(TotalQuantity) AS "Total Quantity"
FROM OrderCount
GROUP BY ROLLUP(CustomerId, OrderId);
```

SQL Example 4.14 Output

	CustomerId	OrderId	Total Quantity
1	1	1	3
2	1	2	13
3	1	5	9
4	1	NULL	25
5	2	3	8
6	2	NULL	8
7	3	6	1
8	3	NULL	1
9	4	4	3
10	4	NULL	3
11	5	7	1
12	5	NULL	1
13	7	8	3
14	7	NULL	3
15	NULL	NULL	41

SQL Example 4.15

Same as SQL Example 4.14. This time replace those NULL rows with "Total" and "Grand Total"

SQL Example 4.15 Analysis

Same as SQL Example 4.14. Add another CASE expression for the OrderId column.

SQL Example 4.15 Statement

```
WITH OrderCount (CustomerId, OrderId, TotalQuantity) AS
(
    SELECT O.CustomerId, O.Orderid, SUM(OD.Quantity)
    FROM Sales.Orders AS O JOIN Sales.OrderDetails AS OD
    ON O.OrderId = OD.OrderId
    GROUP BY O.CustomerId, O.OrderId
)
SELECT CASE WHEN (GROUPING(CustomerId) = 1) THEN 'Grand'
            ELSE ISNULL(CAST(CustomerId AS VARCHAR), 'UNKNOWN')
        END AS CustomerId,
        CASE WHEN (GROUPING(OrderId) = 1) THEN 'Total'
            ELSE ISNULL(CAST(OrderId AS VARCHAR), 'UNKNOWN')
        END AS OrderId,
```

```
    SUM(TotalQuantity) AS "Total Quantity"
FROM OrderCount
GROUP BY ROLLUP(CustomerId, OrderId);
```

SQL Example 4.15 Output

	CustomerId	OrderId	Total Quantity
1	1	1	3
2	1	2	13
3	1	5	9
4	1	Total	25
5	2	3	8
6	2	Total	8
7	3	6	1
8	3	Total	1
9	4	4	3
10	4	Total	3
11	5	7	1
12	5	Total	1
13	7	8	3
14	7	Total	3
15	Grand	Total	41

Review Question 4.53
The _______ sub clause can be used to add a grand total row to the result set and all combinations of values in the selected column(s).
a. CUBE
b. SQUARE
c. GRAND
d. ROLLUP

Review Question 4.54
The _______ sub clause can be used to add a grand total row and a hierarchy of values in the selected columns.
a. CUBE
b. SQUARE
c. GRAND
d. ROLLUP

4.6 Chapter Summary

In this chapter, you explored window functions, a versatile counterpart to aggregate functions, allowing you to retain both detailed data and aggregate results. You also learned about ranking window functions (RANK(), DENSE_RANK(), ROW_NUMBER(), NTILE()) for data ranking and offset window functions

(FIRST_VALUE(), LAST_VALUE(), LAG(), LEAD()) to retrieve neighboring row values. Additionally, you delved into CUBE and ROLLUP subclauses, enabling comprehensive data summarization for advanced analysis and reporting.

4.7 Discussion

Discussion 4.1

In SQL Example 4.1, what happens if you remove the "PARTITION BY EmployeeId"? Explain the purpose of the PARTITION BY clause.

Discussion 4.2

In SQL Example 4.2, what happens if you remove the "ORDER BY OrderId"? Explain the purpose of the ORDER BY clause in window functions.

Discussion 4.3

In SQL Example 4.8, what happens if you remove the "ROWS BETWEEN CURRENT ROW AND UNBOUNDED FOLLOWING"? Explain the purpose of the clause in the statement.

Discussion 4.4

The syntax for the ROWS clause in framing is:

ROWS BETWEEN <start of frame> AND <end of frame>

What are the default values for "start of frame" and "end of frame"? Write two SQL statements, one using the ROWS clause, and the other one not. The two statements should retrieve the same result set.

Discussion 4.5

There are four ranking window functions in T-SQL: RANK(), DENSE_RANK(), ROW_NUMBER(), and NTILE(). Explain the differences of these functions.

Discussion 4.6

We say LAG() and LEAD() are nondeterministic functions. Explain the meaning of "nondeterministic".

Discussion 4.7

In SQL Example 4.14, what happens if the function ROLLUP() is replaced with CUBE()? Use the example to explain the differences between ROLLUP() and CUBE().

4.8 SQL Exercises

Exercise 4.1

Display customer's sales value by month in 2017 and include a running total for each customer. Show customer ID, the month, sales value in that month, and a running total for the customers.

	CustomerId	OrderMonth	Monthly Total	Customer Running Total
1	1	1	1799.97	1799.97
2	1	3	4649.87	6449.84
3	1	5	1499.91	7949.75
4	2	2	2329.92	2329.92
5	3	5	1499.99	1499.99
6	4	4	269.97	269.97

Exercise 4.2

Display the total quantity of all orders each employee handled. Show employee ID and quantity running total.

	EmployeeId	Running Total Quantity
1	2	3
2	3	16
3	4	25
4	5	39
5	6	40
6	7	41

Exercise 4.3

Rank quantity of products in each delivery from high to low quantity.

	DeliveryId	Quantity	Quantity Rank
1	7	25	1
2	5	20	2
3	9	18	3
4	6	15	4
5	8	12	5
6	3	10	6
7	4	10	6
8	2	5	8
9	1	2	9

Exercise 4.4

Same as Exercise 4.3. Rank quantity of products in each delivery from high to low. This time use DENSE_RANK().

	DeliveryId	Quantity	Quantity Rank
1	7	25	1
2	5	20	2
3	9	18	3
4	6	15	4
5	8	12	5
6	3	10	6
7	4	10	6
8	2	5	7
9	1	2	8

Exercise 4.5

Same as Exercise 4.3. Rank quantity of products in each delivery from low to high by assigning a row number to each row in the result set.

	DeliveryId	Quantity	Row number
1	1	2	1
2	2	5	2
3	3	10	3
4	4	10	4
5	8	12	5
6	6	15	6
7	9	18	7
8	5	20	8
9	7	25	9

Exercise 4.6

Same as Exercise 4.5. Rank quantity of products in each delivery from low to high by assigning a tile number in the result set. Make the whole result set into 3 tiles.

	DeliveryId	Quantity	Tile number
1	1	2	1
2	2	5	1
3	3	10	1
4	4	10	2
5	8	12	2
6	6	15	2
7	9	18	3
8	5	20	3
9	7	25	3

Exercise 4.7

Use the four ranking window functions in the same SQL statement to see the differences among the four functions. Use the Purchasing.Deliveries table to rank the quantity delivered. Make the whole result set into 3 tiles.

	DeliveryId	Quantity	Quantity Rank	Quantity Dense Rank	Row number	Tile number
1	1	2	1	1	1	1
2	2	5	2	2	2	1
3	3	10	3	3	3	1
4	4	10	3	3	4	2
5	8	12	5	4	5	2
6	6	15	6	5	6	2
7	9	18	7	6	7	3
8	5	20	8	7	8	3
9	7	25	9	8	9	3

Exercise 4.8

Display total quantity of products in each order. Show Employee ID, order ID, order date, and the total quantity in each order, the first order, and the last order handled by the employee. The sequence of the order is based on the order date.

	EmployeeId	OrderId	OrderDate	TotalQuantity	First Order Quantity	Most Recent Order Quantity
1	2	8	2016-12-23	3	3	3
2	3	2	2017-03-05	13	13	13
3	4	5	2017-05-03	9	9	9
4	5	4	2017-04-13	3	3	3
5	5	3	2017-02-23	8	3	3
6	5	1	2017-01-03	3	3	3
7	6	6	2017-05-08	1	1	1
8	7	7	2016-11-08	1	1	1

Exercise 4.9

Display total quantity of products in each order. Show Employee ID, order ID, order date, and the total quantity in each order, previous order, and the next order handled by the employee. The sequence of the order is based on order date.

	EmployeeId	OrderId	OrderDate	TotalQuantity	Previous Order Quantity	Next Order Quantity
1	2	8	2016-12-23	3	NULL	NULL
2	3	2	2017-03-05	13	NULL	NULL
3	4	5	2017-05-03	9	NULL	NULL
4	5	1	2017-01-03	3	NULL	8
5	5	3	2017-02-23	8	3	3
6	5	4	2017-04-13	3	8	NULL
7	6	6	2017-05-08	1	NULL	NULL
8	7	7	2016-11-08	1	NULL	NULL

Exercise 4.10

Display total quantity of products in each order. Show employee ID, order ID, order date, the total quantity in each order, and the total quantity in the order before the previous order handled by the employee. The sequence of the order is based on the order date.

	EmployeeId	OrderId	OrderDate	TotalQuantity	2 Previous Order Quantity
1	2	8	2016-12-23	3	NULL
2	3	2	2017-03-05	13	NULL
3	4	5	2017-05-03	9	NULL
4	5	1	2017-01-03	3	NULL
5	5	3	2017-02-23	8	NULL
6	5	4	2017-04-13	3	3
7	6	6	2017-05-08	1	NULL
8	7	7	2016-11-08	1	NULL

Exercise 4.11

Display the average quantity of three consecutive deliveries by month. Show delivery ID, month of the delivery, total quantity in that delivery, and the average of three consecutive deliveries.

	DeliveryId	Month	Quantity	Quantity3DeliveryAverage
1	1	10	2	6
2	3	10	10	7
3	4	10	10	13
4	5	10	20	15
5	6	10	15	20
6	7	10	25	17
7	8	10	12	18
8	9	10	18	15
9	2	11	5	5

Exercise 4.12

Display total quantity of each product delivered. Add the grand total for LifeStyle LLC.

	ProductId	Total Quantity
1	1	7
2	2	10
3	3	10
4	4	20
5	5	15
6	6	25
7	7	30
8	NULL	117

Exercise 4.13

Same as Exercise 4.12. This time, change the Null in the last row of the result set to "Total".

	ProductId	Total Quantity
1	1	7
2	2	10
3	3	10
4	4	20
5	5	15
6	6	25
7	7	30
8	Total	117

Exercise 4.14

Display total quantity of each product delivered. Show product ID, delivery ID, a sub total for each product, and the grand total for all products delivered.

	ProductId	DeliveryId	Total Quantity
1	1	1	2
2	1	2	5
3	1	NULL	7
4	2	3	10
5	2	NULL	10
6	3	4	10
7	3	NULL	10
8	4	5	20
9	4	NULL	20
10	5	6	15
11	5	NULL	15
12	6	7	25
13	6	NULL	25
14	7	8	12
15	7	9	18
16	7	NULL	30
17	NULL	NULL	117

Exercise 4.15

Same as Exercise 4.14. This time replace those NULL rows appropriately with "Total" and "Grand Total"

	ProductId	DeliveryId	Total Quantity
1	1	1	2
2	1	2	5
3	1	Total	7
4	2	3	10
5	2	Total	10
6	3	4	10
7	3	Total	10
8	4	5	20
9	4	Total	20
10	5	6	15
11	5	Total	15
12	6	7	25
13	6	Total	25
14	7	8	12
15	7	9	18
16	7	Total	30
17	Grand	Total	117

4.9 Solutions to the Review Questions

4.1 C; 4.2 C; 4.3 A; 4.4 D; 4.5 D; 4.6 C; 4.7 B; 4.8 C; 4.9 B; 4.10 D; 4.11 A; 4.12 C; 4.13 A; 4.14 A; 4.15 B; 4.16 A; 4.17 B; 4.18 C; 4.19 A; 4.20 B; 4.21 C; 4.22 C; 4.23 D; 4.24 D; 4.25 A; 4.26 B; 4.27 C; 4.28 C; 4.29 C; 4.30 C; 4.31 C; 4.32 B; 4.33 A; 4.34 C; 4.35 D; 4.36 D; 4.37 B; 4.38 C; 4.39 B; 4.40 B; 4.41 D; 4.42 A; 4.43 D; 4.44 C; 4.45 C; 4.46 C; 4.47 B; 4.48 C; 4.49 B; 4.50 D; 4.51 C; 4.52 D; 4.53 A; 4.54 D;

CHAPTER 5: STORED PROCEDURES AND USER DEFINED FUNCTIONS

Chapter Learning Objectives

5.1 Describe T-SQL stored procedures, outlining their fundamental purpose and structure.
5.2 Explain the advantages and merits of employing stored procedures in query optimization.
5.3 Develop and execute a T-SQL stored procedure to create functional and efficient database routines.
5.4 Describe user-defined functions (UDFs) and their role in database operations and data processing.
5.5 Construct and employ a T-SQL user-defined function to address a specific data retrieval challenge.

5.1 Introduction to Stored Procedures

In T-SQL, a stored procedure is a pre-compiled set of SQL statements that can be reused as necessary.

Using stored procedures offers several advantages, including:

1. *Improved Performance*: Stored procedures are precompiled, resulting in faster execution compared to ad hoc SQL statements. Additionally, the database management system (DBMS) can reuse execution plans, reducing server resource demands.

2. *Code Reusability*: Stored procedures can be employed by multiple users and client applications, reducing the need for redundant code creation.

3. *Reduced Network Traffic*: Since stored procedures are stored on the server, clients can request the server to execute the procedure instead of transmitting multiple statements. This minimizes the data exchanged between the client and server.

4. *Enhanced Security*: Stored procedures are server-side objects and can have distinct authorization levels from the underlying objects, adding an extra layer of security for sensitive data.

These benefits make stored procedures a valuable tool for enhancing the performance, maintainability, and security of database operations in T-SQL.

Review Question 5.1
A stored procedure in T-SQL is an object that contains a group of SQL statements that are ______ and can be reused any time you need the same group of statements.
a. grouped
b. grouped in a function
c. compiled
d. used

Review Question 5.2
Which of the following is a benefit of using a stored procedure?
a. more concise code
b. make better use of powerful clients
c. easier to learn
d. better performance

Review Question 5.3
Which of the following is a benefit of using a stored procedure?
a. more concise code
b. code reuse
c. can retrieve data from tables and views at the same time
d. no need for indexes

Review Question 5.4
Which of the following is a benefit of using a stored procedure?
a. less network traffic between client and server
b. minimum code execution on the server
c. easier to learn
d. more concise code

Review Question 5.5
Which of the following is a benefit of using a stored procedure?
a. minimum code execution on the server
b. more flexible
c. more powerful clients
d. more secure

Review Question 5.6
What is a stored procedure in T-SQL?
a. A pre-compiled group of SQL statements that can be reused as needed
b. A single SQL statement that is compiled
c. A group of SQL statements that are executed once and discarded
d. A set of SQL statements that are stored on the client

Review Question 5.7
Which of the following is NOT a benefit of using stored procedures?
a. Reduced network traffic

b. Improved performance
c. More code reusability
d. More flexibility

Review Question 5.8
What is one way stored procedures reduce network traffic?
a. By transmitting more data between the client and server
b. By transmitting multiple statements between the client and server
c. By transmitting only the procedure request between the client and server
d. By transmitting no data between the client and server

Review Question 5.9
What is the benefit of enhanced security when using stored procedures?
a. Clients have more control over server objects
b. Servers have more control over client objects
c. Stored procedures have different authorization levels than the underlying objects
d. Stored procedures have the same authorization levels as the underlying objects

Review Question 5.10
What is the primary benefit of the improved performance provided by stored procedures?
a. Reduced server strain
b. Increased client performance
c. More efficient use of server resources
d. Faster execution for ad hoc SQL statements

Review Question 5.11
What is one of the key advantages of using stored procedures in T-SQL?
a. Reduced server resource demands
b. Dynamic execution plans
c. Manual optimization
d. No more network traffic

5.2 Creating, Running, and Deleting Stored Procedures

In T-SQL, the syntax for creating a stored procedure is as follows:

```
CREATE PROCEDURE SchemaName.ProcedureName
@Parameter1 datatype [OUTPUT],
...
@Parameter n datatype [OUTPUT]
AS
SET NOCOUNT ON;

SQL Statement 1
...
SQL Statement n
```

In the initial part of the syntax, the procedure is created with a specified schema name and a unique procedure name. While the keyword PROCEDURE can be abbreviated as PROC, for clarity, it is advisable to use PROCEDURE.

The second part of the syntax lists the parameters that can be employed in the SQL statements. A parameter, as you learned in Chapter 2, is denoted by a name starting with the "@" character and can serve as input, output, or both. If a parameter is used to store the result of the SQL statements, the OUTPUT keyword is added after the data type.

The third part of the syntax, beginning with the keyword AS, contains the SQL statements that the stored procedure will execute. The statement SET NOCOUNT ON; is included to suppress any informational messages returned by the SQL Server, such as "1 record affected" after inserting a row. This enhances the performance of the stored procedure and can be likened to declining a receipt at a restaurant.

It's advisable to first write and test the regular SQL statements independently before converting them into a stored procedure. This approach ensures that the stored procedure functions as intended. When creating a stored procedure, it's important to note that error messages may not be displayed if the SQL statements fail to produce the expected results.

SQL Example 5.1

Create a stored procedure called Sales.OrderValue that returns the total value for each order. Display Order ID, Order date, and Order total.

SQL Example 5.1 Analysis

This is a simple task for writing an SQL statement. The purpose of the example is for you to get familiar with the stored procedure syntax.

SQL Example 5.1 Statement

```
CREATE OR ALTER PROCEDURE Sales.OrderValue
AS
SET NOCOUNT ON;
SELECT O.OrderId, O.OrderDate,
    SUM(OD.Quantity * OD.Price) AS OrderTotal
FROM Sales.Orders AS O JOIN Sales.OrderDetails AS OD
ON O.OrderId = OD.OrderId
GROUP BY O.OrderId, O.OrderDate;
```

SQL Example 5.1 Output

```
Command(s) completed successfully.
```

If you go to the SQL Server, you should see the Sales.OrderValue procedure:

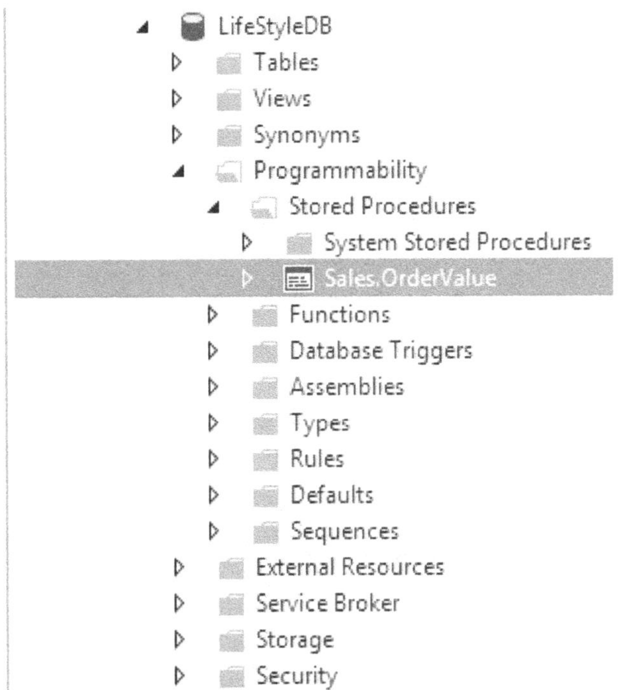

To run the stored procedure you just created, execute the following statement:

```
EXECUTE Sales.OrderValue;
```

The result will be:

	OrderId	OrderDate	OrderTotal
1	1	2017-01-03	1799.97
2	2	2017-03-05	4649.87
3	3	2017-02-23	2329.92
4	4	2017-04-13	269.97
5	5	2017-05-03	1499.91
6	6	2017-05-08	1499.99
7	7	2016-11-08	999.99
8	8	2016-12-23	199.97

To delete a stored procedure, use the following statement:

```
DROP PROCEURE ProcedureName;
```

If you make a mistake in a stored procedure after it has been created, simply editing the statement and running it again will not work as the stored procedure with that name already exists. To resolve this issue, you must drop the stored procedure before creating a new one with the same name.

An alternative solution is to use the "CREATE OR ALTER PROCEDURE" syntax instead of the traditional "CREATE PROCEDURE" when creating the stored procedure, as shown in the previous example.

Review Question 5.12

What are the three portions of a stored procedure syntax?

a. name, parameters, and return

b. name, process, and parameters

c. name, process, and the SQL statements you want for the procedure

d. name, parameters, and the SQL statements you want for the procedure

Review Question 5.13

The _____ in a stored procedure will remove a message returned from the SQL Server.

a. SET IDENTITY ON

b. SET NOCOUNT ON

c. SET NORETURN ON

d. SET NOMESSAGE ON

Review Question 5.14

What is the primary purpose of the "SET NOCOUNT ON;" statement in a T-SQL stored procedure?

a. To display informational messages

b. To improve the performance of the stored procedure

c. To count the number of records affected

d. To execute the SQL statements

Review Question 5.15

Which part of the stored procedure syntax allows parameters to be specified?

a. The part starting with "AS"

b. The part right after the schema and procedure name

c. The part using "CREATE PROCEDURE"

d. The SQL statements section

Review Question 5.16

When is it advisable to test regular SQL statements independently before creating a stored procedure?

a. After creating the stored procedure

b. Before creating the stored procedure

c. During the execution of the stored procedure

d. While editing the stored procedure

Review Question 5.17

What is the purpose of the "DROP PROCEDURE" statement in T-SQL?

a. To create a new stored procedure

b. To execute the SQL statements in the procedure

c. To remove an existing stored procedure

d. To suppress informational messages

Review Question 5.18

If you make a mistake in a stored procedure after it has been created, what must you do to rectify the situation?

a. Edit the statement and run it again

b. Rename the stored procedure

c. Drop the stored procedure and create a new one

d. Ignore the mistake and continue using the existing procedure

Review Question 5.19

What is an alternative solution to handling mistakes in a stored procedure after it has been created?

a. Rename the stored procedure

b. Edit the statement and rerun it

c. Ignore the mistake and continue using the existing procedure

d. Use the "CREATE OR ALTER PROCEDURE" syntax when creating the stored procedure

5.3 Stored Procedures with Parameters

As you learned earlier in the chapter, parameters are defined in the declaration of the stored procedure, immediately following the procedure name. Each parameter is prefixed with an @ symbol and includes a data type. For example:

```
CREATE PROCEDURE dbo.MyProcedure
    @Param1 INT,
    @Param2 NVARCHAR(50)
AS
    -- SQL statements go here
```

In this example, dbo.MyProcedure accepts two parameters: @Param1, which is an integer, and @Param2, which is a string of up to 50 characters.

Once defined, these parameters can be used within the stored procedure just like any other variables. For example, they can be included in SQL statements to filter results, insert data, or update existing records.

When calling a stored procedure with parameters, you must provide values for those parameters. The values are passed in the same order as they are defined in the procedure.

Stored procedures can also have output parameters. These are defined in the same way as input parameters but include the OUTPUT keyword. Output parameters can be used to return data to the calling program.

```
CREATE PROCEDURE dbo.GetEmployeeCount
    @Count INT OUTPUT
AS
    SELECT @Count = COUNT(*) FROM Employees;
```

In this example, dbo.GetStudentCount uses an output parameter to return the total number of records in the Students table. To retrieve the value of an output parameter, you must declare a variable and pass it to the stored procedure using the OUTPUT keyword.

Parameters greatly enhance the flexibility and usefulness of stored procedures in T-SQL by allowing dynamic input and output. They allow for code reuse and can lead to more maintainable and efficient code.

SQL Example 5.2

Create a stored procedure called CustomerOrderTotal that will display a given customer's order total.

SQL Example 5.2 Analysis

Use a parameter to store the customer ID, and then SELECT the order total of the customer's orders. A batch is required to create a stored procedure, so the GO statement must be included in the statement.

SQL Example 5.2 Statement

```
GO
CREATE OR ALTER PROCEDURE Sales.CustomerOrderTotal
    @CustomerId INT
AS
SET NOCOUNT ON;
SELECT O.CustomerId, SUM(OD.Quantity * OD.Price) AS TotalOrder
FROM Sales.Orders AS O JOIN Sales.OrderDetails AS OD
ON O.OrderId = OD.OrderId
WHERE O.CustomerId = @CustomerId
GROUP BY O.CustomerId;
```

SQL Example 5.2 Execute Stored Procedures

```
EXECUTE Sales.CustomerOrderTotal @CustomerId =2;
```

SQL Example 5.2 Output with the Execution

	CustomerId	TotalOrder
1	2	2329.92

SQL Example 5.3

Create a stored procedure named ProductQuantityForCustomerByDate, which will display all products and their corresponding quantities ordered by a specified customer on a specific date. Execute the stored procedure using customer ID 1 and an order date of March 5, 2017.

SQL Example 5.3 Analysis

Use two parameters, one for customer ID and the other for order date.

SQL Example 5.3 Statement

```
GO
CREATE OR ALTER PROCEDURE Sales.ProductQuantityForCustomerByDate
    @CustomerId INT,
    @OrderDate DATE
AS
SET NOCOUNT ON;
SELECT O.CustomerId, O.OrderDate, OD.ProductId, OD.quantity
FROM Sales.Orders AS O JOIN Sales.OrderDetails AS OD
    ON O.OrderId = OD.OrderId
WHERE O.CustomerId = @CustomerId
    AND O.OrderDate = @OrderDate;
```

SQL Example 5.3 Execute Stored Procedures.

```
EXECUTE Sales.ProductQuantityForCustomerByDate
    @CustomerId = 1, @OrderDate = '20170305';
```

SQL Example 5.3 Output with the Execution

	CustomerId	OrderDate	ProductId	quantity
1	1	2017-03-05	1	1
2	1	2017-03-05	2	1
3	1	2017-03-05	4	6
4	1	2017-03-05	6	5

SQL Example 5.4

Create a stored procedure named HighLowSalesPrice, which can identify the product ID of the product sold at the highest price and the product ID of the product sold at the lowest price.

SQL Example 5.4 Analysis

Use two OUTPUT parameters to store the product IDs, one for the highest priced product and the other for the lowest priced product.

SQL Example 5.4 Statement

```
GO
CREATE OR ALTER PROCEDURE Sales.HighLowSalesPrice
    @HighestPriceProductId INT OUTPUT,
    @LowestPriceProductId INT OUTPUT
AS
SET NOCOUNT ON;
SELECT @HighestPriceProductId = ProductId
FROM Sales.OrderDetails
WHERE Price = (SELECT MAX(Price) FROM Sales.OrderDetails);
SELECT @LowestPriceProductId = ProductId
FROM Sales.OrderDetails
WHERE Price = (SELECT MIN(Price) FROM Sales.OrderDetails);
```

SQL Example 5.4 Execute Stored Procedure

```
DECLARE @HighestPriceProductId INT
DECLARE @LowestPriceProductId INT
EXECUTE Sales.HighLowSalesPrice
    @HighestPriceProductId OUTPUT,
    @LowestPriceProductId OUTPUT;
```

```sql
SELECT @HighestPriceProductId AS "Highest Price",
    @LowestPriceProductId AS "Lowest Price";
```

SQL Example 5.4 Output with the Execution

	Highest Price	Lowest Price
1	2	8

SQL Example 5.5

Create a stored procedure named CustomerOrderInformation that accepts a customer ID as input and returns the average amount of the customer's orders and the date of the most recent order.

SQL Example 5.5 Analysis

Utilize one parameter for input (customer ID) and two parameters for output (average order amount and most recent order date).

The primary challenge in this example lies in calculating the average. This process involves two steps: first, the calculation of each order's total, and then, the computation of the average of these individual order totals. To facilitate the initial step, we employ a Common Table Expression (CTE).

Additionally, it's worth noting that the execution statement should use just "1" instead of "@CustomerId = 1". Using "@CustomerId = 1" would imply that all subsequent "@variables" should also have values, which is impractical as these variables are designated for output.

SQL Example 5.5 Statement

```sql
GO
CREATE OR ALTER PROCEDURE Sales.CustomerOrderInformation
    @CustomerId INT,
    @AverageAmount MONEY OUTPUT,
    @MostRecentOrderDate DATE OUTPUT
AS
SET NOCOUNT ON;
WITH CustomerOrder (CustomerId, OrderId, OrderAmount)
AS
(
    SELECT O.CustomerId, O.OrderId, SUM(Quantity * Price)
    FROM Sales.Orders AS O JOIN Sales.OrderDetails AS OD
    ON O.OrderId = OD.OrderId
    GROUP BY O.CustomerId, O.OrderId, O.OrderDate
)
SELECT @AverageAmount = AVG(OrderAmount)
FROM CustomerOrder
```

```
WHERE CustomerId = @CustomerId;
SELECT @MostRecentOrderDate = MAX(OrderDate)
FROM Sales.Orders
WHERE CustomerId = @CustomerId;
```

SQL Example 5.5 Execute Stored Procedure

```
DECLARE @AverageAmount MONEY
DECLARE @MostRecentOrderDate DATE
EXECUTE Sales.CustomerOrderInformation 1,
    @AverageAmount OUTPUT,
    @MostRecentOrderDate OUTPUT;

SELECT CAST (@AverageAmount AS NUMERIC(7, 2))
    AS "Average Order Amount",
    @MostRecentOrderDate
    AS "Most Recent Order Date";
```

SQL Example 5.5 Output with the Execution

	Average Order Amount	Most Recent Order Date
1	2649.92	2017-05-03

SQL Example 5.6

Create a stored procedure named 'OrderTotalPlusTax' designed to take an order ID as input and provide the total order amount, inclusive of tax. A 10% tax applies to orders from customers in states where the state abbreviation's second letter is 'A,' like in GA or CA. Execute the stored procedure using order ID 6.

SQL Example 5.6 Analysis

Declare two variables: @OrderId for input and @TotalPlusTax for output.

To determine the customer's state based on the given order ID, a join operation is necessary between the Customers and Orders tables since the order ID resides in the Orders table, while the customer's state is found in the Customers table.

If the customer's state, as identified, uses a two-letter state abbreviation with "A" as the second letter, a tax rate of 10% is applied.

Next, the order total for the provided order ID must be calculated. This requires a join between the Orders and OrderDetails tables, as the order ID is located in the Orders table, and the order total can be derived from the OrderDetails table.

Finally, the total amount plus tax is computed using the formula: @OrderTotal * (1 + @TaxRate/100).

SQL Example 5.6 Statement

```
GO
CREATE OR ALTER PROCEDURE Sales.OrderTotalPlusTax
    @OrderId INT,
    @TotalPlusTax MONEY OUTPUT
AS
SET NOCOUNT ON;
DECLARE @CustomerState NVARCHAR(20);
DECLARE @TaxRate FLOAT;
DECLARE @OrderTotal MONEY;
SELECT @CustomerState = [State] FROM Sales.Customers AS C
    JOIN Sales.Orders AS O
    ON C.CustomerId = O.CustomerId
    WHERE O.OrderId = @OrderId;
IF (@CustomerState LIKE '_A')
    SET @TaxRate = 10;
ELSE
    SET @TaxRate = 0;
SELECT @OrderTotal = SUM(OD.Quantity * OD.Price)
FROM Sales.Orders AS O
    JOIN Sales.OrderDetails AS OD
    ON O.OrderId = OD.OrderId
    WHERE O.OrderId = @OrderId;
SET @TotalPlusTax = @OrderTotal * ( 1 + @TaxRate/100);
```

SQL Example 5.6 Execute Stored Procedure

```
DECLARE @TotalPlusTax MONEY
EXECUTE Sales.OrderTotalPlusTax 6, @TotalPlusTax OUTPUT;

SELECT CAST(@TotalPlusTax AS NUMERIC(7, 2)) AS Total;
```

SQL Example 5.6 Output with the Execution

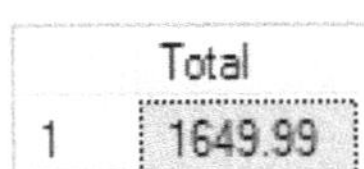

	Total
1	1649.99

Review Question 5.20

Parameters can be used to pass values to a stored procedure at execution time. Which of the following declares such a parameter?

a. OrderId

b. OrderId INT

c. @OrderId

d. @orderId INT

Review Question 5.21
Parameters can be used to store values returned from a stored procedure. Which of the following declares
such a parameter?
a. TotalValue
b. TotalValue MONEY
c. @TotalValue MONEY
d. @TotalValue MONEY OUTPUT

Review Question 5.22
How are parameters defined in a stored procedure in T-SQL?
a. In a separate file
b. Immediately following the procedure name, prefixed with "@" and with a data type
c. Using the "DEFINE" keyword
d. In a comment block

Review Question 5.23
In a stored procedure, what is the purpose of parameters?
a. To write comments in the code
b. To define tables and views
c. To declare data types
d. To provide dynamic input and output

Review Question 5.24
How should you pass values for parameters when calling a stored procedure with parameters?
a. In any order
b. In the order they are defined in the procedure
c. As separate files
d. Within a comment block

Review Question 5.25
What distinguishes output parameters from input parameters in a stored procedure?
a. Output parameters use the OUTPUT keyword
b. Input parameters can be used in SQL statements
c. Output parameters are defined in a separate file
d. Output parameters are used for comments only

Review Question 5.26
How do parameters contribute to the flexibility of stored procedures in T-SQL?
a. By allowing dynamic input and output
b. By defining tables and views
c. By including complex SQL statements
d. By reducing code reuse

Review Question 5.27
What is the recommended format for the execution statement when dealing with both input and output
variables in a T-SQL stored procedure?
a. Use variable names with "@" symbols (e.g., "@CustomerId = 1") for input parameters
b. Use plain values without variable names (e.g., "1") for input parameters
c. Include variable names only for output parameters
d. Use variable names only for input parameters

Review Question 5.28
Why is it impractical to use variable names with "@" symbols for input values in the execution statement of both input and output a T-SQL stored procedure?
a. It improves code clarity
b. It simplifies debugging
c. It implies values for all subsequent "@variables"
d. It allows for better code optimization

5.4 Using Stored Procedures for Data Manipulation

Stored procedures can include SQL statements for inserting, updating, or deleting data. Manipulating data using data manipulation language (DML) can potentially impact the existing data in our sample database tables. To maintain the integrity of your data, it's advisable to create a new table for the examples in this section.

For instance, you can create a new schema named "Chapter5" with a table called "Customers." This new table can contain the same data as the "Sales.Customers" table from our practice database. Here's the SQL statement to accomplish this:

```
CREATE SCHEMA Chapter5Example AUTHORIZATION dbo;
GO
SELECT * INTO Chapter5Example.Customers FROM Sales.Customers;
```

By creating a new schema and table, you can work with the provided examples without affecting your existing data and database tables.

SQL Example 5.7

Create a stored procedure called Chapter5Example.InsertCustomer to insert a new customer name and contact into the Chapter5Example.Customers table. Execute the stored procesure with a new customer called *Nothing Electronics* with the contact name of *Jo J. Bennett.*

SQL Example 5.7 Analysis

There are two input parameters, @CustomerName and @CustomerContact, that will insert data into the customers table.

SQL Example 5.7 Statement

```
GO
CREATE OR ALTER PROCEDURE Chapter5Example.InsertCustomer
    @CustomerName NVARCHAR(50),
```

```
        @CustomerContact NVARCHAR(50)
AS
SET NOCOUNT ON;
INSERT INTO Chapter5Example.Customers
            (CustomerName, Contact)
    VALUES  (@CustomerName, @CustomerContact);
```

SQL Example 5.7 Execute Stored Procedures

```
EXECUTE Chapter5Example.InsertCustomer
    @CustomerName = 'Nothing Electronics',
    @CustomerContact = 'Jo J. Bennett';
```

SQL Example 5.7 Output with the Execution

```
T-SQL    ↑↓    Message

  Command(s) completed successfully.
```

SQL Example 5.7 Verify the Result

Use the SQL statement

```
SELECT * FROM Chapter5Example.Customers;
```

To get the following table (the customer ID for the new record may be different if you try more than once):

CustomerId	CustomerName	StreetAddress	City	State	PostalCode	Country	Contact	Email
1	Just Electronics	123 Broad way	New York	NY	12012	USA	John White	jwhite@je.com
2	Beyond Electronics	45 Cherry Street	Chicago	IL	32302	USA	Scott Green	green@beil.com
3	Beyond Electronics	6767 GameOver Blvd	Atlanta	GA	43347	USA	Alice Black	black1@be.com
4	E Fun	888 Main Ave.	Seattle	WA	69356	USA	Ben Gold	bgold@efun.com
5	Overstock E	39 Garden Place	Los Angeles	CA	32302	USA	Daniel Yellow	dy@os.com
6	E Fun	915 Market st.	London	England	EC1A 1BB	UK	Frank Green	green@ef.com
7	Electronics4U	27 Colmore Row	Birmingham	England	B3 2EW	UK	Grace Smith	smith@e4u.com
8	Cheap Electronics	1010 Easy St	Ottawa	Ontario	K1A 0B1	Canada	NULL	NULL
9	Nothing Electronics	NULL	NULL	NULL	NULL	NULL	Jo J. Bennett	NULL

SQL Example 5.8

Create a stored procedure called Chapter5Example.UpdateCustomer that will update a customer's information based on their name and contact. Add customer address and email only if the customer has a unique name and contact. Execute the stored procedure to update customer: Nothing Electronics, contact: Jo J. Bennett with address of *4429 Heritae Road, Sanger, CA 93657, USA*; email of *jj@ne.com*.

SQL Example 5.8 Analysis

Use an IF statement to check how many records have a matching customer name and contact. If exactly one record found, update the record.

SQL Example 5.8 Statement

```
GO
CREATE OR ALTER PROCEDURE Chapter5Example.UpdateCustomer
    @CustomerName NVARCHAR(50),
    @CustomerContact NVARCHAR(50),
    @StreetAddress NVARCHAR(50),
    @City NVARCHAR(20),
    @State NVARCHAR(20),
    @PostalCode NVARCHAR(10),
    @cOUNTRY NVARCHAR(20),
    @Email NVARCHAR(50)
AS
SET NOCOUNT ON;
DECLARE @NumCustomerFound INT;
SELECT @NumCustomerFound = COUNT(*)
    FROM Chapter5.Customers
    WHERE CustomerName = @CustomerName
    AND Contact = @CustomerContact;
IF (@NumCustomerFound = 1)
UPDATE Chapter5Example.Customers
    SET StreetAddress = @StreetAddress,
        City = @City,
        [State] = @State,
        PostalCode = @PostalCode,
        Country = @Country,
        Email = @Email
WHERE CustomerName = @CustomerName
    AND Contact = @CustomerContact;
```

SQL Example 5.8 Execute Stored Procedures

```
EXECUTE Chapter5Example.UpdateCustomer
    @CustomerName = 'Nothing Electronics',
    @CustomerContact = 'Jo J. Bennett',
    @StreetAddress = '4429 Heritage Road',
    @City = 'Sanger',
    @State = 'CA',
    @PostalCode = '93657',
    @cOUNTRY = 'USA',
    @Email = 'jj@ne.com';
```

SQL Example 5.8 Output with the Execution

```
T-SQL    ↑↓    Message
  Command(s) completed successfully.
```

SQL Example 5.8 Verify the Result

Use the SQL statement

```
SELECT * FROM Chapter5Example.Customers;
```

to get the following table (the customer ID for the new record may be different if you try more than once):

CustomerId	CustomerName	StreetAddress	City	State	PostalCode	Country	Contact	Email
1	Just Electronics	123 Broad way	New York	NY	12012	USA	John White	jwhite@je.com
2	Beyond Electronics	45 Cherry Street	Chicago	IL	32302	USA	Scott Green	green@beil.com
3	Beyond Electronics	6767 GameOver Blvd	Atlanta	GA	43347	USA	Alice Black	black1@be.com
4	E Fun	888 Main Ave.	Seattle	WA	69356	USA	Ben Gold	bgold@efun.com
5	Overstock E	39 Garden Place	Los Angeles	CA	32302	USA	Daniel Yellow	dy@os.com
6	E Fun	915 Market st.	London	England	EC1A 1BB	UK	Frank Green	green@ef.com
7	Electronics4U	27 Colmore Row	Birmingham	England	B3 2EW	UK	Grace Smith	smith@e4u.com
8	Cheap Electronics	1010 Easy St	Ottawa	Ontario	K1A 0B1	Canada	NULL	NULL
9	Nothing Electronics	4429 Heritage Road	Sanger	CA	93657	USA	Jo J. Bennett	jj@ne.com

SQL Example 5.9

Create a stored procedure called Chapter5Example.DeleteCustomer that will delete a customer record based on the customer ID.

SQL Example 5.9 Analysis

Use the SQL DELETE statement in the stored procedure.

SQL Example 5.9 Statement

```
GO
CREATE OR ALTER PROCEDURE Chapter5Example.DeleteCustomer
    @CustomerId INT
AS
SET NOCOUNT ON;
DELETE FROM
    Chapter5Example.Customers
WHERE CustomerId = @CustomerId;
```

SQL Example 5.9 Execute Stored Procedures

```
EXECUTE Chapter5Example.DeleteCustomer @CustomerId = 9;
```

Check the customer ID before executing the above statement. You may have a different customer ID number.

SQL Example 5.9 Output of the Execution

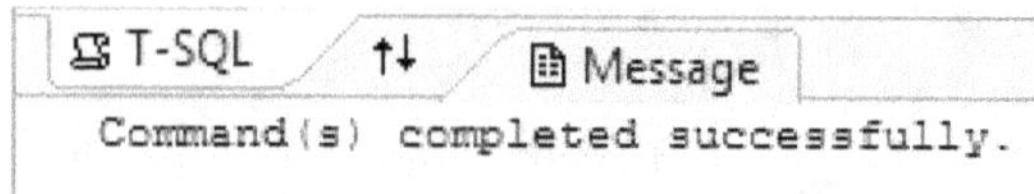

SQL Example 5.9 Verify the Result

Use the SQL statement

```
SELECT * FROM Chapter5Example.Customers;
```

to get the following table:

CustomerId	CustomerName	StreetAddress	City	State	PostalCode	Country	Contact	Email
1	Just Electronics	123 Broad way	New York	NY	12012	USA	John White	jwhite@je.com
2	Beyond Electronics	45 Cherry Street	Chicago	IL	32302	USA	Scott Green	green@beil.com
3	Beyond Electronics	6767 GameOver Blvd	Atlanta	GA	43347	USA	Alice Black	black1@be.com
4	E Fun	888 Main Ave.	Seattle	WA	69356	USA	Ben Gold	bgold@efun.com
5	Overstock E	39 Garden Place	Los Angeles	CA	32302	USA	Daniel Yellow	dy@os.com
6	E Fun	915 Market st.	London	England	EC1A 1BB	UK	Frank Green	green@ef.com
7	Electronics4U	27 Colmore Row	Birmingham	England	B3 2EW	UK	Grace Smith	smith@e4u.com
8	Cheap Electronics	1010 Easy St	Ottawa	Ontario	K1A 0B1	Canada	NULL	NULL

Review Question 5.29
Stored procedure can include _______ statements.
a. SELECT only
b. SELECT and INSERT only
c. SELECT, INSERT, and UPDATE only
d. SELECT, INSERT, UPDATE, and DELETE

Review Question 5.30
Given the following stored procedure:
```
CREATE OR ALTER PROCEDURE Chapter5Example.DeleteCustomer
    @CustomerId INT
AS
SET NOCOUNT ON;
DELETE FROM
    Chapter5Example.Customers
WHERE CustomerId = @CustomerId;
```
What is the correct way to execute the stored procedure?
a. EXECUTE Chapter5Example.DeleteCustomer @CustomerId = 9;
b. EXECUTE Chapter5Example.DeleteCustomer CustomerId = 9;
c. EXECUTE Chapter5Example.DeleteCustomer @9;
d. EXECUTE Chapter5Example.DeleteCustomer = 9;

5.5 User-Defined Functions (UDF)

In our T-SQL journey, we've utilized various built-in functions, like SUM() and CAST(). These built-in functions can accept zero or more parameters, perform processing, and return either a single scalar value (scalar-valued function) or a result set (table-valued function).

User-defined functions (UDFs) offer several advantages. The first benefit is that UDFs provide an effective means of organizing SQL statements.

The second key advantage is improved performance. When a user-defined function is initially called, its execution plan is cached on the server. Subsequent calls to the function benefit from the optimized plan, resulting in time savings. (This topic will be explored further in Chapter 8.)

Here's the syntax for creating scalar-valued UDFs:

```
CREATE FUNCTION FunctionName(Parameter List)
RETURNS DataType
AS
BEGIN
    -- Perform some actions;
END;
```

And here's the syntax for table-valued UDFs:

```
CREATE FUNCTION FunctionName(Parameter List)
RETURNS TABLE
AS
RETURN
(
    -- Perform some actions;
)
```

User-defined functions provide a structured and efficient way to enhance your SQL capabilities and organize your code.

SQL Example 5.10

Create a user defined function called NumOrderByCustomer that will accept a customer ID and return the number of orders the customer placed.

SQL Example 5.10 Analysis

Use the Sales.Orders table to count how many rows there are for the given customer ID.

SQL Example 5.10 Statement

```
GO
CREATE OR ALTER FUNCTION Sales.NumOrderByCustomer(@CustomerId INT)
RETURNS INT
AS
BEGIN
    DECLARE @NumOrders INT;
    SELECT @NumOrders = COUNT(*)
    FROM Sales.Orders
```

```
    WHERE CustomerId = @CustomerId;
    IF (@NumOrders IS NULL)
        SET @NumOrders = 0;
    RETURN @NumOrders;
END;
```

After execution, you should see the following message:

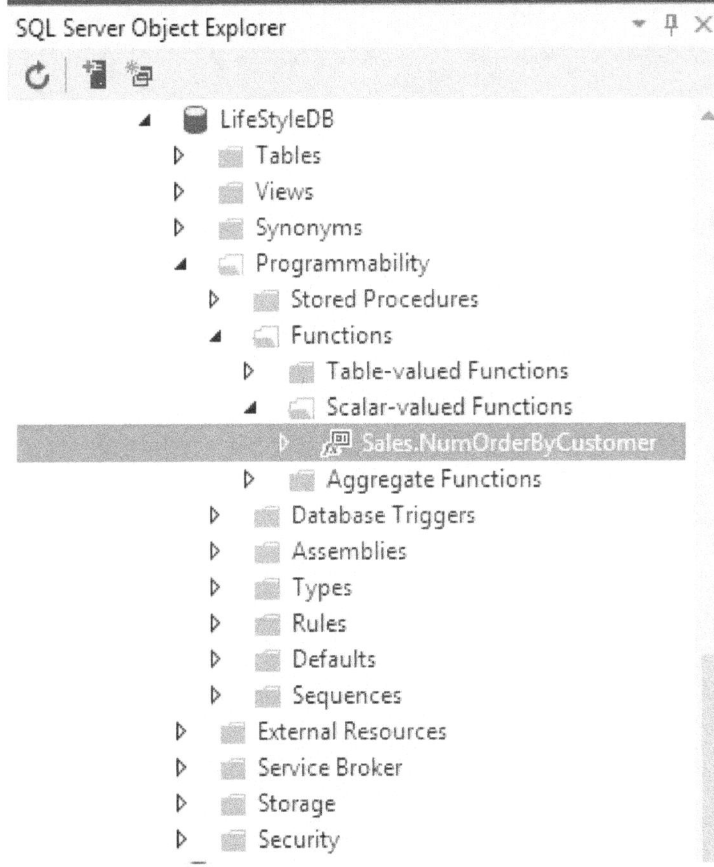

If you want to check whether the function has been created in the SQL Server, visit the "SQL Server Object Explorer" and find Sales.NumOrderByCustomer in the LifeStyleDB as shown in the following figure.

SQL Example 5.10 Use the Function

The function can be employed in various contexts where functions are typically used, such as within a SELECT clause. In this example, we will utilize our newly created function to showcase both the customer ID and the total number of orders placed by the customer.

```
SELECT CustomerId, Sales.NumOrderByCustomer(CustomerId) AS "Number of Orders"
FROM Sales.Customers;
```

The corresponding output looks like this:

	CustomerId	Number of Orders
1	1	3
2	2	1
3	3	1
4	4	1
5	5	1
6	6	0
7	7	1
8	8	0

SQL Example 5.11

Create a user defined function called LifeStyleTotalOrders that will return the total units of products ordered by all customers.

SQL Example 5.11 Analysis

This function will not use any input parameter and will return an int value.

SQL Example 5.11 Statement

```
GO
CREATE OR ALTER FUNCTION Sales.LifeStyleTotalOrders()
RETURNS INT
AS
BEGIN
    DECLARE @TotalNumOrders INT;
    SELECT @TotalNumOrders = SUM(Quantity)
    FROM Sales.OrderDetails
    RETURN @TotalNumOrders;
END;
```

SQL Example 5.11 Use the Function

We will use the previous two functions to display customer ID, number of orders by each customer, and total units of product ordered by all customers.

```
SELECT CustomerId,
    Sales.NumOrderByCustomer(CustomerId) AS "Number of Orders",
    Sales.LifeStyleTotalOrders() AS "Company Total Quantity"
FROM Sales.Customers;
```

SQL Example 5.11 Output with the Use:

	CustomerId	Number of Orders	Company Total Quantity
1	1	3	41
2	2	1	41
3	3	1	41
4	4	1	41
5	5	1	41
6	6	0	41
7	7	1	41
8	8	0	41

SQL Example 5.12

Create a user defined function called ProductsByCustomer that will accept customer ID as input and return product ID, product name and quantity purchased.

SQL Example 5.12 Analysis

In order to return the product name and units of product a customer purchased, we will need to join three tables: Sales.Orders, Sales.OrderDetails, and Purchasing.Products.

SQL Example 5.12 Statement

```
GO
CREATE OR ALTER FUNCTION Sales.ProductsByCustomer(@CustomerId INT)
RETURNS TABLE
AS
RETURN
(
    SELECT O.CustomerId, OD.ProductId, P.ProductName, SUM(OD.quantity) AS "Total Quantity"
    FROM Sales.Orders AS O JOIN Sales.OrderDetails AS OD
    ON O.OrderId = OD.OrderId
    JOIN Purchasing.Products AS P
    ON OD.ProductId = P.ProductId
    WHERE O.CustomerId =@CustomerId
    GROUP BY O.CustomerId, OD.ProductId, P.ProductName
);
```

SQL Example 5.12 Use the Function

```
SELECT * FROM Sales.ProductsByCustomer(2);
```

SQL Example 5.12 Output with the Use

	CustomerId	ProductId	ProductName	Total Quantity
1	2	3	3200 Lumens LED Home Theater Projector	2
2	2	6	Color Laser Printer	1
3	2	7	10" 16GB Android Tablet	2
4	2	8	GPS Android Tablet PC	2
5	2	9	20.2 MP Digital Camera	1

SQL Example 5.13

Create a user-defined function, OrderByCustomerYear, which takes a customer ID and an order year as input and returns order details for that customer in that year. Use the function to fetch data for customer ID 1 in the year 2017, listing order details with a quantity of 1, including order ID, order date, product ID, quantity, and price.

SQL Example 5.13 Analysis

This example demonstrates that the result of a table-valued UDF can be used like a table.

SQL Example 5.13 Statement

```
GO
CREATE OR ALTER FUNCTION Sales.OrderByCustomerYear(@CustomerId INT, @Year INT)
RETURNS TABLE
AS
RETURN
(
    SELECT O.OrderId, O.EmployeeId, O.OrderDate, OD.ProductId, OD.Quantity, OD.Price
    FROM Sales.Orders AS O JOIN Sales.OrderDetails AS OD
    ON O.OrderId = OD.OrderId
    WHERE O.CustomerId = @CustomerId AND YEAR(O.OrderDate) = @Year
);
```

SQL Example 5.13 Use the Function

```
SELECT OrderId, OrderDate, ProductId, Quantity, Price
FROM Sales.OrderByCustomerYear(1, 2017)
WHERE Quantity = 1;
```

SQL Example 5.13 Output with the Use

	OrderId	OrderDate	ProductId	Quantity	Price
1	1	2017-01-03	1	1	1499.99
2	2	2017-03-05	1	1	1499.99
3	2	2017-03-05	2	1	1599.99

Review Question 5.31

A prebuilt scalar-valued function ______.
a. accepts a single value
b. accepts no input
c. returns a single value
d. returns no value

Review Question 5.32
Which of the following is a benefit of using user defined functions?
a. more secure
b. shorter code
c. less traffic between clients and servers
d. better organization of SQL statements.

Review Question 5.33
Which of the following is a benefit of using user defined functions?
a. more secure
b. easier to learn
c. better performance
d. powerful clients

Review Question 5.34
Which of the following cannot be in the RETURNS statement in a user defined function?
a. INT
b. MONEY
c. CURRENCY
d. TABLE

Review Question 5.35
What do built-in functions like SUM() and CAST() in T-SQL primarily return?
a. Scalar values
b. Tables
c. Strings
d. Arrays

Review Question 5.36
What key advantage does the textbook mention about using user-defined functions (UDFs) in T-SQL?
a. More secure SQL statement
b. Improved performance
c. Complex data manipulation
d. Integration with external systems

Review Question 5.37
What key advantage does the textbook mention about using user-defined functions (UDFs) in T-SQL?
a. Organizing SQL statements
b. Improved user experience
c. Complex data manipulation
d. Integration with external systems

Review Question 5.38
How do user-defined functions (UDFs) differ from built-in functions in T-SQL?

a. UDFs cannot accept parameters
b. UDFs are slower than built-in functions
c. UDFs can only return tables
d. UDFs allow for custom processing and can be used to organize code

Review Question 5.39
When is the execution plan of a user-defined function (UDF) cached on the server?
a. Every time the UDF is defined
b. After every call to the UDF
c. When the UDF is initially called
d. When the UDF is executed in a stored procedure

Review Question 5.40
What does the "RETURNS TABLE" indicate in the syntax for creating a table-valued user-defined function (UDF)?
a. It returns a table
b. It returns a scalar value
c. It defines a data type
d. It specifies the function's name

5.6 Differences between Stored Procedures and UDFs

Stored procedures and user-defined functions (UDFs) are fundamental components of T-SQL, and they serve different roles in database development. Here, we'll explore some key distinctions between these two entities:

1. Types of Statements:

A stored procedure can include a variety of SQL statements, both Data Manipulation Language (DML) and Data Query Language (DQL) statements. This means it can have SELECT, INSERT, UPDATE, and DELETE statements, allowing it to modify data in addition to retrieving it.

UDFs are primarily designed for data retrieval. They can only contain SELECT statements and are intended for querying and returning data, not for modifying it.

2. Parameters:

Stored procedures can have both input and output parameters. Output parameters allow the procedure to return values to the calling program.

UDFs can only have input parameters. They are used to accept input values for processing and return results based on those inputs. Output parameters are not supported in UDFs.

3. Usage in Queries:

UDFs offer unique flexibility when used in queries. They can be treated like tables, allowing you to incorporate them directly in SELECT, FROM, WHERE, and HAVING clauses, making them highly versatile for data manipulation.

Stored procedures cannot be used within SELECT, FROM, WHERE, or HAVING clauses of queries. They are typically executed independently and are primarily used for executing sets of statements and procedures.

Review Question 5.41
A stored procedure contains a bunch of SQL statements. Which of the following cannot be part of a stored procedure?
a. SELECT
b. INSERT
c. EDIT
d. DELETE

Review Question 5.42
A user defined function contains a bunch of SQL statements. Which of the following can be part of a user defined function?
a. SELECT
b. INSERT
c. EDIT
d. DELETE

Review Question 5.43
A stored procedure can have _______ parameters.
a. input only
b. output only
c. input and output
d. neither input nor output

Review Question 5.44
A user defined function can have _______ parameters.
a. input only
b. output only
c. input and output
d. neither input nor output

Review Question 5.45
A user defined function can be used like a _______ in many ways.
a. table
b. database
c. SELECT statement
d. INSERT statement

Review Question 5.46

A stored procedure can be used in _______ clause.
a. SELECT
b. WHERE
c. HAVING
d. none of the clause listed

Review Question 5.47
What types of SQL statements can be included in a stored procedure?
a. SELECT only
b. INSERT, UPDATE, and DELETE only
c. Both DML and DQL statements
d. None of the options listed

Review Question 5.48
Which of the following is true about user-defined functions (UDFs) regarding parameters?
a. UDFs can have both input and output parameters.
b. UDFs can only have output parameters.
c. UDFs can only have input parameters.
d. UDFs cannot have any parameters.

Review Question 5.49
In which type of SQL clause can you use user-defined functions (UDFs) as if they were tables?
a. SELECT and FROM clauses
b. WHERE clause
c. HAVING clause
d. None of the clauses listed

Review Question 5.50
What is the primary purpose of stored procedures?
a. Data retrieval
b. Data manipulation
c. Both data retrieval and data manipulation
d. Neither data retrieval nor data manipulation

Review Question 5.51
Can a stored procedure include output parameters?
a. Yes
b. No
c. Only if it contains SELECT statements
d. Only if it contains UPDATE statements

Review Question 5.52
Which of the following statements is true about user-defined functions (UDFs) and their role in database development?
a. UDFs are used for executing sets of statements and procedures.
b. UDFs are primarily designed for data retrieval.
c. UDFs can contain both DML and DQL statements.
d. UDFs can be used in SELECT, INSERT, and HAVING clauses of queries.

5.7 Chapter Summary

In this chapter, you learned about stored procedures, which are frequently used in programming because they are easier to use than a collection of SQL statements, and they are faster since the SQL statements are compiled. You also learned about a similar and useful technique known as user-defined functions. User-defined functions are an effective way to organize code for better understanding and maintenance, especially when working on modular programming.

5.8 Discussion

Discussion 5.1

In any of the examples for creating stored procedures, if you remove the line SET NOCOUTN ON; what differences would you see?

Discussion 5.2

In the SQL Example 5.5 statement, to execute the stored procedure, we issued the following:

```
EXECUTE CustomerOrderInformation 1, @AverageAmount OUTPUT, @MostRecentOrderDate OUTPUT;
```

What happens if you replace the '1' with "@CustomerId = 1" ?

```
EXECUTE CustomerOrderInformation @CustomerId = 1, @AverageAmount OUTPUT, @MostRecentOrderDate OUTPUT;
```

Discussion 5.3

Explain the differences between stored procedures and user defined functions. Sometimes you can use either one of them to solve a problem. In that case, which one would you prefer to use?

5.9 SQL Exercises

Exercise 5.1

Create a stored procedure called Purchasing.DeliveryValue that will return the total value for each product delivered. Include the execution command.

	ProductId	DeliveryTotal
1	1	8199.93
2	2	11999.90
3	3	1299.90
4	4	1599.80
5	5	2099.85
6	6	4249.75
7	7	2219.70

Exercise 5.2

Create a stored procedure called Purchasing.UnitsDelivered that will display a given product's total units delivered. Include the execution command for product ID 7.

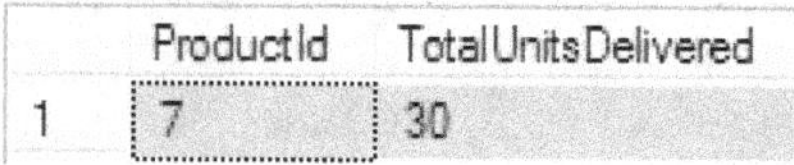

	ProductId	TotalUnitsDelivered
1	7	30

Exercise 5.3

Create a stored procedure called ProductQuantityFromSupplierByDate that will display all products and their corresponding quantity provided by a certain supplier on a certain date.

Include the execution command of the stored procedure for supplier ID 4 on November 1, 2016:

	supplierid	DeliveryDate	ProductId	Quantity
1	4	2016-11-01 10:20:00.0000000	1	5

Exercise 5.4

Create a stored procedure called HighLowDeliveryPrice that can find the product ID for the product that was delivered for the highest price and the product ID of the product that was delivered for the lowest price.

Include the execution command.

	Highest Price	Lowest Price
1	2	7

Exercise 5.5

Create a stored procedure called SupplierDeliveryInformation that will use supplier ID as input and will return the average delivery amount and the most recent delivery date for that supplier.

Include the execution command for supplier ID 2.

	Average Delivery Amount	Most Recent Delivery Date
1	3174.80	2016-10-10 10:30:00.000

Exercise 5.6

Create a stored procedure called DeliveryTotalPlusTax that will accept a delivery ID and return delivery total plus tax. There is a 10% tax on deliveries from suppliers of any foreign country (Non USA country).

Include the execution command for delivery ID 5.

	Total
1	1759.78

Exercise 5.7

The following code is used to provide a Suppliers table in Chapter5Exercise for the practice of Exercises 5.7 to 5.9:

```
GO
CREATE SCHEMA Chapter5Exercise AUTHORIZATION dbo;
GO
SELECT * INTO Chapter5Exercise.Suppliers FROM Purchasing.Suppliers;
```

Create a stored procedure called InsertSupplier that can be used to insert a new supplier name into the Chapter5Exercise.Suppliers table.

Include the execution command for a supplier named "Augur".

Use the following statement to confirm that the result is correct (Supplier ID may be different.)

```
SELECT * FROM Chapter5Exercise.Suppliers;
```

	SupplierId	SupplierName	StreetAddress	City	State	PostalCode	Country
1	1	Pine Apple	1 Pine Apple St.	Idanha	CA	87201	USA
2	2	IMB	123 International Blvd	Los Angeles	CA	89202	USA
3	3	Lonovo	33 Beijin Square	Beijing	Beijing	100201	China
4	4	Samsong	1 Electronics Road	Yeongtong	Suwon	30174	South Korea
5	5	Canan	12 Camera St	Ota	Tokyo	100-0121	Japan
6	6	Augur	NULL	NULL	NULL	NULL	NULL

Exercise 5.8

Create a stored procedure called Chapter5Exercise.UpdateSupplier that will update a supplier based on a given name. Add supplier address only if the supplier has a unique name.

Include the execution command for updating the supplier called "Augur" with the following address:

1000 Augur Parkway,

Redwood Shores, CA 94065

USA

Use the following statement to confirm the result is correct (Supplier ID may be different.)

```
SELECT * FROM Chapter5Exercise.Suppliers;
```

	SupplierId	SupplierName	StreetAddress	City	State	PostalCode	Country
1	1	Pine Apple	1 Pine Apple St.	Idanha	CA	87201	USA
2	2	IMB	123 International Blvd	Los Angeles	CA	89202	USA
3	3	Lonovo	33 Beijin Square	Beijing	Beijing	100201	China
4	4	Samsong	1 Electronics Road	Yeongtong	Suwon	30174	South Korea
5	5	Canan	12 Camera St	Ota	Tokyo	100-0121	Japan
6	6	Augur	1000 Augur Parkway	Redwood Shores	CA	94065	USA

Exercise 5.9

Create a stored procedure called Chapter5Exercise.DeleteSupplier that will delete a supplier record based on its supplier ID.

Include the execution command for deleting the newly added supplier from Exercise 5.7 (supplierID of 6 in the book, your newly added supplierID may be different)

Use the following statement to confirm that the result is correct.

```
SELECT * FROM Chapter5Exercise.Suppliers;
```

	SupplierId	SupplierName	StreetAddress	City	State	PostalCode	Country
1	1	Pine Apple	1 Pine Apple St.	Idanha	CA	87201	USA
2	2	IMB	123 International Blvd	Los Angeles	CA	89202	USA
3	3	Lonovo	33 Beijin Square	Beijing	Beijing	100201	China
4	4	Samsong	1 Electronics Road	Yeongtong	Suwon	30174	South Korea
5	5	Canan	12 Camera St	Ota	Tokyo	100-0121	Japan

Exercise 5.10

Create a user defined function called Purchasing.NumDeliveryBySupplier that will accept the supplier ID and return the number of deliveries from that supplier.

Use the Purchasing.NumDeliveryBySupplier function in an SQL statement to generate a result like this:

	SupplierId	Number of Deliveries
1	1	0
2	2	2
3	3	1
4	4	5
5	5	1

Exercise 5.11

Create a user defined function called Purchasing.LifeStyleTotalDeliveries that will return the total units of product delivered to LifeStyle from all suppliers.

Use the Purchasing.NumDeliveryBySupplier (see Exercise 5.10) and Purchasing.LifeStyleTotalDeliveries (this exercise) functions in an SQL statement to generate a result like this:

	SupplierId	Number of Deliveries	Company Delivery Quantity
1	1	0	117
2	2	2	117
3	3	1	117
4	4	5	117
5	5	1	117

Exercise 5.12

Create a user defined function called Purchasing.ProductsBySupplier that will accept supplier ID as input and return product ID, product name and quantity delivered from the supplier.

Use the Purchasing.ProductsBySupplier function in an SQL statement to generate a result like this:

	supplierid	ProductId	ProductName	Total Quantity
1	4	1	65-Inch 4K Ultra HD Smart TV	7
2	4	2	60-Inch 4K Ultra HD Smart LED TV	10
3	4	7	10" 16GB Android Tablet	30

Exercise 5.13

Create a user defined function called Purchasing.DeliveryBySupplierMonth that will accept supplier ID and delivery month as input and return delivery details for that supplier in that month.

Use the Purchasing.DeliveryBySupplierMonth function in an SQL statement to generate a result like this (ID=4 and Month=10):

	DeliveryId	DeliveryDate	ProductId	Quantity	Price
1	1	2016-10-01 09:30:00.0000000	1	2	1099.99
2	3	2016-10-02 11:10:00.0000000	2	10	1199.99
3	8	2016-10-11 11:10:00.0000000	7	12	79.99
4	9	2016-10-12 09:50:00.0000000	7	18	69.99

5.10 Solutions to the Review Questions

5.1 C; 5.2 D; 5.3 B; 5.4 A; 5.5 D; 5.6 A; 5.7 D; 5.8 C; 5.9 C; 5.10 C; 5.11 A; 5.12 D; 5.13 B; 5.14 B; 5.15 B; 5.16 B; 5.17 C; 5.18 C; 5.19 D; 5.20 D; 5.21 D; 5.22 B; 5.23 D; 5.24 B; 5.25 A; 5.26 A; 5.27 B; 5.28 C; 5.29 D; 5.30 A; 5.31 C; 5.32 D; 5.33 C; 5.34 C; 5.35 A; 5.36 B; 5.37 A; 5.38 D; 5.39 C; 5.40 A; 5.41 C; 5.42 A; 5.43 C; 5.44 A; 5.45 A; 5.46 D; 5.47 C; 5.48 C; 5.49 A; 5.50 C; 5.51 A; 5.52 B;

CHAPTER 6: TRANSACTIONS AND ERROR HANDLING

Chapter Learning Objectives

6.1 Apply the use of transactions in T-SQL to solve real-world scenarios.
6.2 Describe and differentiate the four essential properties of a transaction.
6.3 Implement error handling within a transaction to address exceptions and ensure data integrity.
6.4 Illustrate instances of deadlock in database systems and identify the factors leading to deadlock.

6.1 Introduction to Transactions

In SQL, a transaction represents a collective set of SQL statements that must either all be executed successfully or none executed at all. Imagine a scenario where there are 10 SQL statements within a transaction, and if, for any reason, one of them cannot be executed, we want that none of the 10 SQL statements will be executed.

To illustrate this concept, consider a business that keeps track of the quantity on hand for a particular product. When a customer purchases one unit of this product, the order data (representing the purchase of one unit) should be inserted into the customer orders table, and simultaneously, the quantity on hand for that product should be decreased by one. The objective here is to ensure that both actions, the recording of the purchase and the decrement of the quantity, are executed together. If, by any chance, one action is recorded while the other is not, it would result in a compromise of the database's integrity.

There are four fundamental properties that define a transaction: atomicity, consistency, isolation, and durability, collectively referred to as ACID:

Atomicity: In essence, atomicity ensures that the transaction is an indivisible unit of work, meaning that either all changes within the transaction occur or none of them do. If an issue arises before the transaction is completed, or more precisely, before it is committed, SQL Server has the capability to reverse the changes.

Consistency: This property implies that a transaction should not transition the database from one integrity state to another in a way that violates its constraints. For instance, after inserting a new record, the primary key must still be unique, and foreign keys must remain valid.

Isolation: Isolation guarantees that the data accessed during a transaction remains consistent with its state at the beginning of the transaction. If data is retrieved while other data is being updated, it should reflect the valid state before the update and an invalid state after. Isolation ensures that transactions access only consistent data.

Durability: Durability stipulates that data saved in the database must remain unchanged even in the face of unexpected events. Before making permanent changes to the database, any alterations to the data are initially recorded in a transaction log. SQL Server is then capable of either replaying these changes from the log to the database (redo) or reverting them (undo). Once a transaction is committed, the data is permanently saved.

By default, SQL Server treats each individual SQL statement as a transaction, implying that it is automatically committed after execution. To initiate a transaction, use the "BEGIN TRANSACTION" (or "BEGIN TRAN") statement. To conclude a transaction and commit it, use "COMMIT TRANSACTION," while for ending a transaction without committing, use "ROLLBACK TRANSACTION."

Before working on the examples in this chapter, let's create a schema and a table to avoid interfering with our original database. Execute the following SQL statement:

```
use LifeStyleDB;

CREATE SCHEMA Chapter6Example AUTHORIZATION dbo;
GO

SELECT * INTO Chapter6Example.Orders FROM Sales.Orders;
```

This will make a copy of orders table for pratice. Then, take a look at the Chapter6Example.Orders table by issuing:

```
SELECT * FROM Chapter6Example.Orders;
```

You should see the result table like this:

	OrderId	CustomerId	EmployeeId	OrderDate
1	1	1	5	2017-01-03
2	2	1	3	2017-03-05
3	3	2	5	2017-02-23
4	4	4	5	2017-04-13
5	5	1	4	2017-05-03
6	6	3	6	2017-05-08
7	7	5	7	2016-11-08
8	8	7	2	2016-12-23

SQL Example 6.1

First, issue the following SQL statement:

```
DELETE FROM Chapter6Example.Orders
    WHERE CustomerId = 1;
```

Then, issue the following SQL statement again:

```
SELECT * FROM Chapter6Example.Orders;
```

You should see the result table like this:

	OrderId	CustomerId	EmployeeId	OrderDate
1	3	2	5	2017-02-23
2	4	4	5	2017-04-13
3	6	3	6	2017-05-08
4	7	5	7	2016-11-08
5	8	7	2	2016-12-23

The question is, can you undo the three rows you just deleted? The answer is no. By default, every SQL statement will be committed. That is, the result set is saved to the database.

Next, let's delete all orders handled by Employee 5 by issuing the following SQL statements:

```
BEGIN TRANSACTION
    DELETE FROM Chapter6Example.Orders
    WHERE EmployeeId = 5;
```

Then, take a look at the Chapter6.Orders table to see what's in it:

```
SELECT * FROM Chapter6Example.Orders;
```

You should see the result like this:

	OrderId	CustomerId	EmployeeId	OrderDate
1	6	3	6	2017-05-08
2	7	5	7	2016-11-08
3	8	7	2	2016-12-23

No surprise. The two rows handled by Employee 5 are gone. The question is: Can you undo the two rows just deleted? The answer is: Yes, you can rollback a transaction if you use BEGIN TRANSACTION.

Next, issue the following statement:

```
ROLLBACK TRANSACCTION;
```

Finally, check the table with the following statement:

```
SELECT * FROM Chapter6Example.Orders;
```

The result data set looks like:

	OrderId	CustomerId	EmployeeId	OrderDate
1	3	2	5	2017-02-23
2	4	4	5	2017-04-13
3	6	3	6	2017-05-08
4	7	5	7	2016-11-08
5	8	7	2	2016-12-23

SQL Example 6.2

Write a transaction to delete all orders handled by Employee 5 in the Chapter6Example.Orders table. This time don't allow the data to be undone.

SQL Example 6.2 Analysis

Instead of ROLLBACK TRANSACTION, use COMMIT TRANSACTION that will save the change to the database.

SQL Example 6.2 Statement

```
BEGIN TRANSACTION
    DELETE FROM Chapter6Example.Orders
    WHERE EmployeeId = 5;
COMMIT TRANSACTION
```

SQL Example 6.2 Output

If you issue the following SQL statement:

```
SELECT * FROM Chapter6Example.Orders;
```

You will see the result set like this:

	OrderId	CustomerId	EmployeeId	OrderDate
1	6	3	6	2017-05-08
2	7	5	7	2016-11-08
3	8	7	2	2016-12-23

There is no way to undo the delete. If you try to undo the delete with the following:

```
ROLLBACK TRANSACTION;
```

You will receive the error message similar to the following:

T-SQL   ↑↓   ▦ Results   ▤ Message

```
Msg 3903, Level 16, State 1, Line 16
The ROLLBACK TRANSACTION request has no corresponding BEGIN TRANSACTION.
```

Review Question 6.1
A ______ is a group of SQL statements that you want to be executed or none to be executed.
a. view
b. stored procedure
c. transaction
d. user defined function

Review Question 6.2
A transaction is a(n) ______ unit of work, ensuring that all changes within the transaction either fully occur or are completely rolled back.
a. atomic
b. consistent
c. isolated
d. durable

Review Question 6.3
One property of transaction is ______, which means that the transaction may change the database state from one integrity state to another.
a. atomicity
b. consistency
c. isolation
d. durability

Review Question 6.4
If you retrieve data while some data is updating, the data is valid before updating. The data is invalid after updating. ______ ensures that transactions access only consistent data.
a. atomicity
b. consistency
c. isolation
d. durability

Review Question 6.5
The ______ means that data saved in the database should be the same even after something unexpected happens.
a. atomicity
b. consistency
c. isolation
d. durability

Review Question 6.6

By default, SQL Server treats _____ as a transaction.
a. all related SQL statements
b. each individual SQL statement
c. no individual SQL statement
d. one group of SQL statements

Review Question 6.7
For each transaction in SQL Server, to end a transaction with commit use _____.
a. COMMIT
b. COMMIT TRANSACTION
c. SAVE
d. SAVE TRANSACTION.

Review Question 6.8
For each transaction in SQL Server, to end a transaction without commit, use _____.
a. UNDO
b. UNDO TRANSACTION
c. ROLLBACK
d. ROLLBACK TRANSACTION

Review Question 6.9
Once a transaction is committed, _______.
a. you can rollback with rollback
b. you cannot rollback
c. you can find the statement in the trash can
d. you can undo the transaction with UNDO

Review Question 6.10
Without using a transaction, if you accidentally delete a record, you _________.
a. can undo it by issuing ROLLBACK TRANSACTION
b. can undo it by issuing UNDO Delete
c. don't need to undo as long as you don't COMMIT
d. cannot execute a sql statement to take the record back

Review Question 6.11
What is the primary purpose of a transaction in SQL?
a. To execute SQL statements individually
b. To ensure all SQL statements within it are executed successfully or none at all
c. To allow flexibility in executing SQL statements
d. To improve database performance

Review Question 6.12
In the context of a transaction, what does atomicity mean?
a. The ability to execute SQL statements individually
b. Ensuring all changes within the transaction occur together or not at all
c. The flexibility of executing transactions
d. Improving data retrieval performance

Review Question 6.13
Which of the following is a fundamental property of a transaction and is often abbreviated as ACID?

a. Reliability
b. Consistency
c. Flexibility
d. Efficiency

Review Question 6.14
What does the property of "consistency" in a transaction ensure?
a. The transaction is efficient and quick
b. The database transitions between integrity states smoothly
c. The primary key remains unique
d. The foreign keys remains unique

Review Question 6.15
What does the property of "isolation" in a transaction guarantee?
a. Data is accessed without consistency
b. Data remains unchanged during the transaction
c. Data is isolated from the rest of the database
d. Data accessed during a transaction remains consistent with its initial state

Review Question 6.16
What is the role of "durability" in a transaction?
a. Making SQL statements flexible
b. Enhancing data retrieval speed
c. Ensuring that data remains unchanged even after unexpected events
d. Accelerating database operations

Review Question 6.17
By default, how does SQL Server treat individual SQL statements?
a. As flexible transactions
b. As uncommitted transactions
c. As automatically committed transactions
d. As transactions without rollback options

Review Question 6.18
What SQL statement is used to mark the beginning of a transaction in SQL Server?
a. BEGIN TRANSACTION
b. INITIATE TRANSACTION
c. START TRANSACTION
d. OPEN TRANSACTION
Review Question 6.19
How can you end a transaction with a commitment in SQL Server?
a. END TRANSACTION
b. FINALIZE TRANSACTION
c. COMMIT TRANSACTION
d. CLOSE TRANSACTION

Review Question 6.20
What statement is used to end a transaction without committing it in SQL Server?
a. END TRANSACTION
b. FINALIZE TRANSACTION

c. ROLLBACK TRANSACTION
d. CLOSE TRANSACTION

6.2 Transaction with Exception Handling

The syntax for a T-SQL transaction typically follows this structure:

```
BEGIN TRANSACTION
    BEGIN TRY
        --Perform operations here;
        COMMIT TRANSACTION;
    END TRY
    BEGIN CATCH
        ROLLBACK TRANSACTION;
    END CATCH
GO
```

In the above syntax, the SQL statements you wish to execute should be enclosed within the "Perform operations here" block. If these statements are successfully executed, the COMMIT TRANSACTION statement that follows the block will save the changes and conclude the transaction. However, if an error occurs during execution, the control will shift to the BEGIN CATCH block, where the ROLLBACK TRANSACTION statement is triggered, reverting all changes and terminating the transaction.

SQL Example 6.3

Reset the Chapter6Example tables before proceeding. Execute the following code to create three tables (Orders, OrderDetails, and Products) along with their associated primary keys and foreign keys in the Chapter6Example schema. You'll encounter this code multiple times throughout this chapter:

```
DROP TABLE IF EXISTS Chapter6Example.OrderDetails;
SELECT * INTO Chapter6Example.OrderDetails FROM Sales.OrderDetails;
DROP TABLE IF Exists Chapter6Example.Orders;
SELECT * INTO Chapter6Example.Orders FROM Sales.Orders;
DROP TABLE IF EXISTS Chapter6Example.Products;
SELECT * INTO Chapter6Example.Products FROM Purchasing.Products;
ALTER TABLE Chapter6Example.Orders
    Add CONSTRAINT pk_Chapter6Example_Orders PRIMARY KEY (OrderId);
ALTER TABLE Chapter6Example.OrderDetails
    Add CONSTRAINT pk_Chapter6Example_OrderDetails PRIMARY KEY (OrderId,
ProductId);
ALTER TABLE Chapter6Example.Products
    Add CONSTRAINT pk_Chapter6Example_Products PRIMARY KEY (ProductId);
ALTER TABLE Chapter6Example.OrderDetails
    ADD CONSTRAINT fk_Chapter6Example_OrderDetails_Orders
    FOREIGN KEY (OrderId)
    REFERENCES Chapter6Example.Orders(OrderId);
```

```
ALTER TABLE Chapter6Example.OrderDetails
    ADD CONSTRAINT fk_Chapter6Example_OrderDetails_Products
    FOREIGN KEY (ProductId)
    REFERENCES Chapter6Example.Products(ProductId);
```

Add an order for Customer 2 on January 1, 2017. The order has two products in it: 2 units of Product 3 for $169.99 each and 1 unit of Product 4 for $99.99. The order was handled by Employee 3.

SQL Example 6.3 Analysis

If you only intend to insert a row into the Sales.Orders table and two rows into the Sales.OrderDetails table, there's nothing new. However, we aim to group these three INSERT statements into a transaction to avoid having a partially completed order.

SQL Example 6.3 Statement

```
BEGIN TRANSACTION;
BEGIN TRY
  DECLARE @neworderid AS INT;
  INSERT INTO Chapter6Example.Orders
      (CustomerId, EmployeeId, orderdate)
    VALUES
      (2, 3, '20170101');
  SET @neworderid = SCOPE_IDENTITY();
INSERT INTO Chapter6Example.OrderDetails (orderid, productid, Price, Quantity)
    VALUES(@neworderid, 3, 169.99, 2);
INSERT INTO Chapter6Example.OrderDetails (orderid, productid, Price, quantity)
    VALUES(@neworderid, 4, 99.99, 1);
COMMIT TRANSACTION;
END TRY
BEGIN CATCH
  ROLLBACK TRANSACTION;
END CATCH
GO
```

SQL Example 6.3 Check the Data

Issue the following SELECT statements to check if the data is correctly inserted:

```
SELECT * FROM Chapter6.orders
    WHERE CustomerId = 2
    AND EmployeeId = 3
    AND orderdate = '20170101';
SELECT * FROM Chapter6.OrderDetails
    WHERE orderid > 8;
```

Example 6.3 Output with Check the Data SELECT Statement

	OrderId	CustomerId	EmployeeId	OrderDate
1	9	2	3	2017-01-01

	OrderId	ProductId	Price	quantity
1	9	3	169.99	2
2	9	4	99.99	1

SQL Example 6.4

Before proceeding, reset the Chapter6 tables. Execute the code block at the beginning of Example 6.3, which drops three tables and adds primary key and foreign key constraints.

Next, create an order for Customer 2 on January 1, 2017, consisting of two units of Product 3 priced at $169.99 each and one unit of Product 14 priced at $99.99. The order was handled by Employee 3.

SQL Example 6.4 Analysis

The sole distinction between this example and the previous one is the replacement of 1 unit of Product 4 with 1 unit of Product 14. Since Product 14 does not exist in the Products table, we anticipate an error, and consequently, none of the three INSERT statements will be executed.

SQL Example 6.4 Statement

```
BEGIN TRANSACTION;
BEGIN TRY
  DECLARE @neworderid AS INT;
  INSERT INTO Chapter6.Orders
      (CustomerId, EmployeeId, orderdate)
    VALUES
      (2, 3, '20170101');
  SET @neworderid = SCOPE_IDENTITY();
  INSERT INTO Chapter6.OrderDetails (orderid, productid, Price, Quantity)
    VALUES(@neworderid, 3, 169.99, 2);
  INSERT INTO Chapter6.OrderDetails (orderid, productid, Price, quantity)
    VALUES(@neworderid, 14, 99.99, 1);
COMMIT TRANSACTION;
END TRY
BEGIN CATCH
  ROLLBACK TRANSACTION;
END CATCH
GO
```

SQL Example 6.4 Output

Even though the following output may show two of the three INSERTs successfully executed, if you check the data with the following "Example 6.4 Check the Data", you won't see any rows inserted.

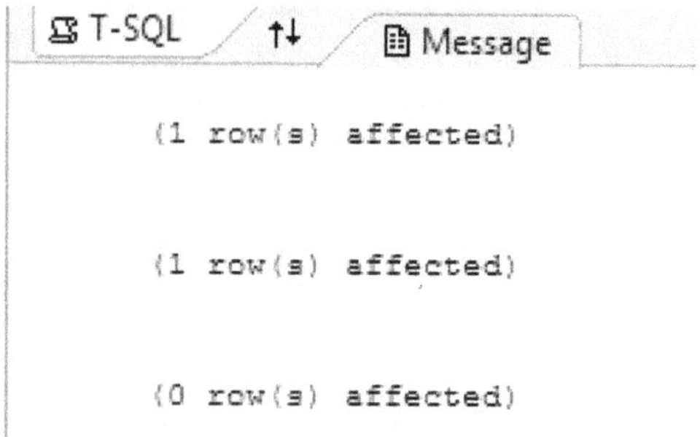

SQL Example 6.4 Check the Data

Issue the following SELECT statements to check if the data was correctly inserted:

```sql
SELECT * FROM Sales.orders
    WHERE CustomerId = 2
    AND EmployeeId = 3
    AND orderdate = '20170101';
SELECT * FROM Sales.OrderDetails
    WHERE orderid > 8;
```

SQL Example 6.4 Check the Data Output (blank tables)

Review Question 6.21
A transaction often includes a try … catch statement. A COMMIT TRANSACTION line should be _____.
a. anywhere inside the try block
b. anywhere inside the catch block
c. the last line in the try block
d. the last line in the catch block

Review Question 6.22
A transaction often includes a try … catch statement. A ROLLBACK TRANSACTION line should be ____.
a. anywhere inside the try block
b. the last line in the try block
c. right after the line that might throw an exception
d. inside the catch block

Review Question 6.23
What is the purpose of the "BEGIN TRANSACTION" statement in T-SQL?

a. To initiate a new database connection.
b. To execute SQL statements.
c. To start a new transaction.
d. To retrieve data from a database.

Review Question 6.24
Where should SQL statements you want to execute within a transaction be placed in the syntax?
a. Within the BEGIN CATCH block.
b. In the "ROLLBACK TRANSACTION" block.
c. After the "BEGIN TRY" line.
d. After the "GO" statement.

Review Question 6.25
What happens if the SQL statements in the "TRY" block are successfully executed?
a. The transaction is automatically committed.
b. The transaction remains open indefinitely.
c. The transaction is rolled back.
d. The transaction is explicitly committed using "COMMIT TRANSACTION."

Review Question 6.26
What is the purpose of the "ROLLBACK TRANSACTION" statement in T-SQL?
a. To create a new database transaction.
b. To execute SQL statements.
c. To revert changes and terminate a transaction.
d. To save changes made in a transaction.

Review Question 6.27
What does the "BEGIN CATCH" block in the syntax handle?
a. SQL statement execution.
b. Database connections.
c. Error handling.
d. Committing the transaction.

Review Question 6.28
What is the function of the "GO" statement at the end of the T-SQL transaction syntax?
a. It marks the end of the T-SQL batch.
b. It executes all SQL statements before and after the "GO" in one batch.
c. It is the same as "RUN" command.
d. It rolls back the transaction.

Review Question 6.29
If the following is the output of an T-SQL transaction that inserts 3 rows, it is most likely _______.
(1 row(s) affected)
(1 row(s) affected)
(0 row(s) affected)
a. the first two rows are inserted, but the third row insertion failed
b. two of the three rwos are inserted, but not all three rows
c. all three rows are inserted, but the third row value may be wrong
d. none of the rows are inserted

6.3 Nested Transactions and Savepoints

Transactions in SQL Server can be nested, meaning you can start a new transaction within an existing outer transaction. The nested inner transaction is dependent on the outer - if the outer transaction rolls back, the inner nested transaction will also roll back, even if it was committed. For example:

```
BEGIN TRANSACTION Outer
BEGIN TRANSACTION Inner
-- SQL statements
COMMIT TRANSACTION Inner
ROLLBACK TRANACTION Outer
```

Here, Inner will be committed but then rolled back when Outer is rolled back. The SQL statements within Inner will not be committed even though Inner was committed explicitly.

Savepoints provide more granular control over parts of a transaction. A savepoint marks a point within a transaction that can be rolled back to, without aborting the entire transaction.

For example:

```
BEGIN TRANSACTION
SAVE TRANSACTION Savepoint1
-- SQL statements
SAVE TRANSACTION Savepoint2
-- More SQL statements
ROLLBACK TRANSACTION Savepoint2
COMMIT TRANSACTION
```

In this case, "ROLLBACK TRANSACTION Savepoint2" will undo the SQL statements after SAVE TRANSACTION Savepoint2 but before ROLLBACK TRANSACTION Savepoint2. The COMMIT TRANSACTION will then commit the entire transaction, including any changes made before SAVE TRANSACTION Savepoint1 and after ROLLBACK TRANSACTION Savepoint2.

Savepoints allow partial rollbacks within a transaction, unlike nested transactions which are all-or-nothing. This provides finer control over transaction scopes.

SQL Example 6.5

Reset the Chapter6Example tables before proceeding. Execute the code block at the beginning of Example 6.3, which drops three tables and adds primary keys and foreign key constraints.

Next, delete order IDs 3 and 5 from the Chapter6Example.OrderDetails table using two nested transactions. In the outer transaction, delete order ID 3, and in the inner transaction, delete order ID 5. Commit the inner transaction while rolling back the outer transaction. Which delete statement gets committed?

SQL Example 6.5 Analysis

Just one rollback will undo any nested transaction.

SQL Example 6.5 Statement

```
BEGIN TRANSACTION
    DELETE FROM Chapter6Example.OrderDetails WHERE OrderId = 3;
    BEGIN TRANSACTION
        DELETE FROM Chapter6Example.OrderDetails WHERE OrderId = 5;
    COMMIT TRANSACTION
ROLLBACK TRANSACTION;
```

SQL Example 6.5 Output with SELECT

After executing the statement, you may notice the output shows a total of 7 rows affected:

```
(5 row(s) affected)
(2 row(s) affected)
```

Use the following SQL statement to verify which statement is committed:

```
SELECT * FROM Chapter6Example.OrderDetails;
```

You should still see 19 rows in the Chapter6Example.OrderDetails table, with no rows removed. What happens if you swap the positions of the COMMIT and ROLLBACK lines? Remember that ROLLBACK will undo any transactions. Consequently, the COMMIT command will not correspond to any "BEGIN TRANSACTION".

SQL Example 6.6

Reset the Chapter6Example tables before continuing. Execute the code block at the beginning of Example 6.3, which drops three tables and adds primary keys and foreign key constraints.

Next, in a transaction, delete all order details from the Chapter6Example.OrderDetails table with order IDs of 3 and 5, one statement at a time, with a save point in between. Then, rollback to the save point. Finally, commit the change. Which delete statement is committed?

SQL Example 6.6 Analysis

This example illustrates that a rollback does not always reset the transaction to its beginning. Rollback only undoes statements made after a save point. If a commit immediately follows the rollback, any statements preceding the save point will be committed.

SQL Example 6.6 Statement

```
BEGIN TRANSACTION
    DELETE FROM Chapter6.OrderDetails WHERE OrderId = 3;
    SAVE TRANSACTION SavePoint
    DELETE FROM Chapter6.OrderDetails WHERE OrderId = 5;
ROLLBACK TRANSACTION SavePoint;
COMMIT TRANSACTION;
```

SQL Example 6.6 Output with SELECT

Use the following SQL statement to check which statement is committed:

```
SELECT * FROM Chapter6.OrderDetails;
```

You may notice that rows with OrderId =3 are gone and rows with OrderId=5 are still there.

Review Question 6.30
If you want to commit partial transaction, use the ______.
a. partial transaction
b. incomplete transaction
c. book mark
d. savepoint

Review Question 6.31
What happens to a nested inner transaction when the outer transaction is rolled back?
a. The inner transaction is automatically committed.
b. The inner transaction is rolled back along with the outer transaction.
c. The inner transaction remains open and unaffected.
d. The inner transaction is saved as a separate transaction.

Review Question 6.32
What does a savepoint within a transaction allow you to do?
a. Abort the entire transaction.
b. Commit specific changes within the transaction.
c. Roll back the entire transaction to a certain point.
d. Create a new nested transaction.

Review Question 6.33
In the given example with a savepoint, what happens after executing "ROLLBACK TRANSACTION Savepoint2"?

```
BEGIN TRANSACTION
SAVE TRANSACTION Savepoint1
-- SQL statements
```

```
SAVE TRANSACTION Savepoint2
-- More SQL statements
ROLLBACK TRANSACTION Savepoint2
COMMIT TRANSACTION
```
a. The entire transaction is rolled back.
b. Only the changes after "SAVE TRANSACTION Savepoint2" are rolled back.
c. The transaction is committed.
d. The entire transaction is saved as a separate transaction.

Review Question 6.34
What is the key difference between nested transactions and savepoints?
a. Savepoints allow partial rollbacks, while nested transactions are all-or-nothing.
b. Nested transactions provide finer control over transaction scopes.
c. Savepoints are used for rolling back the entire transaction.
d. Nested transactions can be nested indefinitely.

Review Question 6.35
Can a savepoint be used to create a new nested transaction?
a. Yes, a savepoint functions as a nested transaction.
b. No, savepoints and nested transactions are unrelated concepts.
c. Yes, but only in certain circumstances.
d. No, savepoints are used solely for error handling.

Review Question 6.36
What is the outcome of executing "COMMIT TRANSACTION" in the provided savepoint example?
```
BEGIN TRANSACTION
SAVE TRANSACTION Savepoint1
-- SQL statements
SAVE TRANSACTION Savepoint2
-- More SQL statements
ROLLBACK TRANSACTION Savepoint2
COMMIT TRANSACTION
```
a. The entire transaction is rolled back.
b. The entire transaction is committed, including all changes.
c. The transaction is aborted.
d. Only the changes before "SAVE TRANSACTION Savepoint2" are committed.

6.4 Error Handling

Prior to SQL Server 2000, the primary method for error handling was the @@Error system function. This function returns an integer value representing the error code. A value of 0 indicates no error. The value of @@Error is automatically set to 0 once a statement is successfully executed. However, you should exercise caution when using the @@Error function. For instance, if a faulty statement is followed by a successful one, the @@Error value will be reset to 0. This might not always align with your intentions.

Another error-handling technique at your disposal is the RAISEERROR statement. It enables you to throw exceptions at runtime, offering the flexibility for custom error handling. An example of its usage is as follows:

```
RAISERROR('This is a custom error message.', 11, 127);
```

In this example, 'This is a custom error message' represents the error message string, 11 is the error level number, and 127 is the state value.

The default message code number is 50000. You can specify any number between 13000 and 2147483647, excluding 50000.

The error level number indicates the severity of the error. Values between 0 and 10 are typically used for informational purposes. Values between 11 and 18 indicate errors, while values between 19 and 25 signify fatal errors.

The state value is a user-defined number that aids in message identification for debugging. This number is often employed to pinpoint the location of the error. For example, using state 1 to indicate the first RAISERROR and state 2 for the second RAISERROR helps programmers locate the issue more efficiently. The state value can range from 1 to 127.

The third technique for error handling is the TRY...CATCH statement. You've already seen how this statement was used in transactions earlier in this chapter. In this section, you will learn how it can be applied in stored procedures.

SQL Example 6.7

Before proceeding, reset the Chapter6Example.Orders table by dropping it and populating it again:

```
DROP TABLE Chapter6Example.Orders;
SELECT * INTO Chapter6Example.Orders FROM Sales.Orders;
```

Next, create a transaction to insert a new order row into the Chapter6Example.Orders table using fictitious data. Save the @@Error system function value in a variable named @ErrorResult. If @ErrorResult is 0, the transaction will be committed; otherwise, it will be rolled back."

SQL Example 6.7 Statement

```
DECLARE @ErrorResult VARCHAR(100);
BEGIN TRANSACTION
```

```
SET IDENTITY_INSERT Chapter6Example.Orders ON
    INSERT INTO Chapter6Example.Orders
        (OrderId, CustomerId, EmployeeId, OrderDate)
        VALUES
        (10, 3, 6, '20170101')
SET @ErrorResult = @@ERROR;
IF (@ErrorResult = 0)
BEGIN
    PRINT 'Success!';
    COMMIT TRANSACTION;
END
ELSE
BEGIN
    PRINT 'Insert failed.';
    ROLLBACK TRANSACTION;
END
```

Example 6.7 Output

```
Success!
```

Note: Sometimes, you may encounter the following error: `'IDENTITY_INSERT is already ON for table LifeStyleDB.Chapter6Example.XXXXX.'` You will need to execute the following command to turn it off:

```
SET IDENTITY_INSERT Chapter6Example.XXXXX OFF
```

SQL Example 6.8

This example is similar to SQL Example 6.7, with the difference being the removal of the OrderId and its corresponding value '10'. You should expect to see 'Insert failed.' in the output.

SQL Example 6.8 Statement

```
DECLARE @ErrorResult VARCHAR(100);
BEGIN TRANSACTION
SET IDENTITY_INSERT Chapter6Example.Orders ON
    INSERT INTO Chapter6Example.Orders
        (CustomerId, EmployeeId, OrderDate)
        VALUES
        (3, 6, '20170101')
SET @ErrorResult = @@ERROR;
IF (@ErrorResult = 0)
BEGIN
    PRINT 'Success!';
```

```
   COMMIT TRANSACTION;
END
ELSE
BEGIN
   PRINT 'Insert failed.';
   ROLLBACK TRANSACTION;
END
```

SQL Example 6.8 Output

```
Msg 545, Level 16, State 1, Line 173
Explicit value must be specified for
Insert failed.
```

SQL Example 6.9

This example demonstrates how to create a custom error code using the same scenario as the previous one.

SQL Example 6.9 Statement

```
DECLARE @ErrorResult VARCHAR(100);
BEGIN TRANSACTION
SET IDENTITY_INSERT Chapter6Example.Orders ON
   INSERT INTO Chapter6Example.Orders
      (CustomerId, EmployeeId, OrderDate)
      VALUES
      (3, 6, '20170101')
SET @ErrorResult = @@ERROR;
IF (@ErrorResult = 0)
BEGIN
   PRINT 'Success!';
   COMMIT TRANSACTION;
END
ELSE
BEGIN
   RAISERROR('Insert failed.', 17, 127);
   ROLLBACK TRANSACTION;
END
```

SQL Example 6.9 Output

```
Msg 545, Level 16, State 1, Line 193
Explicit value must be specified for identity
Msg 50000, Level 17, State 127, Line 205
Insert failed.
```

SQL Example 6.10

This example utilizes TRY...CATCH for the execution of a stored procedure.

Create a stored procedure named 'TableError' to retrieve data from a fictitious table name not in the database. While the stored procedure won't raise any complaints, executing it will result in an error that can be managed using TRY...CATCH.

SQL Example 6.10 Statement

```
GO
CREATE OR ALTER PROCEDURE TableError
AS
    SELECT * FROM NoSuchTable;
GO

BEGIN TRY
    EXECUTE TableError;
END TRY
BEGIN CATCH
    SELECT
        ERROR_NUMBER() AS "Error Number",
        ERROR_MESSAGE() AS "Error Message";
END CATCH;
```

SQL Example 6.10 Output

	Error Number	Error Message
1	208	Invalid object name 'NoSuchTable'.

Review Question 6.37
The ______ system function returns an integer value representing the error code
a. Error
b. @Error
c. @@Error
d. @@@Error

Review Question 6.38
You can use ______ statement to handle error. It allows you to throw an exception at runtime.
a. ERROR
b. RAISERROR
c. @ERROR
d. @RAISERROR

Review Question 6.39
Given RAISERROR('This is a custom error message.', 11, 127), what is the default error code number?
a. 0
b. 11

c. 127

d. 50000

Review Question 6.40

Given RAISERROR('This is a custom error message.', 11, 127), what is the level number?

a. 0

b. 11

c. 127

d. 50000

Review Question 6.41

Given RAISERROR('This is a custom error message.', 11, 127), what is the state number?

a. 0

b. 11

c. 127

d. 50000

Review Question 6.42

What is the primary method of error handling before SQL Server 2000?

a. RAISEERROR statement

b. TRY...CATCH statement

c. @@Error system function

d. Custom error messages

Review Question 6.43

What value does the @@Error system function return when there is no error?

a. 0

b. 11

c. 127

d. 50000

Review Question 6.44

What is the purpose of the RAISEERROR statement in T-SQL?

a. To suppress errors in the code

b. To automatically commit transactions

c. To throw exceptions at runtime

d. To set the state value for debugging

Review Question 6.45

What is the default message code number for RAISEERROR?

a. 0

b. 11

c. 127

d. 50000

Review Question 6.46

What does the state value help with in error handling and debugging?

a. It represents the severity of the error.

b. It specifies the error message code number.

c. It identifies the location of the error.

d. It indicates whether the error is fatal.

Review Question 6.47
What is the purpose of the TRY...CATCH statement in error handling?
a. To automatically commit transactions
b. To throw exceptions at runtime
c. To suppress errors in the code
d. To manage errors and exceptions in a structured way

Review Question 6.48
What is the purpose of the "SET IDENTITY_INSERT" command mentioned in the note?
```
SET IDENTITY_INSERT Chapter6Example.Orders ON
```
a. To turn on the identity column for a table.
b. To insert new records into a table.
c. To insert your own explicit values into the identity column of that table.
d. To activate the primary key constraint.

Review Question 6.49
When might you encounter the error message mentioned in the note?
```
'IDENTITY_INSERT is already ON for table LifeStyleDB.Chapter6Example.XXXXX.'
```
a. When trying to enable the identity column for a table.
b. When inserting records into any table.
c. When you can insert your own explicit values into the identity column of that table.
d. When the identity column is already turned off for a specific table.

6.5 Blocking

When one user is updating a row while another user is attempting to read data from the same row, SQL Server takes measures to ensure data consistency, often by blocking the second user's request. Nevertheless, blocking can lead to deadlocks and a decline in database performance. A simple scenario illustrating a deadlock situation involves two sessions attempting to use resources held by each other. For instance, let's consider one session with a transaction that targets two rows, Row1 and Row2, and another session with a transaction that accesses the same two rows but in a different order, Row2 and then Row1. If the first session is immediately followed by the second session, Row1 becomes blocked due to the first session's actions, and Row2 is blocked due to the second session's activities.

As a result, the first session is unable to complete its transaction because Row2 is blocked. Similarly, the second session cannot finish its transaction due to the blocking of Row1. These scenarios can result in database contention and performance degradation.

Let's see an example. Begin by opening three "New Query" tabs as shown in the following figure. These tabs will have default names: "SQLQuery1.sql," "SQLQuery2.sql," and "SQLQuery3.sql." Keeping these default names will make it easier to follow the instructions. Your Visual Studio should look like this:

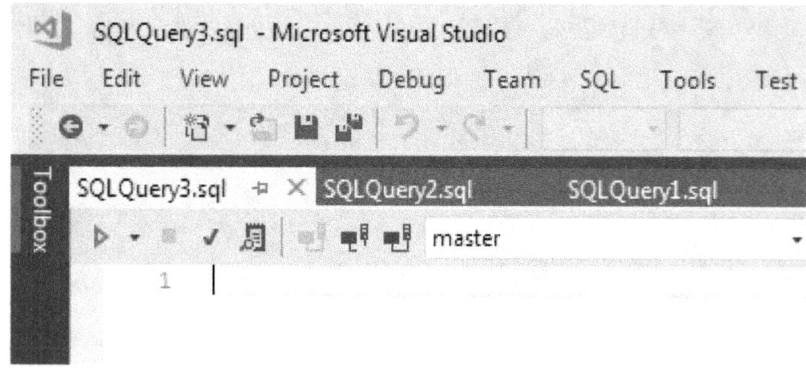

Now, click on the "SQLQuery1.sql" tab and execute the code as shown in the following figure:

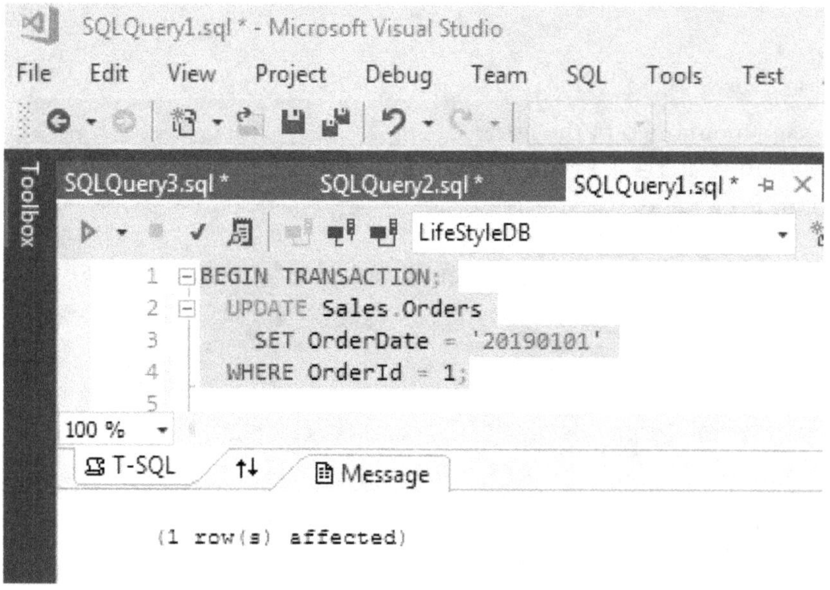

Note that we are intentionally not completing the transaction with either COMMIT or ROLLBACK. This will lock that particular row.

Next, in the "SQLQuery2.sql" tab, enter the following code and execute it:

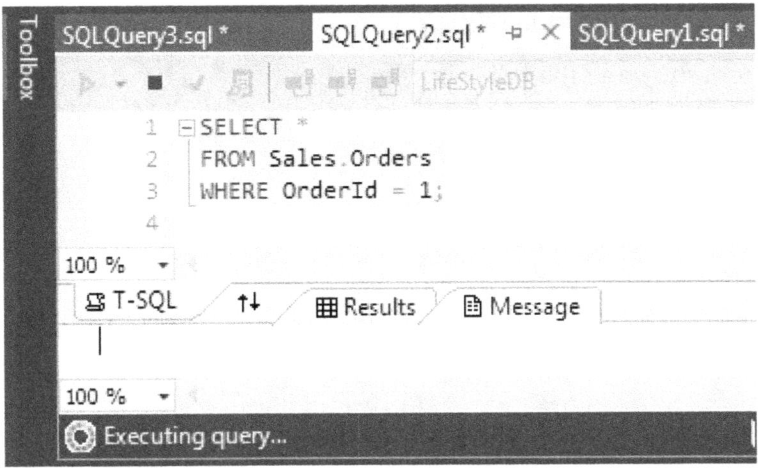

Note the blank result and the busy "Executing query..." symbol at the bottom left. However, if you change OrderId = 1 to OrderId = 2, it will work.

In the "SQLQuery3.sql" tab, type in the following code and execute it:

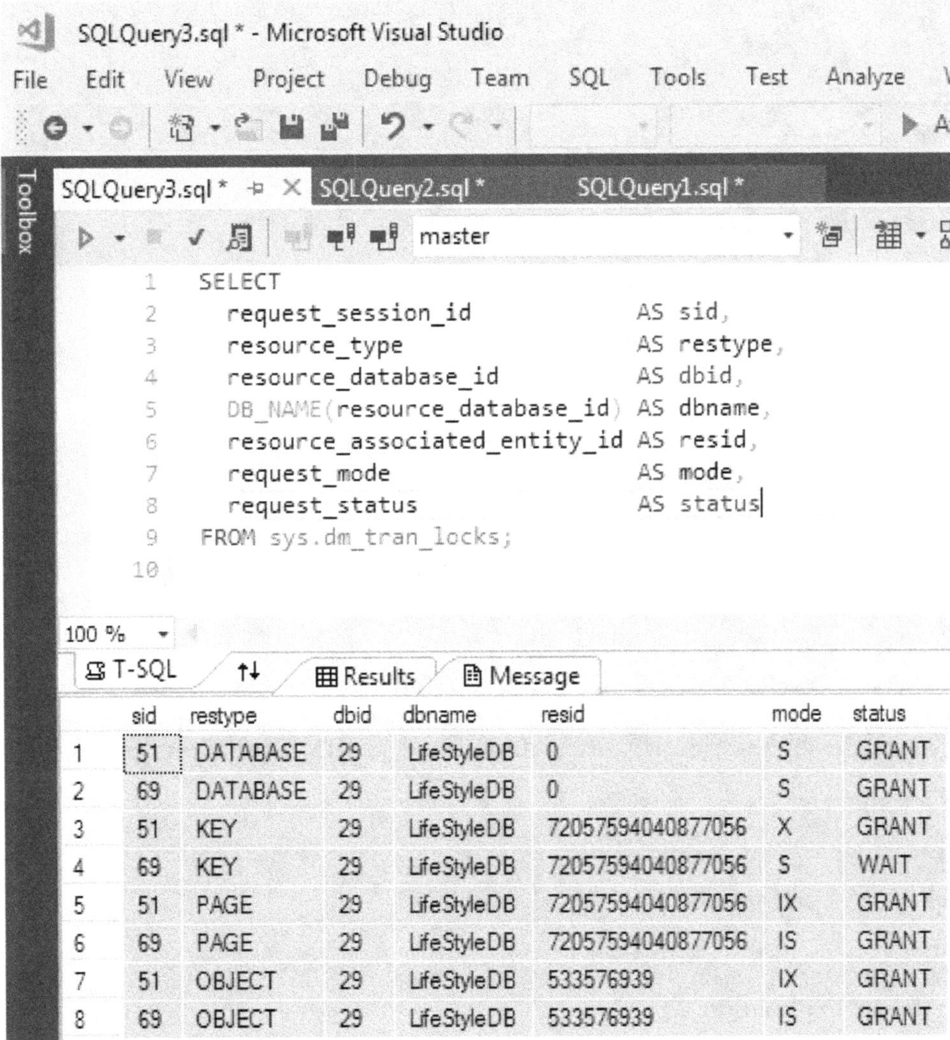

Now, return to the "SQLQuery2.sql" tab and cancel the execution by clicking on the "Cancel Execution (Alt+Break)" square and stopping the execution as shown in the following figure:

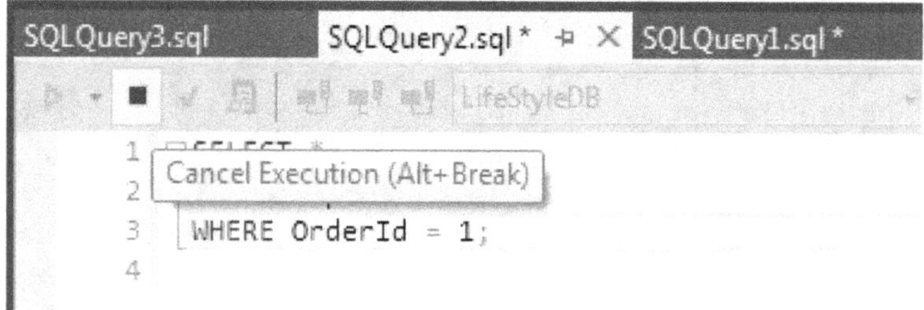

Next, go back to "SQLQuery3.sql" and execute the same query:

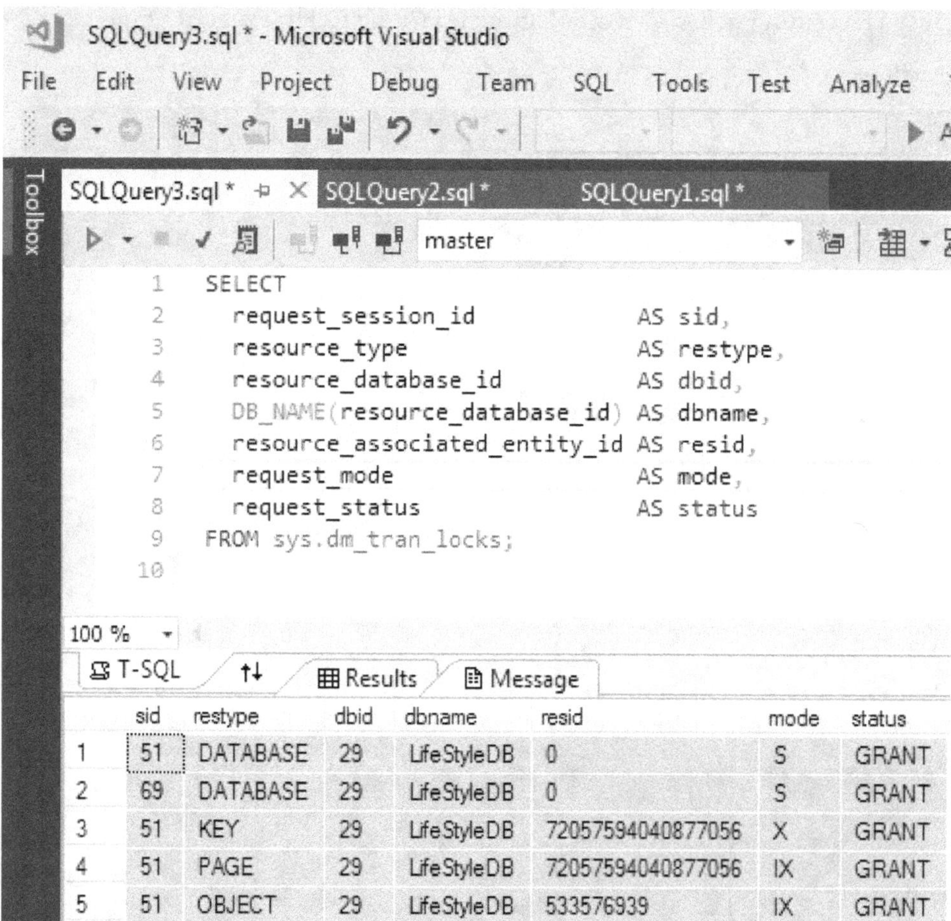

Each database connection is associated with a session ID, often abbreviated as SID. To find out the sid for a connection, issue the following statement:

```
SELECT @@spid FROM sys.dm_exec_connections;
```

I found that my SQLQuery1.sql sid is 51 and my SQLQuery2.sql sid is 69.

Regarding the resource types, here's an explanation:

"Database" represents the database as a resource. In the example, it's "LifeStyleDB."

"Page" signifies a single page within a data file, and it serves as a container for storing database file information. The standard page size in SQL Server is 8KB. If a file size exceeds 8KB (after accounting for some administrative overhead), it will require more than one page. In both "SQLQuery1.sql" and "SQLQuery2.sql" sessions, only one page is involved in each session.

"Rid" stands for "Row ID," which represents one or more rows in an index.

"Object" denotes a database object, which can be a table, view, index, stored procedure, extended stored procedure, or any object with an object ID.

Regarding the "Mode," there are four possible values:

"S" (Shared): A shared lock reserves a resource, such as a page or row, for reading only. Other processes cannot update resources that are shared locked, but multiple processes can hold shared locks for the same resource simultaneously.

"X" (Exclusive): An exclusive lock reserves a resource, such as a page or row, for exclusive use by a single transaction. DML statements require exclusive locks. An exclusive lock is not possible if another process holds a shared or exclusive lock on the same resource simultaneously. Furthermore, when an exclusive lock is set for a resource, no other lock can be placed on the same resource.

The "I" in both "IS" and "IX" stands for "intent to lock." An intent lock indicates an intention to lock the next lower-level resource in the database hierarchy. In the example, there is an "IX" on a page, which will result in an "X" on a "RID." This prevents other processes from locking the page before obtaining the desired locks on the row.

SQL Example 6.11

The purpose of this exercise is to generate a deadlock. Start two sessions to update the order date in the Sales.Orders table by incrementing it by one day. The first session will update order ID 1 and then order ID 2, while the second session will update order ID 2 first and then order ID 1.

SQL Example 6.11 Sesion1 Statement in the first session

```
GO
DECLARE @retry INT;
SET @retry = 5;
WHILE (@retry > 0)
BEGIN
    BEGIN TRY
        BEGIN TRANSACTION;
            UPDATE Sales.Orders
            SET OrderDate = DATEADD(DAY, 1, OrderDate)
            WHERE OrderId = 1;
        WAITFOR DELAY '00:00:15';
            UPDATE Sales.Orders
```

```
            SET OrderDate = DATEADD(DAY, 1, OrderDate)
            WHERE OrderId = 2;
        SET @retry = 0;
        COMMIT TRANSACTION;
    END TRY
    BEGIN CATCH
        IF (ERROR_NUMBER() = 1205)
            BEGIN
                PRINT 'Dead lock in session 1';
                SET @retry = @retry - 1;
            END
        ELSE
            SET @retry = -1;
        IF XACT_STATE() <> 0
            ROLLBACK TRANSACTION;
    END CATCH;
END;
GO
```

SQL Example 6.11 Session2 Statement in second session

```
GO
DECLARE @retry INT;
SET @retry = 5;
WHILE (@retry > 0)
BEGIN
    BEGIN TRY
        BEGIN TRANSACTION;
            UPDATE Sales.Orders
            SET OrderDate = DATEADD(DAY, 1, OrderDate)
            WHERE OrderId = 2;
        WAITFOR DELAY '00:00:7';
            UPDATE Sales.Orders
            SET OrderDate = DATEADD(DAY, 1, OrderDate)
            WHERE OrderId = 1;
        SET @retry = 0;
        COMMIT TRANSACTION;
    END TRY
    BEGIN CATCH
        IF (ERROR_NUMBER() = 1205)
            BEGIN
                PRINT 'Dead lock in session 2.';
                SET @retry = @retry - 1;
            END
        ELSE
            SET @retry = -1;
        IF XACT_STATE() <> 0
            ROLLBACK TRANSACTION;
    END CATCH;
END;
GO
```

Execute "session 1" immediately followed by seecute "session 2" and wait for a few seconds to see result.

SQL Example 6.11 Session1 Output

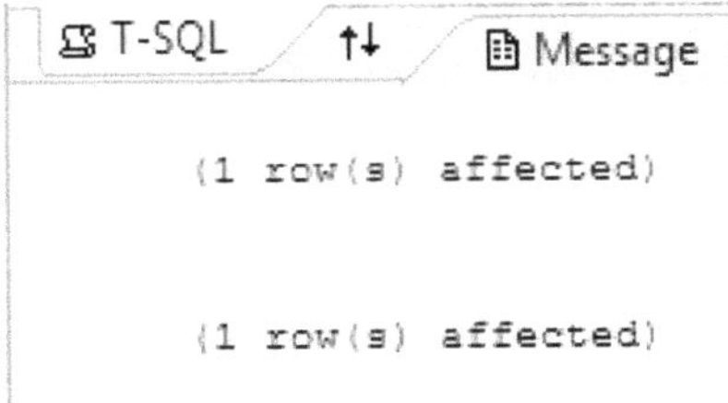

SQL Example 6.11 Session2 Output

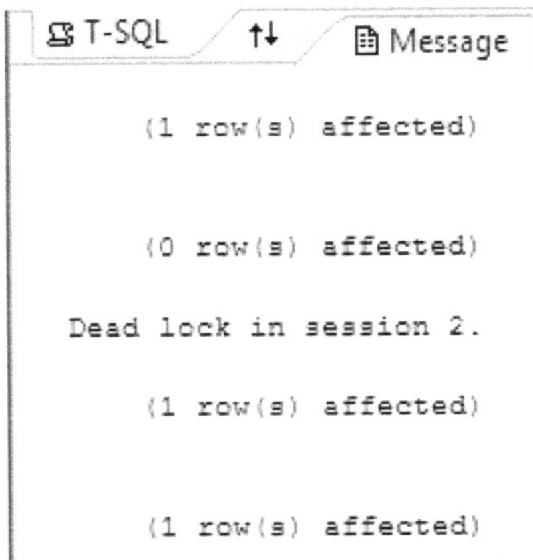

In SQL Example 6.11, Session2 was chosen by SQL Server as victim of the deadlock.

Review Question 6.50
What happens if one user is updating a row while another user is trying to read the data from the same row? To avoid the second user reading inconsistent data, the SQL Server will block the ______.
a. first user
b. second user
c. neither user
d. both users

Review Question 6.51
Two sessions trying to use the resource held by each other may result in ______.
a. conflict
b. crash
c. deadlock
d. one session is blocked

Review Question 6.52
A(n) ______ reserves a resource (e.g. page, or row) for reading only. Other processes cannot update the resources.
a. shared lock
b. exclusive lock
c. intent to shared lock
d. intent to exclusive lock

Review Question 6.53
A(n) ______ reserves a resource (e.g. page or row) for exclusive use of a single transaction.
a. shared lock
b. exclusive lock
c. intent to shared lock
d. intent to exclusive lock

6.6 Chapter Summary

In this chapter, you have learned about T-SQL transactions and their significance. We discussed the four properties of a transaction that aid in determining which statements should be included in one. Additionally, you explored the three techniques for error handling in T-SQL. The final part of this chapter delves into how SQL Server manages deadlocks with blocking. You can retrieve information about currently active lock manager resources in SQL Server from 'sys.dm_tran_locks.' This information is often invaluable for identifying and addressing the deadlocks that may impact SQL Server performance.

6.7 Discussion

Discussion 6.1

What is transaction? Do we have to use a transaction? Why or why not?

Discussion 6.2

What are the four properties of a transaction? Explain each with an example.

Discussion 6.3

@@Error is a system function that will return the error code for the current transaction. Why you should be careful when using it?

Discussion 6.4

Explain how the RAISERROR statement is used.

Discussion 6.5

Explain how the TRY … CATCH statement is used.

Discussion 6.6

What is deadlock? Use two examples to explain deadlock, one from everyday life and the other from database usage.

Discussion 6.7

In Section 6.5 Blocking, SQLQuery3.sql shows the database resource status. You may notice that there is only one RID in each session. Now change something in SQLQuery1.sql to make the output of the query in SQLQuery3.sql display multiple RIDs. Explain why.

Discussion 6.8

There are four different types of blocking modes discussed in this chapter. They are shared, exclusive, intended share, and intended exclusive. Explain the modes.

6.8 SQL Exercises

Exercise 6.1

Execute the following statement to create a schema called Chapter6Exercise and a table called Employees with data from HR.Employees.

```
CREATE SCHEMA Chapter6Exercise AUTHORIZATION dbo;
GO
SELECT * INTO Chapter6Exercise.Employees FROM HR.Employees;
```

Then write an SQL statement to update employee ID 7's date of birth to Oct. 5, 1987. Finally write SQL statement to undo it.

Exercise 6.2

Write an SQL statement to update employee ID 7's date of birth to Oct 5, 1987 as a transaction and finalize it in the database.

Exercise 6.3

Execute the following SQL statement to add a table called Orders to the Chapter6Exercise schema of the database.

```
SELECT * INTO Chapter6Exercise.Orders FROM Sales.Orders;
```

Then write a transaction to add a new employee with two orders handled in 2018. The customer ID in both orders is 3 and the dates are January 5 and February 6. The employee name is William Hardy. Birth date is March 5, 1987 and hired date is March 7, 2018. Leave all fields without data provided blank.

EmployeeId	FirstName	LastName	BirthDate	HireDate	HomeAddress	City	State	PostalCode	Phone	ManagerId
1	Alex	Hall	1990-02-03	2015-08-09	85 Main Ln	New Canton	VA	23123	(434) 290-3322	NULL
2	Dianne	Hart	1978-12-03	2010-08-01	209 Social Hall Blvd	New Canton	VA	23123	(434) 290-1122	1
3	Maria	Law	1988-07-13	2012-08-21	258 Blinkys St	New Canton	VA	23123	(434) 531-5673	1
4	Alice	Law	1988-12-13	2012-04-22	300 Vista Valley Blvd	Buckingham	VA	23123	(434) 531-1010	1
5	Black	Hart	1982-11-09	2015-04-12	1 Old Fifteen St	Buckingham	VA	23123	(434) 531-1034	2
6	Christina	Robinson	1978-07-13	2014-06-15	217 Chapel St	New Canton	VA	23123	NULL	2
7	Nicholas	Pinkston	1977-10-05	2013-05-22	26 N James Madison Rd	Buckingham	VA	23123	NULL	3
8	William	Hardy	1987-03-05	2018-03-07	NULL	NULL	NULL	NULL	NULL	NULL

OrderId	CustomerId	EmployeeId	OrderDate
1	1	5	2017-01-05
2	1	3	2017-03-07
3	2	5	2017-02-23
4	4	5	2017-04-13
5	1	4	2017-05-03
6	3	6	2017-05-08
7	5	7	2016-11-08
8	7	2	2016-12-23
9	3	8	2018-01-05
10	3	8	2018-02-06

Exercise 6.4

Write a transaction to add a new employee with two orders handled in 2018. The customer ID in both orders is 3 and the dates are January 5 and February 30. The employee name is William Hardy. Birth date is March 5, 1987 and hired date is March 7, 2018. Leave all fields without data provided blank.

The only difference between Exercise 6.4 and Exercise 6.3 is the change of second order date from February 6 to February 30.

Execute the following two SQL statements to confirm that no new records are inserted into either table.

```
SELECT * FROM Chapter6Exercise.Employees;
SELECT * FROM Chapter6Exercise.Orders;
```

Exercise 6.5

Delete employee IDs 3 and 5 from Chapter6Exercise.Employees table in two nested transactions. In the outer transaction delete employee ID 3 and in the inner transaction, delete employee ID 5. Commit the inner transaction while rolling back the outer transaction. Which delete statement is committed?

Exercise 6.6

In a transaction, delete employee ID 4 from Chapter6Exercise.Employees table. Then set a save point.

Continue to delete employee ID 6 from Chapter6Exercise.Employees. Next, rollback to the save point. Finally, commit the change. Which delete statement is committed?

Exercise 6.7

Create a transaction to insert a new employee row into the Chapter6Exercise.Employees table with made up data. Save @@Error system function value in a variable called @ErrorResult. If @ErrorResult is 0, the transaction will be committed. Otherwise, it will be rolled back.

Exercise 6.8

This exercise uses the same statements as Exercise 6.7 except for removing the first name. You should see the "Insert failed." In the output.

Exercise 6.9

This exercise uses the same statements as Exercise 6.8. Instead of PRINT error message, use RAISERROR statement with a custom error message.

Exercise 6.10

Create a stored procedure called SchemaError to retrieve data from a fake schema name that is not in the database. The stored procedure will not complain, but the execution of the stored procedure will result in an error that can be handled with TRY … CATCH.

Display error number and error message.

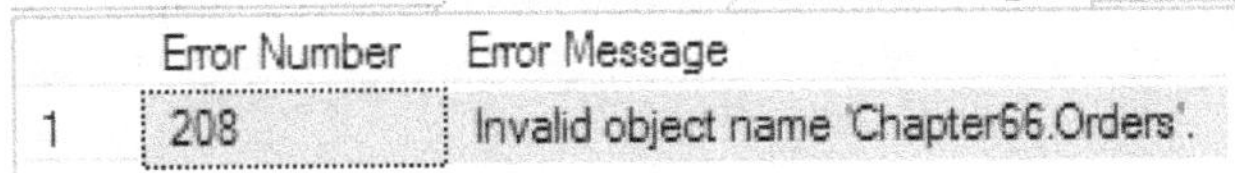

	Error Number	Error Message
1	208	Invalid object name 'Chapter66.Orders'.

Exercise 6.11

Simulate a deadlock with updating two rows of Chapter6Exercise.Employees with two sessions.

6.9 Solutions to the Review Questions

6.1 C; 6.2 A; 6.3 B; 6.4 C; 6.5 D; 6.6 B; 6.7 B; 6.8 D; 6.9 B; 6.10 D; 6.11 B; 6.12 B; 6.13 B; 6.14 B; 6.15 D; 6.16 C; 6.17 C; 6.18 A; 6.19 C; 6.20 C; 6.21 C; 6.22 D; 6.23 C; 6.24 C; 6.25 D; 6.26 C; 6.27 C; 6.28 A; 6.29 D; 6.30 D; 6.31 B; 6.32 C; 6.33 B; 6.34 A; 6.35 B; 6.36 D; 6.37 C; 6.38 B; 6.39 D; 6.40 B; 6.41 C; 6.42 C; 6.43 A; 6.44 C; 6.45 D; 6.46 C; 6.47 D; 6.48 C; 6.49 C; 6.50 B; 6.51 C; 6.52 A; 6.53 B;

CHAPTER 7: TRIGGERS AND ALTER TABLE

Chapter Learning Objectives

7.1 Identify the distinctions between triggers and stored procedures.
7.2 Explain the purpose and demonstrate the use of DML triggers.
7.3 Explain the purpose and demonstrate the use of DDL triggers.
7.4 Apply the knowledge to modify columns of a table.
7.5 Apply the knowledge to modify constraints of a table.

7.1 Introduction to Triggers

In Chapter 5, you acquired the skills to create and implement stored procedures. Now, in this chapter, we delve into the world of triggers, a specialized category of stored procedures designed to automatically respond to specific events within a database. Triggers are invaluable tools in database management as they enable you to execute predefined actions in reaction to events like record insertions. For instance, you can employ a trigger to automatically create an audit trail by storing a copy of each newly inserted record in a separate table.

It's worth noting that, while a trigger is fundamentally a type of stored procedure, it differs in execution. You don't explicitly execute triggers; instead, they are bound to specific events. SQL Server recognizes two primary event categories: data manipulation events (including INSERT, UPDATE, and DELETE) and data definition events (such as CREATE TABLE).

One essential consideration is that if you delete the table or view (only on INSTEAD OF triggers explained in the next section) upon which a trigger depends, the trigger itself will also be removed.

To define a trigger that activates after a specific event, the syntax is as follows:

```
CREATE TRIGGER TriggerName
ON TableName
AFTER INSERT[, UPDATE][, DELETE]
AS
BEGIN
    SET NOCOUNT ON;
    -- Your trigger logic here
END;
```

Before you proceed with the practice examples in this chapter, create a schema named "Chapter7Example" authorized by the "dbo" role. Next, create two tables: one named "Students" and the other named "StudentsAudit." You can achieve this by executing the following SQL statements:

```
use LifeStyleDB;
GO
CREATE SCHEMA Chapter7Example AUTHORIZATION dbo;
GO
DROP TABLE IF EXISTS Chapter7Example.Students;
CREATE TABLE Chapter7Example.Students
(
    StudentId    INT IDENTITY,
    StudentName  NVARCHAR(100) NOT NULL,
    StudentGpa   DECIMAL(3,2) NULL,
    CONSTRAINT pk_Students PRIMARY KEY(StudentId)
);

DROP TABLE IF EXISTS Chapter7Example.StudentsAudit;
CREATE TABLE Chapter7Example.StudentsAudit
(
    AuditId      INT IDENTITY,
    StudentId    INT NOT NULL,
    StudentName  NVARCHAR(100) NOT NULL,
    StudentGpa   DECIMAL(3,2) NULL,
    AuditAction  NVARCHAR(100) NOT NULL,
    AuditTimestamp DATETIME2(3) NOT NULL DEFAULT(SYSDATETIME()),
    LoginName SYSNAME NOT NULL DEFAULT(ORIGINAL_LOGIN()),
    CONSTRAINT pk_StudentsAudit PRIMARY KEY(AuditId)
);
```

SQL Example 7.1

Create a trigger named "trgStudentsInsert" within the "Chapter7Example" schema, which will automatically insert a record into the "Chapter7Example.StudentsAudit" table whenever a new student record is inserted into the "Chapter7Example.Students" table.

SQL Example 7.1 Analysis

The "Chapter7Example.StudentsAudit" table includes additional columns compared to the "Chapter7Example.Students" table. The "AuditAction" column stores a custom message describing the action that initiates the insertion of records into the "StudentsAudit" table. "AuditTimestamp" captures the system time, while "LoginName" denotes the user's name.

SQL Example 7.1 Statement

```
GO
CREATE OR ALTER TRIGGER Chapter7Example.trgStudentsInsert
ON Chapter7Example.Students
AFTER INSERT
AS
SET NOCOUNT ON;
INSERT INTO Chapter7Example.StudentsAudit
    (StudentId, StudentName, StudentGpa, AuditAction)
    SELECT StudentId, StudentName, StudentGpa, 'Insert a new student'
    FROM INSERTED;
GO
```

SQL Example 7.1 Invoke the Trigger by Inserting Two New Students

```
INSERT INTO Chapter7Example.Students(StudentName, StudentGpa)
    VALUES ('Ken Allen', 3.3);
INSERT INTO Chapter7Example.Students(StudentName, StudentGpa)
    VALUES ('Donna Harber', 3.4);
```

SQL Example 7.1 Confirm Output

Execute the following two SELECT statements to confirm that the trigger works.

```
SELECT * FROM Chapter7Example.Students;
SELECT * FROM Chapter7Example.StudentsAudit;
```

StudentId	StudentName	StudentGpa
1	Ken Allen	3.30
2	Donna Harber	3.40

AuditId	StudentId	StudentName	StudentGpa	AuditAction	AuditTimestamp	LoginName
1	1	Ken Allen	3.30	Insert a new student	2017-12-09 15:41:40.124	LS\Scott
2	2	Donna Har...	3.40	Insert a new student	2017-12-09 15:41:40.136	LS\Scott

SQL Example 7.2

Create a trigger named "trgStudentsUpdate" within the "Chapter7Example" schema. This trigger will automatically insert a record into the "Chapter7Example.StudentsAudit" table when a student's record in the "Chapter7Example.Students" table is updated. Specifically, if a student's name is modified, the Audit Action message should be "student name updated." If a student's GPA is modified, the Audit Action message should be "student GPA updated." If both the name and GPA of a student are modified, the Audit Action message should be "both student name and GPA updated."

SQL Example 7.2 Analysis

To proceed with this example, ensure that you have existing records in the "Students" table. If the table is empty, you can practice Example 7.1 to insert records before continuing. Additionally, declare a variable named "@AuditAction" to allow for the storage of different messages based on the actions performed, such as modifying the name, modifying the GPA, or both.

SQL Example 7.2 Statement

```
GO
CREATE OR ALTER TRIGGER Chapter7Example.trgStudentsUpdate
ON Chapter7Example.Students
AFTER UPDATE
AS
SET NOCOUNT ON;
DECLARE @auditAction NVARCHAR(100);
SET @auditAction = '';
IF UPDATE (StudentName)
    SET @auditAction += 'student name updated';
IF UPDATE (StudentGpa)
    SET @auditAction += 'student gpa updated';
IF UPDATE (StudentName) AND UPDATE(StudentGpa)
    SET @auditAction = 'Both student name and gpa updated';
INSERT INTO Chapter7Example.StudentsAudit
    (StudentId, StudentName, StudentGpa, AuditAction)
    SELECT StudentId, StudentName, StudentGpa, @AuditAction
    FROM INSERTED;
GO
```

SQL Example 7.2 Invoke the Trigger by Updating Students Three Times

```
UPDATE Chapter7Example.Students
    SET StudentName = 'Alice Allen'
WHERE StudentName = 'Ken Allen'
    AND StudentGpa = 3.3;

UPDATE Chapter7Example.Students
    SET StudentGpa = 3.9
WHERE StudentName = 'Donna Harber'
    AND StudentGpa = 3.4;
```

```
UPDATE Chapter7Example.Students
    SET StudentName = 'Donna Harper',
        StudentGpa = 3.8
WHERE StudentName = 'Donna Harber'
    AND StudentGpa = 3.9;
```

SQL Example 7.2 Confirm Output

Run the following two SELECT statements to confirm that the trigger works.

```
SELECT * FROM Chapter7.Students;
SELECT * FROM Chapter7.StudentsAudit;
```

StudentId	StudentName	StudentGpa
1	Alice Allen	3.30
2	Donna Harper	3.80

AuditId	StudentId	StudentName	StudentGpa	AuditAction	AuditTimestamp	LoginName
1	1	Ken Allen	3.30	Insert a new student	2017-12-09 15:41:40.124	LS\Scott
2	2	Donna Harber	3.40	Insert a new student	2017-12-09 15:41:40.136	LS\Scott
3	1	Alice Allen	3.30	student name updated	2017-12-09 16:17:09.931	LS\Scott
4	2	Donna Harber	3.90	student gpa updated	2017-12-09 16:24:28.543	LS\Scott
5	2	Donna Harper	3.80	Both student name and gpa updated	2017-12-09 16:27:26.162	LS\Scott

SQL Example 7.3

Create a trigger called Chapter7Example.trgStudentsDelete that will automatically insert a record into the Chapter7Example.StudentsAudit table when a student's record in the Chapter7Example.Students table is deleted.

SQL Example 7.3 Analysis

The only difference between this one and the previous two examples is that the previous two examples both use the "INSERTED" table while this one uses "DELETED" table.

SQL Example 7.3 Statement

```
GO
CREATE OR ALTER TRIGGER Chapter7Example.trgStudentsDelete
ON Chapter7Example.Students
AFTER DELETE
AS
SET NOCOUNT ON;
INSERT INTO Chapter7Example.StudentsAudit
    (StudentId, StudentName, StudentGpa, AuditAction)
    SELECT StudentId, StudentName, StudentGpa, 'Delete a student'
    FROM DELETED;
GO
```

SQL Example 7.3 Invoke the Trigger by Deleting a Student Row

```
DELETE FROM Chapter7Example.Students
    WHERE StudentName = 'Alice Allen'
        AND StudentGpa = 3.3;
```

SQL Example 7.3 Confirm Output

Run the following two SELECT statements to confirm that the trigger works.

```
SELECT * FROM Chapter7Example.Students;
SELECT * FROM Chapter7Example.StudentsAudit;
```

StudentId	StudentName	StudentGpa
2	Donna Harper	3.80

AuditId	StudentId	StudentName	StudentGpa	AuditAction	AuditTimestamp	LoginName
1	1	Ken Allen	3.30	Insert a new student	2017-12-09 16:47:39.947	LS\Scott
2	2	Donna Harber	3.40	Insert a new student	2017-12-09 16:47:39.948	LS\Scott
3	1	Alice Allen	3.30	student name updated	2017-12-09 16:49:02.046	LS\Scott
4	2	Donna Harber	3.90	student gpa updated	2017-12-09 16:49:06.267	LS\Scott
5	2	Donna Harper	3.80	Both student name a...	2017-12-09 16:49:14.384	LS\Scott
6	1	Alice Allen	3.30	Delete a student	2017-12-09 19:29:53.712	LS\Scott

Note, in SQL Server, the INSERTED table is a virtual table that is automatically created and managed by SQL Server. It is used to keep copies of the affected rows during INSERT and UPDATE statements. The INSERTED table mirrors the structure of the table that owns the trigger. Every time you perform an INSERT or UPDATE statement, the new data is stored in the INSERTED table. Also, the table used within a trigger to capture the old values before an UPDATE and DELETE operations in SQL Server is the DELETED table.

Review Question 7.1
A(n) _______ is a special type of stored procedure that executes automatically in response to certain events, such as when a record is inserted into a table.
a. special procedure
b. auto procedure
c. trigger
d. auto trigger

Review Question 7.2
A trigger is bound to specific _______.
a. CTE
b. view model

c. stored procedure
d. event

Review Question 7.3
SQL Server supports two types of events: ______ events such as INSERT, UPDATE, and DELETE, and ______ events such as CREATE TABLE.
a. data select, data delete
b. data manipulation, data definition
c. data select, data definition
d. date manipulation, data delete

Review Question 7.4
When you delete the table or view that a trigger is based on, ______.
a. an error shows up
b. you must delete the trigger before deleting the table or view
c. the trigger will be deleted
d. the trigger will still work on related tables or views

Review Question 7.5
When you update a record in a table, the affected records are stored in a table called ______.
a. inserted
b. updated
c. deleted
d. selected

Review Question 7.6
What is the primary purpose of a trigger in SQL Server?
a. To execute stored procedures
b. To create new tables
c. To automatically respond to specific events
d. To perform data backups

Review Question 7.7
How does a trigger differ in execution from a stored procedure?
a. Triggers are explicitly executed, while stored procedures are automatically executed.
b. Triggers are bound to events, while stored procedures are not.
c. Triggers are used for data definition, while stored procedures are used for data manipulation.
d. Triggers cannot execute SQL statements, while stored procedures can.

Review Question 7.8
Which of the following events is the data definition events recognized by SQL Server for triggers?
a. CREATE TABLE
b. DELETE
c. INSERT
d. UPDATE

Review Question 7.9
What happens to a trigger when you delete the table or view it is dependent on?
a. The trigger is automatically deleted as well.
b. The trigger remains but becomes inactive.

c. The trigger generates an error.

d. The trigger triggers an automatic backup.

Review Question 7.10

What is the purpose of declaring a variable called "@AuditAction"?

```
CREATE OR ALTER TRIGGER Chapter7Example.trgStudentsUpdate
ON Chapter7Example.Students
AFTER UPDATE
AS
SET NOCOUNT ON;
DECLARE @auditAction NVARCHAR(100);
SET @auditAction = '';
IF UPDATE (StudentName)
    SET @auditAction += 'student name updated';
IF UPDATE (StudentGpa)
    SET @auditAction += 'student gpa updated';
IF UPDATE (StudentName) AND UPDATE(StudentGpa)
    SET @auditAction = 'Both student name and gpa updated';
INSERT INTO Chapter7Example.StudentsAudit
    (StudentId, StudentName, StudentGpa, AuditAction)
    SELECT StudentId, StudentName, StudentGpa, @AuditAction
    FROM INSERTED;
```

a. To control the execution of triggers

b. To track the trigger's execution time

c. To store different messages based on actions performed

d. To store user login information

Review Question 7.11

Which table is used within a trigger to capture the old values before an UPDATE operation?

a. INSERTED

b. UPDATED

c. OLD

d. DELETED

Review Question 7.12

What is the main difference between the "INSERTED" and "DELETED" tables in triggers?

a. "INSERTED" stores new data, and "DELETED" stores old data.

b. "INSERTED" stores old data, and "DELETED" stores new data.

c. "INSERTED" stores data for INSERT operations, and "DELETED" stores data for DELETE operations.

d. There is no difference between them.

Review Question 7.13

What is the purpose of the "SET NOCOUNT ON;" statement in trigger examples?

a. To prevent any output from the trigger

b. To count the number of trigger executions

c. To record the timestamp of trigger execution

d. To disable the trigger

Review Question 7.14

Which virtual table in SQL Server is used to keep copies of affected rows during INSERT and UPDATE statements?

a. DELETED

b. TABLEINFO
c. UPDATED
d. INSERTED

Review Question 7.15
What is the primary purpose of the DELETED table in SQL Server triggers?
a. To store the new data
b. To create new tables
c. To capture old values before UPDATE and DELETE operations
d. To execute stored procedures

Review Question 7.16
Which virtual table mirrors the structure of the table that owns the trigger in SQL Server?
a. TABLEINFO
b. UPDATED
c. INSERTED
d. MIRROR

Review Question 7.17
Which type of trigger can be based on either a table or a view in SQL Server?
a. "After" trigger
b. "Instead of" trigger
c. "Before" trigger
d. "On Trigger" trigger

Review Question 7.18
What type of trigger can only be based on a table in SQL Server?
a. "After" trigger
b. "Instead of" trigger
c. "Before" trigger
d. "On Trigger" trigger

7.2 INSTEAD OF Triggers

In Section 7.1, you learned that when an event occurs in a database, certain actions are typically performed in response to that event. For instance, after inserting a new row into a student's table, you might want to save all the data along with some additional information to a StudentsAudit table. This is achieved through "AFTER" triggers, which are executed after the event has taken place.

However, there's another type of trigger in SQL Server that operates differently, known as "INSTEAD OF" triggers. These triggers provide you with a unique capability: you can specify what should happen instead of the default INSERT, UPDATE, or DELETE operation. This means you have the flexibility to include custom logic that can selectively accept or reject parts of a row, effectively altering the way data is handled during these operations.

Syntax for an INSTEAD OF Trigger:

```
CREATE TRIGGER TriggerName
ON TableName
INSTEAD OF INSERT[, UPDATE][, DELETE]
AS
BEGIN
    SET NOCOUNT ON;
    -- Custom logic or actions go here
END;
```

Here's where INSTEAD OF triggers truly shine: you can intercept the standard data modification operations and replace them with your custom logic. This can be particularly useful when dealing with views, where you might want to implement complex validation or custom handling of data before it's actually modified in the underlying tables. INSTEAD OF triggers give you the power to control the behavior of data modifications, offering a higher level of flexibility and customization in your database operations.

SQL Example 7.4

Reset the Chapter7Example.Students table and Chapter7Example.StudentsAudit table by removing all data. You can simply re-run the SQL statements provided at the beginning of this chapter to recreate these two tables. Now, let's create a trigger named 'trgStudentInsertCheckGPA' that will validate a student's GPA before inserting a new row into the student's table. If a student's GPA falls outside the range of 0.0 to 4.0, an error message will be raised, and the record won't be inserted. However, if the GPA is within the valid range, the record will be successfully inserted.

SQL Example 7.4 Analysis

The main distinction between Example 7.4 and Example 7.1 lies in the replacement of 'AFTER INSERT' with 'INSTEAD OF INSERT' in the SQL statement. Furthermore, you can incorporate additional code logic, such as the 'RAISEERROR' function, and specify how the data should be inserted into the StudentsAudit table.

SQL Example 7.4 Statement

```
GO
CREATE OR ALTER TRIGGER Chapter7Example.trgStudentsInsertCheckGPA
ON Chapter7Example.Students
```

```
INSTEAD OF INSERT
AS
SET NOCOUNT ON;
DECLARE @studentId AS INT;
DECLARE @newGpa AS DECIMAL(3, 2);
SELECT @newGpa = StudentGpa FROM INSERTED;
BEGIN
    IF(@newGpa > 4.0 OR @newGpa < 0.0)
        BEGIN
            RAISERROR('GPA must be between 0 and 4.0', 16, 1);
            ROLLBACK;
        END
    ELSE
        BEGIN
            INSERT INTO Chapter7Example.Students
                (StudentName, StudentGpa)
                SELECT StudentName, StudentGpa
                FROM INSERTED;
            SET @studentId = SCOPE_IDENTITY();
            INSERT INTO Chapter7Example.StudentsAudit
                (StudentId, StudentName, StudentGpa, AuditAction)
                SELECT @studentId, studentName, studentGpa,
                'Insert a new student'
                FROM inserted;
            PRINT('Record inserted');
        END
END
```

SQL Example 7.4 Invoke the Trigger by Inserting Two Students

The first student has a GPA within the acceptable range, while the second student has a GPA that falls outside the specified range.

```
INSERT INTO Chapter7Example.Students
    (StudentName, StudentGpa)
    VALUES ('Ken Allen', 3.3);
INSERT INTO Chapter7Example.Students
    (StudentName, StudentGpa)
    VALUES ('Donna Harber', 4.4);
```

SQL Example 7.4 Output

```
T-SQL    ↑↓    ⊞ Results    ▤ Message

   Record inserted

       (1 row(s) affected)

   Msg 50000, Level 16, State 1, Procedure trgStudentsInsertCheckGPA, Line 173
   GPA must be between 0 and 4.0
   Msg 3609, Level 16, State 1, Line 165
   The transaction ended in the trigger. The batch has been aborted.
```

SQL Example 7.4 Confirm Output

Execute the following two SELECT statements to confirm that the trigger works.

```
SELECT * FROM Chapter7Example.Students;
SELECT * FROM Chapter7Example.StudentsAudit;
```

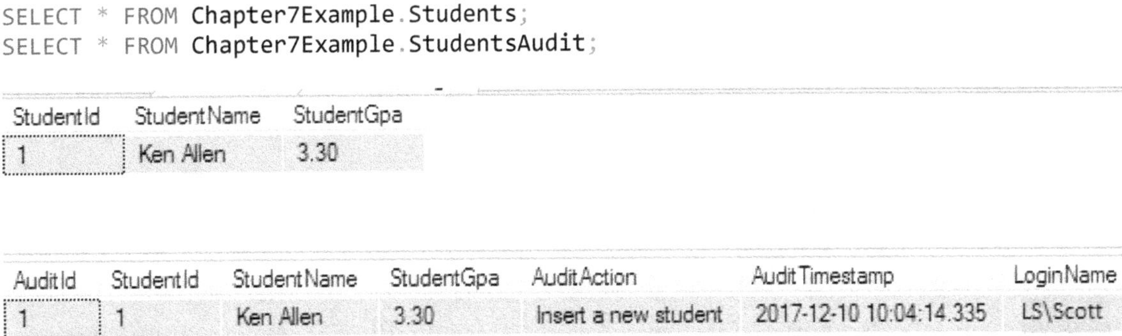

StudentId	StudentName	StudentGpa
1	Ken Allen	3.30

AuditId	StudentId	StudentName	StudentGpa	AuditAction	AuditTimestamp	LoginName
1	1	Ken Allen	3.30	Insert a new student	2017-12-10 10:04:14.335	LS\Scott

SQL Example 7.5

Create a trigger named 'trgStudentUpdateCheckGPA' that validates a student's GPA before updating a row in the student's table. If a student's GPA falls outside the range of 0.0 to 4.0, an error message will be raised. Otherwise, the record will be updated.

SQL Example 7.5 Analysis

The term 'INSERTED' is frequently mentioned in this chapter. You can conceptualize it as a temporary table that temporarily stores newly modified data. When an UPDATE statement is executed, it effectively updates the data within this 'INSERTED' table.

SQL Example 7.5 Statement

```
GO
CREATE OR ALTER TRIGGER Chapter7Example.trgStudentsUpdateCheckGPA
ON Chapter7Example.Students
INSTEAD OF UPDATE
AS
SET NOCOUNT ON;
DECLARE @studentId AS INT;
DECLARE @newGpa AS DECIMAL(3, 2);
DECLARE @studentName AS NVARCHAR(100);
SELECT @newGpa = studentGpa
    FROM INSERTED;
SELECT @studentName = studentName
    FROM INSERTED;
SELECT @studentId = studentId
    FROM INSERTED;
BEGIN
    IF(@newGpa > 4.0 OR @newGpa < 0.0)
        BEGIN
            RAISERROR('GPA must be between 0 and 4.0', 16, 1);
            ROLLBACK;
        END
    ELSE
        BEGIN
            UPDATE Chapter7Example.Students
                SET StudentGpa = @newGpa
                WHERE StudentName = @studentName;
            INSERT INTO Chapter7Example.StudentsAudit
```

```
        (StudentId, StudentName, StudentGpa, AuditAction)
        SELECT @studentId, StudentName, StudentGpa, 'Update GPA'
        FROM INSERTED;
        PRINT('Record updated');
    END
END
```

SQL Example 7.5 Invoke the Trigger by Updating Twice

The first UPDATE statement reflects a correct GPA, whereas the second UPDATE statement involves a GPA that falls outside the specified range.

```
UPDATE Chapter7Example.Students
    SET StudentGpa = 4.0
    WHERE StudentName = 'Ken Allen'
    AND StudentGpa = 3.3;

UPDATE Chapter7Example.Students
    SET StudentGpa = 5.0
    WHERE StudentName = 'Ken Allen'
    AND StudentGpa = 4.0;
```

SQL Example 7.5 Output

```
T-SQL    ↑↓    ▦ Results    ▤ Message
  Msg 50000, Level 16, State 1, Procedure trgStudentsUpdateCheckGPA, Line 241
  GPA must be between 0 and 4.0
  Msg 3609, Level 16, State 1, Line 224
  The transaction ended in the trigger. The batch has been aborted.
```

SQL Example 7.5 Confirm Output

Execute the following two SELECT statements to confirm that the trigger works.

```
SELECT * FROM Chapter7Example.Students;
SELECT * FROM Chapter7Example.StudentsAudit;
```

StudentId	StudentName	StudentGpa
1	Ken Allen	4.00

AuditId	StudentId	StudentName	StudentGpa	AuditAction	AuditTimestamp	LoginName
1	1	Ken Allen	3.30	Insert a new student	2017-12-10 10:04:14.335	LS\Scott
2	1	Ken Allen	4.00	Update GPA	2017-12-10 10:33:52.331	LS\Scott

SQL Example 7.6

Create a trigger named 'trgStudentsDeleteCheckGPA' that validates a student's GPA before deleting a row from the student's table. If a student's GPA is not null, an error message will be raised, and the record won't be deleted. This ensures that students with a numeric GPA are not allowed to be removed from the student's table.

SQL Example 7.6 Analysis

The DELETED keyword is akin to the INSERTED keyword. You can visualize DELETED as a table that stores all values intended for deletion.

SQL Example 7.6 Statement

```
GO
CREATE OR ALTER TRIGGER Chapter7Example.trgStudentsDeleteCheckGPA
ON Chapter7Example.Students
INSTEAD OF DELETE
AS
SET NOCOUNT ON;
DECLARE @studentId AS INT;
DECLARE @studentGpa AS DECIMAL(3, 2);
DECLARE @studentName AS NVARCHAR(100);
SELECT @studentGpa = StudentGpa
    FROM DELETED;
SELECT @studentName = StudentName
    FROM DELETED;
SELECT @studentId = StudentId
    FROM DELETED;
BEGIN
    IF(@studentGpa IS NOT NULL)
        BEGIN
            RAISERROR('Cannot delete a student with gpa', 16, 1);
            ROLLBACK;
        END
    ELSE
        BEGIN
            DELETE FROM Chapter7Example.Students
                WHERE StudentName = @studentName;
            INSERT INTO Chapter7Example.StudentsAudit
                (StudentId, StudentName, StudentGpa, AuditAction)
                SELECT @studentId, StudentName, StudentGpa,
                'Record deleted'
                FROM DELETED;
            PRINT('Record deleted');
        END
END
```

SQL Example 7.6 Invoke the Trigger by Deleting a student with GPA

```
DELETE FROM Chapter7Example.Students
    WHERE StudentName = 'Ken Allen'
    AND StudentGpa = 4.0;
```

SQL Example 7.6 Output for Failed to delete a Student with GPA

```
Msg 50000, Level 16, State 1, Procedure trgStudentsDeleteCheckGPA, Line 290
```

```
Cannot delete a student with gpa
Msg 3609, Level 16, State 1, Line 273
The transaction ended in the trigger. The batch has been aborted.
```

SQL Example 7.6 Invoke the Trigger by Deleting a Student without GPA

First, you need to insert a new student without GPA into the Chapter7Example.Students table:

```
INSERT INTO Chapter7Example.Students
    (StudentName) VALUES ('Donna Harber');
```

Next, you can delete this new student who does not have any GPA yet.

```
DELETE FROM Chapter7Example.Students
    WHERE StudentName = 'Donna Harber';
```

SQL Example 7.6 Confirm Output

StudentId	StudentName	StudentGpa
1	Ken Allen	4.00

AuditId	StudentId	StudentName	StudentGpa	AuditAction	AuditTimestamp	LoginName
1	1	Ken Allen	3.30	Insert a new student	2017-12-10 10:04:14.335	LS\Scott
2	1	Ken Allen	4.00	Update GPA	2017-12-10 10:33:52.331	LS\Scott
3	2	Donna Harber	NULL	Insert a new student	2017-12-10 17:06:29.144	LS\Scott
4	2	Donna Harber	NULL	Record deleted	2017-12-10 17:07:09.833	LS\Scott

Review Question 7.19
INSTEAD OF INSERT statement of a trigger can be used to ______ the data before inserting a new record.
a. validate
b. preview
c. update
d. update or delete

Review Question 7.20
When you delete records from a table, the deleted records are stored in a table called ______.
a. inserted
b. updated
c. deleted
d. selected

Review Question 7.21
What is the primary function of "AFTER" triggers in SQL Server?
a. Rejecting parts of a row during INSERT, UPDATE, or DELETE operations.
b. Executing custom logic before an event takes place.
c. Validating data after it has been modified.
d. Running custom actions instead of the default operations.

Review Question 7.22
What distinguishes "INSTEAD OF" triggers from "AFTER" triggers in SQL Server?
a. "INSTEAD OF" triggers are executed after the event.
b. "INSTEAD OF" triggers cannot be used with views.
c. "INSTEAD OF" triggers allow you to control data modifications by custom logic.
d. "INSTEAD OF" triggers are limited to INSERT operations.

Review Question 7.23
Which type of trigger is suitable for implementing complex validation and custom data handling for views?
a. "AFTER" triggers
b. "INSTEAD OF" triggers
c. "DELETE" triggers
d. "UPDATE" triggers

Review Question 7.24
In T-SQL, which keyword is commonly used and can be visualized as a temporary table for temporarily storing newly modified data?
a. INSERTED
b. DELETED
c. UPDATE
d. RAISEERROR

Review Question 7.25
Which keyword in SQL Server can be visualized as a temporary table that stores all values intended for deletion?
a. INSERTED
b. SELECT
c. DELETE
d. DELETED

7.3 Database-Level Triggers

In the previous sections, we delved into the creation of Data Manipulation Language (DML) triggers that operate at the table level. These triggers respond to specific events occurring within a table, such as INSERT, UPDATE, or DELETE operations. However, in addition to table-level triggers, T-SQL also offers the capability to create triggers that operate at the database level, responding to events that affect the entire database. One such example is DDL triggers.

For instance, when a significant database-level event occurs, like the creation of a new table within the database, a trigger designed for database-level operations can be invoked. This allows you to implement customized actions or logic in response to such database-wide events, extending the flexibility and power of T-SQL triggers to address a broader scope of actions within the database environment.

SQL Example 7.7

Create a DDL trigger named 'trgAddNewTable' that displays the message 'Contact DBA if you want to create a new table' and performs a rollback. This trigger is designed to prevent the execution of any CREATE TABLE statement.

SQL Example 7.7 Analysis

Similar to a DML trigger, which is associated with a table, a DDL trigger is often associated with a database. In this example, we use the syntax 'ON DATABASE FOR CREATE_TABLE.

SQL Example 7.7 Statement

```
GO
CREATE OR ALTER TRIGGER trgAddNewTable
ON DATABASE
FOR CREATE_TABLE
AS
    RAISERROR ('Contact DBA if you want to create the table!',10, 1)
    ROLLBACK;
```

SQL Example 7.7 Invoke the Trigger by Executing CREATE TABLE

```
CREATE TABLE Chapter7Example.NewStudents
(
    StudentId INT IDENTITY,
    StudentName NVARCHAR(100) NOT NULL,
    StudentGpa DECIMAL(3,2) NULL,
    CONSTRAINT pk_NewStudents PRIMARY KEY(StudentId)
);
```

SQL Example 7.7 Output for CREATE TABLE

```
T-SQL      ↑↓      ⊞ Results      🖹 Message                          ═══
  Contact DBA if you want to create the table!
  Msg 3609, Level 16, State 2, Line 301
  The transaction ended in the trigger. The batch has been aborted.
```

SQL Example 7.7 Drop the Trigger

```
    DROP TRIGGER trgAddNewTable
    ON DATABASE;
```

Review Question 7.26

A _____ trigger most likely works at the table level. The trigger is fired when an event happens at a table.
a. DDL
b. DCL

c. DML

d. MML

Review Question 7.27

A _______ trigger works at the database level. The trigger is fired when an event happens at a database. For example, when a new table is created, a trigger can be executed.

a. DDL

b. DCL

c. DML

d. MML

Review Question 7.28

What distinguishes DDL triggers from DML triggers in T-SQL?

a. DDL triggers operate at the table level, while DML triggers work at the database level.

b. DDL triggers are used for INSERT, UPDATE, or DELETE operations, while DML triggers respond to CREATE TABLE events.

c. DDL triggers are used for database-level operations, while DML triggers work at the table level.

d. DDL triggers are primarily used for SELECT queries, while DML triggers handle database-wide actions.

Review Question 7.29

When might you want to use a DDL trigger in T-SQL?

a. When you need to respond to specific data manipulation events within a table.

b. When you want to create a trigger for SELECT queries.

c. When you want to customize actions in response to database-level events.

d. When you want to restrict the use of INSERT statements.

Review Question 7.30

What database-level event does the DDL trigger 'trgAddNewTable' in the following code respond to?

```
CREATE OR ALTER TRIGGER trgAddNewTable
ON DATABASE
FOR CREATE_TABLE
AS
    RAISERROR ('Contact DBA if you want to create the table!',10, 1)
    ROLLBACK;
```

a. RAISERROR function

b. ROLLBACK command

c. DELETE operation

d. CREATE TABLE operation

Review Question 7.31

In the following code, what action does the trigger 'trgAddNewTable' take if a CREATE TABLE statement is executed?

```
CREATE OR ALTER TRIGGER trgAddNewTable
ON DATABASE
FOR CREATE_TABLE
AS
    RAISERROR ('Contact DBA if you want to create the table!',10, 1)
    ROLLBACK;
```

a. It creates a new table with the specified name unless an error is raised.

b. It displays a message and continues with the transaction.

c. It raises an error message and performs a rollback.

d. It automatically commits the transaction.

Review Question 7.32
How can you drop a DDL trigger in T-SQL?
a. Use the 'DELETE TRIGGER' statement.
b. Execute 'DROP TRIGGER' followed by the trigger name.
c. Modify the trigger to be inactive.
d. Disable the trigger from the database settings.

7.4 Drop, Alter, Disable, and Enable Triggers

In the previous sections, we learned how to create triggers to automate actions based on specific events in our database. However, in real-world scenarios, there might come a time when you need to manage these triggers efficiently. SQL Server provides several ways to do this.

In the previous example, you have used the DROP TRIGGER statement to remove a trigger. This action effectively deletes the trigger and all its associated properties. The trigger is permanently gone from the database.

But what if you only need to make changes to an existing trigger without losing the properties and permissions you've already set? In such cases, you can use the ALTER TRIGGER statement to modify an existing trigger while retaining its established properties. All examples in this chapter include the ALTER TRIGGER statement.

There might be scenarios where you want to temporarily prevent a trigger from executing without deleting it. To achieve this, SQL Server offers the DISABLE TRIGGER and ENABLE TRIGGER statements. You can disable a trigger when you don't want it to take any actions. Later, you can re-enable it when it's needed again. Here is the syntax for doing that:

```
-- Example of disabling a trigger
DISABLE TRIGGER TriggerName ON TableName;
-- Example of enabling a trigger
ENABLE TRIGGER TriggerName ON TableName;
```

When modifying or disabling triggers, remember that these actions can impact the functionality of your database applications. Always exercise caution and thoroughly test any changes in a non-production environment before applying them in a live system. Proper trigger management ensures that your database operates efficiently and accurately, and it's an essential part of database maintenance and development.

SQL Example 7.8

Update the trigger you previously created in SQL Example 7.4,

'Chapter7Example.trgStudentsInsertCheckGPA,' to permit a GPA range between 0.0 and 5.0.

SQL Example 7.8 Analysis

Retyping the two lines of code in SQL Example 7.4 to drop the trigger and then create a new trigger with the same name might seem like an easier solution. However, in practice, this approach can lead to issues. For instance, when you drop the trigger in this manner, you lose all the constraints and permissions associated with it. On the other hand, using the 'ALTER TRIGGER' command allows you to retain all the existing settings and properties.

SQL Example 7.8 Statement

```
ALTER TRIGGER Chapter7Example.trgStudentsInsertCheckGPA
ON Chapter7Example.Students
INSTEAD OF INSERT
AS
SET NOCOUNT ON;
DECLARE @studentId AS INT;
DECLARE @newGpa AS DECIMAL(3, 2);
SELECT @newGpa = StudentGpa FROM INSERTED;
BEGIN
    IF(@newGpa > 5.0 OR @newGpa < 0.0)
        BEGIN
            RAISERROR('GPA must be between 0 and 5.0', 16, 1);
            ROLLBACK;
        END
    ELSE
        BEGIN
            INSERT INTO Chapter7Example.Students
                (StudentName, StudentGpa)
                SELECT StudentName, StudentGpa
                FROM INSERTED;
            SET @studentId = SCOPE_IDENTITY();
            INSERT INTO Chapter7Example.StudentsAudit
                (StudentId, StudentName, StudentGpa, AuditAction)
                SELECT @studentId, studentName, studentGpa,
                'Insert a new student'
                FROM inserted;
            PRINT('Record inserted');
        END
END
```


SQL Example 7.9

First, disable the trigger you created in Example 7.4 and altered in Example 7.8,

'Chapter7Example.trgStudentsInsertCheckGPA.' After disabling it, attempt to insert a new student with a

GPA of 7.6. Will the INSERT statement work? Next, enable the trigger and try to insert a new student with a GPA of 7.6. Will the INSERT statement work?

SQL Example 7.9 Statement to Disable the Trigger

```
GO
DISABLE TRIGGER Chapter7Example.trgStudentsInsertCheckGPA
    ON Chapter7Example.Students;
```

SQL Example 7.9 Insert a new student with a GPA of 7.6 without an issue

```
INSERT INTO Chapter7Example.Students
    (StudentName, StudentGpa)
    VALUES ('Ralph Moore', 7.6);
```

SQL Example 7.9 Statement to Enable the Trigger

```
GO
ENABLE TRIGGER Chapter7Example.trgStudentsInsertCheckGPA
    ON Chapter7Example.Students;
```

If you now try to insert Ralph Moore with 7.6 GPA, you will see the following error message:

```
T-SQL    ↑↓    ⊞ Results    ▤ Message
 Msg 50000, Level 16, State 1, Procedure trgStudentsInsertCheckGPA, Line 359
 GPA must be between 0 and 5.0
 Msg 3609, Level 16, State 1, Line 348
 The transaction ended in the trigger. The batch has been aborted.
```

Review Question 7.33
The _______ statement allows you to modify an existing trigger without losing those properties you already established on the trigger.
a. DROP TRIGGER
b. ALTER TRIGGER
c. ENABLE TRIGGER
d. DISABLE TRIGGER

Review Question 7.34
If you just want to disable a trigger without deleting it, you can use the _______.
a. DROP TRIGGER
b. ALTER TRIGGER
c. ENABLE TRIGGER
d. DISABLE TRIGGER

Review Question 7.35
What is the primary purpose of the ALTER TRIGGER statement in SQL Server?
a. To permanently delete a trigger.

b. To temporarily disable a trigger.
c. To modify an existing trigger while retaining its properties.
d. To create a new trigger.

Review Question 7.36
How can you temporarily prevent a trigger from executing without deleting it in SQL Server?
a. By using the ALTER TRIGGER statement.
b. By using the DISABLE TRIGGER statement.
c. By using the DROP TRIGGER statement.
d. By using the ENABLE TRIGGER statement.

Review Question 7.37
What are the potential consequences of re-creating a trigger by dropping it and creating a new one with the same name?
a. The trigger remains unchanged.
b. All constraints and permissions on the trigger are lost.
c. The trigger becomes more efficient.
d. The trigger retains its properties.

7.5 ALTER TABLE: Modifying Table Structures

In the previous chapters, we explored the powerful world of triggers and how they can automate actions in response to specific database events. Now, let's shift our focus to a closely related topic that plays a crucial role in database management: the "ALTER TABLE" statement.

The "ALTER TABLE" statement empowers you to make structural changes to an existing table. These changes can involve adding, dropping, modifying, or renaming columns within the table. Whether you need to accommodate new data requirements or refine the structure of your database, "ALTER TABLE" provides the flexibility to adapt your tables to evolving needs.

Examples of ALTER TABLE

To illustrate the capabilities of the "ALTER TABLE" statement, we will work with the "Chapter7Example.Students" table. Before we begin, let's reset the table to its initial state using the following SQL statements:

```sql
GO
DROP TABLE IF EXISTS Chapter7Example.Students;
CREATE TABLE Chapter7Example.Students
(
    StudentId INT IDENTITY,
    StudentName NVARCHAR(100) NOT NULL,
    StudentGpa DECIMAL(3,2) NULL,
```

```
    CONSTRAINT pk_Students PRIMARY KEY(StudentId)
);
```

SQL Example 7.10

Add two columns to the Chapter7Example.Students table: one named 'BirthDate' with a Date data type, and the other named 'ApplicationDate' with a DateTime2 data type.

SQL Example 7.10 Statement

```
ALTER TABLE Chapter7Example.Students
    ADD BirthDate DATE NULL,
        ApplicationDate DATETIME2 NULL;
```

SQL Example 7.10 Confirm the Output

The following statement (a built-in stored procedure) will allow you to check if the columns are added:

```
sp_help 'Chapter7Example.Students';
```

SQL Example 7.11

Change the 'StudentName' column in the Chapter7Example.Students table to NVARCHAR(200) and allow NULL values.

SQL Example 7.11 Statement

```
ALTER TABLE Chapter7Example.Students
    ALTER COLUMN StudentName NVARCHAR(200) NULL;
```

SQL Example 7.12

Drop the BirthDate column from the Chapter7Example.Students table

SQL Example 7.12 Statement

```
ALTER TABLE Chapter7Example.Students
    DROP COLUMN BirthDate;
```

SQL Example 7.13

Rename the StudentName column in the Chapter7Example.Students table to FullName.

SQL Example 7.13 Analysis

You may receive a warning on changing the column name, but SQL Server will change it anyway.

SQL Example 7.13 Statement

```
sp_rename 'Chapter7Example.Students.StudentName', 'FullName', 'COLUMN';
```

Review Question 7.38
The _______ statement allows you to add, drop, modify, and rename a column of a table.
a. ADD TABLE
b. DROP TABLE
c. MODIFY TABLE
d. ALTER TABLE

Review Question 7.39
Which of the following statements add a new column called BirthDate to a table with existing data in it.
a. `ADD BirthDate`
b. `ADD BirthDate DATE NULL`
c. `ADD COLUMN BirthDate`
d. `ADD COLUMN BirthDate DATE NULL`

Review Question 7.40
Which of the following statements modify the StudentName column in a table to NVARCHAR(200) and allow NULL?
a. `Modify StudentName NVARCHAR(200) NULL`
b. `Modify COLUMN StudentName NVARCHAR(200) NULL`
c. `ALTER StudentName NVARCHAR(200) NULL`
d. `ALTER COLUMN StudentName NVARCHAR(200) NULL`

Review Question 7.41
What is the primary purpose of the "ALTER TABLE" statement in T-SQL?
a. To add new rows to a table.
b. To modify data within a table.
c. To make structural changes to an existing table.
d. To create new tables.

Review Question 7.42
What is the purpose of the "sp_help 'Chapter7Example.Students'" statement in SQL?
a. It drops columns from a table.
b. It renames columns in a table.
c. It checks if the new columns have been added to the table.
d. It updates existing rows in the table.

Review Question 7.43
In the following code, what change is made to the 'StudentName' column in the "Chapter7Example.Students" table?
```
ALTER TABLE Chapter7Example.Students ALTER COLUMN StudentName NVARCHAR(200) NULL;
```
a. The column is dropped.
b. The column is renamed.
c. The column data type is modified.
d. The column is not allowed to contain NULL values.

Review Question 7.44
What does the following SQL code demonstrate?
```
sp_rename 'Chapter7Example.Students.StudentName', 'FullName', 'COLUMN';
```
a. Modifying the 'StudentName' column.
b. Adding new columns to the table.
c. Renaming the table itself.
d. Dropping the entire table.

7.6 Alter Table Constraints

In this section, you will delve into the intricacies of modifying table constraints, particularly focusing on default value constraints and foreign key constraints.

Default value constraints are essential for ensuring that your data maintains a certain level of consistency. You may need to modify a column with a default value constraint for various reasons, such as adapting to evolving business requirements. When altering a column with a default value constraint, it's important to remember that dropping and re-adding the constraint is the standard procedure.

For instance, consider a scenario where you have a 'RegistrationDate' column in a 'Students' table with a default value constraint of the current date. If you need to change the default value to the start of the academic year due to a new school policy, you would follow the process of dropping the existing constraint and adding a new one with the updated default value.

Foreign key constraints establish relationships between tables, ensuring data integrity and referential consistency. There are several specifications to consider when modifying foreign key constraints, each with its implications:

No Action (Default): This setting prevents the deletion of a record in the parent table if corresponding child records exist. For example, in a database where advisors have associated students, attempting to delete an advisor with linked students would result in an error, preserving data integrity.

ON DELETE/UPDATE SET NULL: Changing the specification to "SET NULL" means that when a parent record is deleted or updated, all corresponding child records will have the foreign key column set to NULL. In our 'Students' and 'Advisors' example, if an advisor is deleted, all corresponding student records would have their advisor ID set to NULL.

ON DELETE/UPDATE SET DEFAULT: Similar to "SET NULL," this specification sets the foreign key column to the default value when the parent record is deleted or updated. It's important to ensure that the default constraint exists and has a valid default value in the parent table.

ON DELETE/UPDATE CASCADE: The CASCADE specification should be used with caution. With this setting, when a record in the parent table is removed, all corresponding records in the child table are also deleted. In other words, it propagates the deletion throughout the associated records. This can have a significant impact on your data and should be implemented with care.

Understanding how to navigate these specifications and apply them effectively is crucial for maintaining data consistency and ensuring that your database structure aligns with your organization's evolving needs. Remember to test any changes in a controlled environment before implementing them in a production system to avoid unintended consequences. Properly managing constraints is a fundamental aspect of database maintenance and development.

You will require two tables for the examples in this section. Execute the following statements to create the tables and insert one advisor and two students:

```sql
DROP TABLE IF EXISTS Chapter7Example.Students;
DROP TABLE IF EXISTS Chapter7Example.Advisors;
CREATE TABLE Chapter7Example.Advisors
(
    AdvisorId INT IDENTITY,
    AdvisorName NVARCHAR(100) NOT NULL,
    Office NVARCHAR(50) NULL,
    CONSTRAINT pk_Advisors PRIMARY KEY(AdvisorId)
);
CREATE TABLE Chapter7Example.Students
(
    StudentId INT IDENTITY,
    StudentName NVARCHAR(100) NOT NULL,
    StudentGpa DECIMAL(3,2) NULL,
    AdvisorId INT NULL,
    CONSTRAINT pk_Students PRIMARY KEY(StudentId),
    CONSTRAINT fk_Students_Advisors
    FOREIGN KEY (AdvisorId)
    REFERENCES Chapter7Example.Advisors(AdvisorId)
);
SET IDENTITY_INSERT Chapter7Example.Advisors ON;
INSERT INTO Chapter7Example.Advisors
    (AdvisorId, AdvisorName, Office)
    VALUES
    (1, 'Ralph Moore', 'Tiger 301');
SET IDENTITY_INSERT Chapter7Example.Advisors OFF;
INSERT INTO Chapter7Example.Students
    (StudentName, StudentGpa, AdvisorId)
```

```
    VALUES
    ('Ken Allen', 3.4, 1);
INSERT INTO Chapter7Example.Students
    (StudentName, StudentGpa, AdvisorId)
    VALUES
    ('Donna Harber', 3.5, 1);
```

SQL Example 7.14

Delete the advisor ID 1 in the Chapter7Example.Advisors table using the following statement:

```
DELETE FROM Chapter7Example.Advisors WHERE AdvisorId = 1;
```

There will be an error message because there are two students with AdvisorId of 1. You are not allowed to delete the Advisor with ID of 1. Now, modify the foreign key constraint so that when an advisor is deleted, the AdvisorId in the Students table will be set to NULL.

SQL Example 7.14 Statement

First drop the fk_Students_Advisors constraint in the Chapter7Example.Students table:

```
ALTER TABLE Chapter7Example.Students DROP CONSTRAINT fk_Students_Advisors;
```

Then, add the constraint back with ON DELETE SET NULL (ON UPDATE SET NULL works similarly)

```
ALTER TABLE Chapter7Example.Students
    ADD CONSTRAINT fk_Students_Advisors
    FOREIGN KEY (AdvisorId)
    REFERENCES Chapter7Example.Advisors (AdvisorId)
    ON DELETE SET NULL;
```

Try to delete the advisorId 1:

```
DELETE FROM Chapter7Example.Advisors WHERE AdvisorId = 1;
```

SQL Example 7.14 Confirm the Advisor Deleted and AdvisorId Set to NULL

Run the following two SELECT statements to confirm that the modified constraint works.

```
SELECT * FROM Chapter7Example.Advisors;
SELECT * FROM Chapter7Example.Students;
```

AdvisorId	AdvisorName	Office

	StudentId	StudentName	StudentGpa	AdvisorId
1	1	Ken Allen	3.40	NULL
2	2	Donna Har...	3.50	NULL

SQL Example 7.15

Before proceeding with this exercise, execute the SQL statements at the beginning of this section to reset the two tables and their relationship. This practice consists of two tasks:

Modify the 'AdvisorId' column in the 'Chapter7Example.Students' table to allow a default value of 100.

Adjust the foreign key constraint in the 'Chapter7Example.Students' table so that when an advisor is deleted, the corresponding student's 'AdvisorId' is automatically set to 100.

SQL Example 7.15 Statement

Modify the AdvisorId column in the Chapter7Example.Students table:

```
ALTER TABLE Chapter7Example.Students
    ADD CONSTRAINT DEF_AdvisorId
    DEFAULT 100 FOR AdvisorId;
```

Drop the fk_Students_Advisors foreign key constraint:

```
ALTER TABLE Chapter7Example.Students
    DROP CONSTRAINT fk_Students_Advisors;
```

Add back the fk_Students_Advisors constraint (ON UPDATE SET DEFAULT works similarly):

```
ALTER TABLE Chapter7Example.Students
    ADD CONSTRAINT fk_Students_Advisors
    FOREIGN KEY (AdvisorId)
    REFERENCES Chapter7Example.Advisors (AdvisorId)
    ON DELETE SET DEFAULT;
```

Try to delete the advisorId 1:

```
DELETE FROM Chapter7Example.Advisors WHERE AdvisorId = 1;
```

You will encounter an error message because the default value 'AdvisorId 100' does not exist in the 'Chapter7Example.Advisors' table. To resolve this, execute the following statement to insert a new advisor with 'AdvisorId 100':

```
SET IDENTITY_INSERT Chapter7Example.Advisors ON;
INSERT INTO Chapter7Example.Advisors
    (AdvisorId, AdvisorName, Office)
    VALUES
    (100, 'Staff', 'Tiger 100');
SET IDENTITY_INSERT Chapter7Example.Advisors OFF;
```

Execute the delete for AdvisorId 1 in the 'Advisors' table once more to observe that the 'AdvisorId' in the 'Students' table has been successfully set to 100.

SQL Example 7.15 Confirm AdvisorId Is Set to 100

Run the following two SELECT statements to confirm that the modified constraint works.

```
SELECT * FROM Chapter7Example.Advisors;
SELECT * FROM Chapter7Example.Students;
```

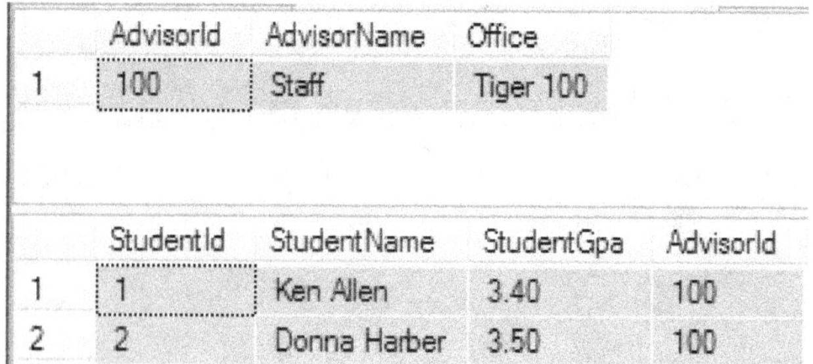

SQL Example 7.16

Before proceeding with this example, execute the SQL statements at the beginning of this section to reset the two tables and their relationship. Modify the 'fk_Students_Advisors' foreign key constraint so that when an advisor is deleted, all corresponding student records are also deleted (please note that this is a potentially risky example, but the technique can be occasionally useful).

SQL Example 7.16 Statement

Drop the fk_Students_Advisors foreign key constraint:

```
ALTER TABLE Chapter7Example.Students DROP CONSTRAINT fk_Students_Advisors;
```

Add back the fk_Students_Advisors constraint (ON UPDATE CASCADE works similarly):

```
ALTER TABLE Chapter7Example.Students
    ADD CONSTRAINT fk_Students_Advisors
    FOREIGN KEY (AdvisorId)
    REFERENCES Chapter7.Advisors (AdvisorId)
    ON DELETE CASCADE;
```

Try to delete the advisorId 1:

```
DELETE FROM Chapter7Example.Advisors WHERE AdvisorId = 1;
```

SQL Example 7.16 Confirm

Run the following two SELECT statements to confirm that the modified constraint works.

```
SELECT * FROM Chapter7Example.Advisors;
SELECT * FROM Chapter7Example.Students;
```

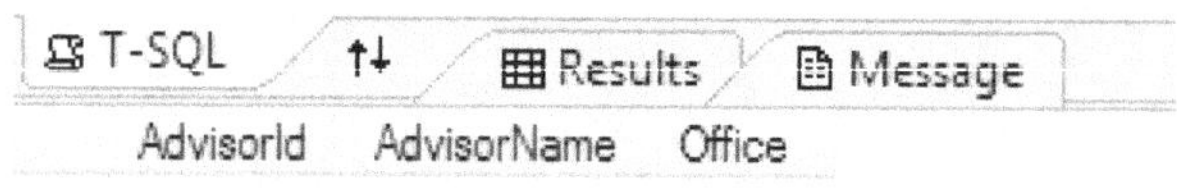

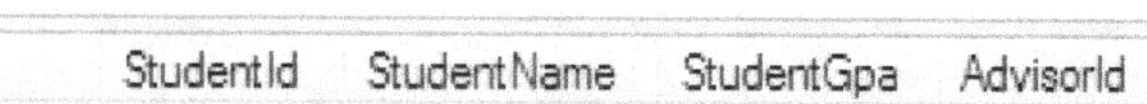

Review Question 7.45

Which of the following statements allow you to change a table constraint?
a. ALTER CONSTRAINT
b. UPDATE CONSTRAINT
c. CHANGE CONSTRAINT
d. DROP and ADD CONSTRAINT

Review Question 7.46
The foreign key of a table is _______.
a. a constraint
b. a field with unique values
c. a field that contains data from another country
d. always a single field

Review Question 7.47
When a _______ constraint setting is in place, attempting to delete a record in the parent table will result in an error if there are one or more corresponding child records.
a. default/no action
b. on delete set null
c. on delete set default
d. on delete cascade

Review Question 7.48
When using the _______ constraint setting, deleting a parent record will lead to all associated child records having a null value for the foreign key column.
a. default/no action
b. on delete set null
c. on delete set default
d. on delete cascade

Review Question 7.49
When applying the _______ constraint setting, removing a parent record will result in all related child records having the default value for the foreign key column.
a. default/no action
b. on delete set null
c. on delete set default
d. on delete cascade

Review Question 7.50
When using the _______ constraint setting, deleting a record in the parent table will lead to the removal of all associated records in the child table.
a. default/no action
b. on delete set null
c. on delete set default
d. on delete cascade

Review Question 7.51
What is the standard procedure for altering a column with a default value constraint in T-SQL?
a. Use the "ALTER COLUMN" statement
b. Modify the constraint in place
c. Drop and re-add the constraint

d. Create a new table

Review Question 7.52
Which foreign key constraint specification prevents the deletion of a parent record if corresponding child records exist?
a. ON DELETE/UPDATE SET NULL
b. ON DELETE/UPDATE SET DEFAULT
c. ON DELETE/UPDATE CASCADE
d. No Action (Default)

Review Question 7.53
What happens when you change the foreign key constraint specification to "ON DELETE/UPDATE CASCADE"?
a. Child records are set to NULL
b. Parent records are set to NULL
c. All corresponding child records are deleted
d. Child records are updated with a default value

Review Question 7.54
If you need to change the default value for a column with a default value constraint, what process should you follow?
a. Modify the constraint in place
b. Use the "ALTER COLUMN" statement
c. Drop the column and recreate it
d. Drop the existing constraint and add a new one

Review Question 7.55
In a scenario where you change the foreign key specification to "ON DELETE/UPDATE SET NULL," what happens to child records when a parent record is deleted?
a. Child records are set to a NULL value
b. Child records are updated with a new value
c. Child records are deleted
d. Child records remain unchanged

Review Question 7.56
What should you do before implementing changes to constraints in a production database?
a. Apply changes directly in the production system
b. Test changes in a controlled environment
c. Make changes without testing
d. Implement changes during peak usage hours

7.7 Chapter Summary

In this chapter, you have gained the knowledge of creating, modifying, disabling, and enabling triggers.

Triggers are essentially automatically executed stored procedures. You can create DML or DDL triggers that are automatically executed in response to DML or DDL events. These triggers can be designed to execute after the event takes place, or they can take over the event and perform custom actions instead. You have also explored the process of making alterations to a table, which involves adding, deleting, and modifying column definitions. Additionally, you've learned how to rename columns. Lastly, you've acquired the ability to adjust a table's constraints as needed.

7.8 Questions

Question 7.1

A trigger is a stored procedure. A stored procedure can be executed by EXECUTE StoredProcedureName. Can you do the same for a trigger? Why or why not?

Question 7.2

Compare and contrast the syntax of a trigger and a stored procedure. What are the similarities and what are the differences? Focus on the functionalities of each. For example, an insert stored procedure usually has a list of parameters. Can an insert trigger have the same list of parameters? Why or why not?

Question 7.3

When creating a trigger, you often use INSERTED and DELETED. What are these?

Question 7.4

List and explain the steps involved in alter table constraints. Why didn't the creators of alter table constraints make alter table constraints similar to alter table columns?

Question 7.5

List and explain the four possible specifications of a table foreign key constraint.

7.9 SQL Exercises

Exercise 7.1

Create a schema called Chapter7Exercise authorized with dbo. Then, create two tables: one is called Courses and the other is called CoursesAudit. You will use these tables for Exercises 7.1 through 7.6. Use the following SQL statements to accomplish this:

```sql
GO
CREATE SCHEMA Chapter7Exercise AUTHORIZATION dbo;
GO
DROP TABLE IF EXISTS Chapter7Exercise.Courses;
CREATE TABLE Chapter7Exercise.Courses
(
    CourseId INT IDENTITY,
    CourseNumber NCHAR(6) NOT NULL,
    CourseTitle NVARCHAR(255) NULL,
       MaxSeats INT NOT NULL,
    CONSTRAINT pk_Courses PRIMARY KEY(CourseId)
);

DROP TABLE IF EXISTS Chapter7Exercise.CoursesAudit;
CREATE TABLE Chapter7Exercise.CoursesAudit
(
    AuditId INT IDENTITY,
    CourseId INT NOT NULL,
    CourseNumber NCHAR(6) NOT NULL,
    CourseTitle NVARCHAR (255) NULL,
       MaxSeats INT NOT NULL,
    AuditAction NVARCHAR(100) NOT NULL,
    AuditTimestamp DATETIME2(3) NOT NULL DEFAULT(SYSDATETIME()),
    LoginName SYSNAME NOT NULL DEFAULT(ORIGINAL_LOGIN()),
    CONSTRAINT pk_CoursesAudit PRIMARY KEY(AuditId)
);
```

Next, create a trigger called Chapter7Exercise.trgCoursesInsert that will automatically insert a record into the Chapter7Exercise.CoursesAudit table when a new course is inserted into the Chapter7Exercise.Courses table.

Exercise 7.2

Create a trigger called Chapter7Exercise.trgCoursesUpdate that will automatically insert a record into the Chapter7Exercise.CoursesAudit table when a course record in the Chapter7Exercise.Courses table is updated. Specifically, if a course number is modified, the Audit Action message should be "course number updated". If a course title is modified, the Audit Action message should be "course title updated". If both number and title of a course are modified, the Audit Action message should be "both course number and title updated".

Exercise 7.3

Create a trigger called Chapter7Exercise.trgCoursesDelete that will automatically insert a record into the Chapter7Exercise.CoursesAudit table when a course in the Chapter7Exercise.Courses table is deleted.

Exercise 7.4

Reset the Chapter7Exercise.Courses table and Chapter7Exercise.CoursesAudit table back to no data. You can just re-execute the SQL statements from Exercise 7.1 to recreate the two tables.

Write a trigger called trgCourseInsertCheckSeat that will validate maximum seats before inserting a row into the courses table. If the max seats is less than 10, an error message will be raised. Otherwise, the record will be inserted.

Exercise 7.5

Write a trigger called trgCourseUpdateCheckSeat that will validate a course's maximum seats before updating a row in the Courses Table. If the max seats is less than 10, an error message will be raised. Otherwise, the record will be updated.

Exercise 7.6

Write a trigger called trgCoursesDeleteCheckSeat that will validate a course's maximum seats before deleting a row in the courses table. If a course's max seat is more than 100, an error message will be raised. Otherwise, the record will be deleted. We won't allow a course with a large class size to be deleted from the courses table.

Exercise 7.7

Create a DDL trigger called trgDeleteTable that will display a message "Contact DBA if you want to delete a table." Then rollback. This trigger will ban any DROP TABLE statement to be executed.

Exercise 7.8

Modify the trigger you created in Exercise 7.4, Chapter7Exercise.trgCourseInsertCheckSeat, so that the minimum acceptable max seat is 5 instead of 10.

Exercise 7.9

First, disable the trigger you created in Exercise 7.4 and altered in Exercise 7.8: Chapter7Exercise.trgCourseInsertCheckSeat. Insert a new course with a max seat of 2.
Next, enable the trigger and try to insert a new course with a max seat of 2.

Exercise 7.10

Add two columns to the Chapter7Exercise.Courses table. One column called SeatTaken of INT data type. The other column called location of NVARCHAR(10) data type.

Exercise 7.11

Modify the CourseTitle column in Chapter7Exercise.Courses table to NVARCHAR(50) and does not allow NULL.

Exercise 7.12

Drop the location column from the Chapter7Exercise.Courses table.

Exercise 7.13

Rename the CourseTitle column in the Chapter7Exercise.Courses table to CourseName.

Exercise 7.14

You need two tables for the practice of Exercises 7.14 to 7.16. Execute the following statements to create the two tables:

```sql
IF OBJECT_ID(N'Chapter7Exercise.Courses') IS NOT NULL
    DROP TABLE Chapter7Exercise.Courses;
IF OBJECT_ID(N'Chapter7Exercise.Instructors') IS NOT NULL
    DROP TABLE Chapter7Exercise.Instructors;
CREATE TABLE Chapter7Exercise.Instructors
(
    InstructorId INT IDENTITY,
    InstructorName NVARCHAR(100) NOT NULL,
    Office NVARCHAR(50) NULL,
    CONSTRAINT pk_Instructors PRIMARY KEY(InstructorId)
);
CREATE TABLE Chapter7Exercise.Courses
(
    CourseId INT IDENTITY,
    CourseNumber NVARCHAR(10) NOT NULL,
    CourseTitle NVARCHAR(200) NULL,
    InstructorId INT NULL,
    CONSTRAINT pk_Courses PRIMARY KEY(CourseId),
    CONSTRAINT fk_Courses_Instructors
    FOREIGN KEY (InstructorId)
    REFERENCES Chapter7Exercise.Instructors(InstructorId)
);
SET IDENTITY_INSERT Chapter7Exercise.Instructors ON;
INSERT INTO Chapter7Exercise.Instructors
    (InstructorId, InstructorName, Office)
    VALUES
    (1, 'Ralph Moore', 'Tiger 301');
SET IDENTITY_INSERT Chapter7Exercise.Instructors OFF;
INSERT INTO Chapter7Exercise.Courses
    (CourseNumber, CourseTitle, InstructorId)
    VALUES
    ('CS101', 'Introduction to Database', 1);
INSERT INTO Chapter7Exercise.Courses
    (CourseNumber, CourseTitle, InstructorId)
    VALUES
    ('CS102', 'Advanced T-SQL', 1);
```

Can you delete the Instructor Id 1? If not, modify the foreign key constraint of the Chapter7Exercise.Courses so that when an instructor is deleted, the InstructorId in the Courses table will be set to NULL.

Exercise 7.15

Execute the SQL statements at the beginning of Exercise 7.14 to reset the two tables and their relationship before this exercise.

There are two tasks in this exercise:

First, change the InstructorId column in Chapter7Exercise.Courses table so that it can have default InstructorId value of 100.

Second, modify the foreign key constraint of Chapter7Exercise.Courses table so that when an instructor is deleted, the corresponding course's InstructorId automatically changes to 100.

Exercise 7.16

Execute the SQL statements at the beginning of Exercise 7.14 to reset the two tables and their relationship before this exercise.

Modify the fk_Courses_Instructors foreign key constraint so that when an instructor is deleted, all corresponding course records are deleted as well.

7.10 Solutions to the Review Questions

7.1 C; 7.2 D; 7.3 B; 7.4 C; 7.5 A; 7.6 C; 7.7 B; 7.8 A; 7.9 A; 7.10 C; 7.11 D; 7.12 A; 7.13 A; 7.14 D; 7.15 C; 7.16 C; 7.17 B; 7.18 A; 7.19 A; 7.20 C; 7.21 C; 7.22 C; 7.23 B; 7.24 A; 7.25 D; 7.26 C; 7.27 A; 7.28 C; 7.29 C; 7.30 D; 7.31 C; 7.32 B; 7.33 B; 7.34 D; 7.35 C; 7.36 B; 7.37 B; 7.38 D; 7.39 D; 7.40 D; 7.41 C; 7.42 C; 7.43 C; 7.44 A; 7.45 D; 7.46 A; 7.47 A; 7.48 B; 7.49 C; 7.50 D; 7.51 C; 7.52 D; 7.53 C; 7.54 D; 7.55 A; 7.56 B;

CHAPTER 8: QUERY TUNING AND PROJECTS

Chapter Learning Objectives

8.1 Describe the post-submission processes for an SQL statement batch.
8.2 Analyze graphical execution plans effectively.
8.3 Distinguish between estimated and actual execution plans.

8.1 Introduction to Query Tuning

After a batch of SQL statements is transmitted from a client to the server, the server faces the dual objectives of executing the statements as efficiently as possible while safeguarding the database's integrity. Key components of SQL Server participating in this process include the relational engine and the storage engine, as illustrated in the following figure:

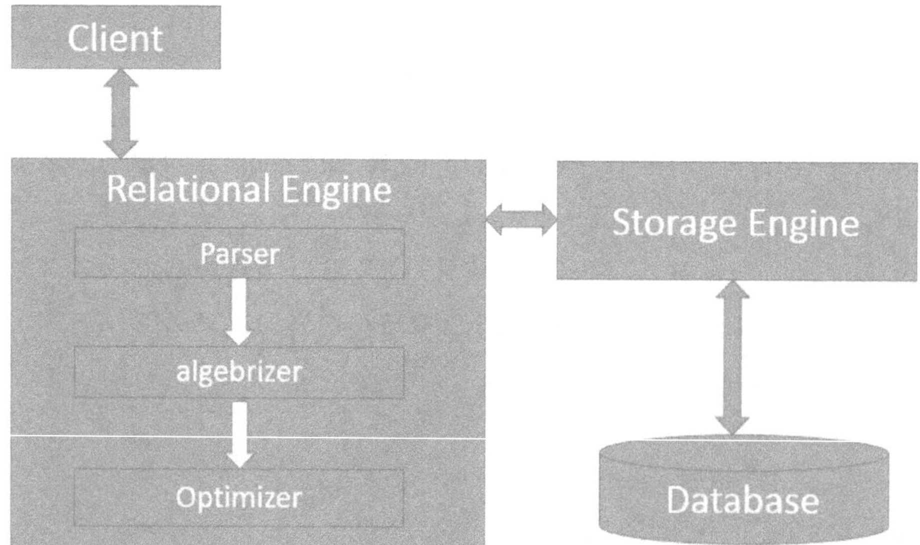

Within the relational engine, the SQL statements undergo three essential processes: parsing, algebrizing, and optimization.

Parsing: The parser process scrutinizes the syntax of the submitted SQL statement. If errors are detected, an error message is returned to the client. If the statement is error-free, a parse tree, outlining the logical steps to execute the query, is generated. The following figure shows a parser error:

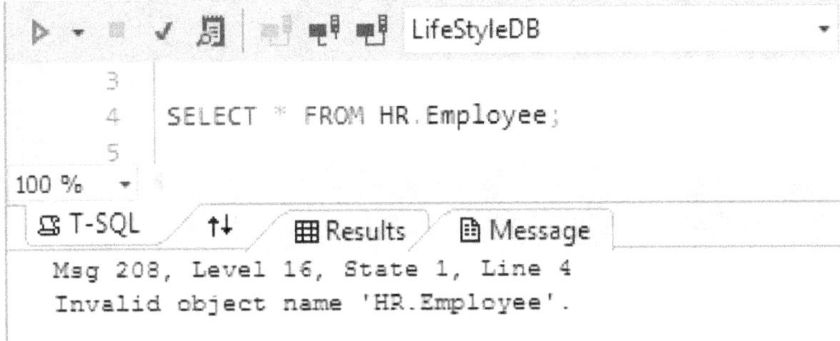

Algebrizing: The algebrizer takes the parse tree as input, performing a semantic check to verify the existence of elements like column names, table names, and other database objects. It also identifies data types in the query. If errors are identified, an error message is returned. If no errors are found, the algebrizer produces a binary code known as a query processor tree. The following figure shows a semantic error on a statement.

Optimization: The query optimizer works with the query processor tree to determine the most efficient way to retrieve the required data. The optimizer employs a cost-based approach, assessing the CPU processing and I/O time required. The data size, distribution of column values (gathered from data statistics), and other factors impact the cost. The optimizer may generate multiple cost plans, with the goal of selecting the most efficient one. However, in cases with an excessive number of plans, it may opt for a less efficient plan to save evaluation time. Reusing execution plans is a significant advantage of stored procedures and user-defined functions, as you learned in Chapter 5, as it reduces the workload on the optimizer.

The output of the optimizer is a query execution plan, which signals the end of the relational engine's role. The execution plan is passed to the storage engine, which follows it for data manipulation. To optimize query performance, a deep understanding of these processes is crucial, as efficient query execution relies on the collaboration between the relational and storage engines.

Review Question 8.1
After a batch of SQL statements is sent from a client to the server, the server has two objectives: ______.
a. to execute the statements in a secure way and to maintain the integrity of the database
b. to execute the statements in a secure way and to execute the statements in the shortest possible amount of time
c. to maintain the integrity of the database and to execute the statements in a secure way
d. to execute the statements in the shortest possible amount of time and to maintain the integrity of the database

Review Question 8.2
There are two major components of SQL Server involved in the process of executing a statement: ______.
a. the process engine and the storage engine
b. the process engine and the logic engine

c. the relational engine and the storage engine.
d. the relational engine and the logic engine

Review Question 8.3
There are three processes in the relational engine that the batch of SQL statements has to go through _____.
a. syntax, security, and optimizer
b. parser, security, and optimizer
c. syntax, parser, and security
d. parser, algebrizer, and optimizer.

Review Question 8.4
The _____ process of SQL Server relational engine checks the syntax of the submitted SQL statement.
a. parser
b. algebrizer
c. optimizer
d. security

Review Question 8.5
The _____ process of SQL Server relational engine performs a semantic check to make sure things such as the column names, table names, and other database objects exist.
a. parser
b. algebrizer
c. optimizer
d. security

Review Question 8.6
Which process of SQL Server relational engine identifies all data types in the submitted query?
a. parser
b. algebrizer
c. optimizer
d. security

Review Question 8.7
The input for which process of SQL Server relational engine is a parse tree?
a. parser
b. algebrizer
c. optimizer
d. security

Review Question 8.8
The output of which process of SQL Server relational engine is a query processor tree?
a. parser
b. algebrizer
c. optimizer
d. security

Review Question 8.9
The query _____ accepts the query processor tree as input and finds the best way to retrieve the needed data.
a. parser

b. algebrizer
c. optimizer
d. security

Review Question 8.10
All queries you submit for execution must go through the _______ of SQL Server relational engine to reach the goal of shortest possible execution time.
a. parser
b. algebrizer
c. optimizer
d. security

Review Question 8.11
The output of the optimizer is _______.
a. a parse tree
b. a query processor tree
c. a query execution plan
d. a query optimization plan

Review Question 8.12
When there are _______ plans to choose from, the optimizer may believe it is not worth the time to evaluate all these plans and thus just pick a _______ efficient plan to save the time needed to evaluate all plans.
a. too many, more
b. few, more
c. too many, less
d. few, less

Review Question 8.13
The query execution plan from one SQL statement _______.
a. may be used for another SQL statement
b. will unlikely be used for another SQL statement
c. may be used for another SQL statement if the programmer prefer
d. will never be used for another SQL statement

Review Question 8.14
The query execution plan is sent to the _______ engine for execution.
a. relational
b. storage
c. execution
d. SQL

Review Question 8.15
What are the two main objectives when processing a batch of SQL statements in SQL Server?
a. Data integrity and query optimization
b. Query optimization and report generation
c. Data integrity and cost estimation
d. Data retrieval and query compilation

Review Question 8.16
In the SQL Server's relational engine, which of the following is the correct order of processes that SQL

statements go through?
a. Parsing, optimization, algebrizing
b. Parsing, algebrizing, optimization
c. Optimization, parsing, algebrizing
d. Algebrizing, parsing, optimization

Review Question 8.17
What is the role of the parsing process in SQL Server?
a. It generates a query execution plan.
b. It checks the syntax of submitted SQL statements.
c. It creates binary code from the parse tree.
d. It validates data types in the query.

Review Question 8.18
What is the output of the algebrizer process in SQL Server's relational engine?
a. Query execution plan
b. Binary code called a query processor tree
c. Error message
d. Semantic check results

Review Question 8.19
What approach does the SQL Server optimizer use to determine the most efficient way to retrieve data?
a. Rule-based optimization
b. Heuristic-based optimization
c. Cost-based optimization
d. Performance-based optimization

Review Question 8.20
What is the role of a query execution plan in SQL Server?
a. It checks the data integrity of the database.
b. It generates the query processor tree.
c. It guides the relational engine in parsing.
d. It signals the end of the relational engine's role.

Review Question 8.21
How can stored procedures and user-defined functions benefit query performance?
a. They optimize the storage engine.
b. They reduce the workload on the optimizer.
c. They streamline the parsing process.
d. They generate more efficient SQL statements.

Review Question 8.22
What does the SQL Server optimizer consider when assessing the cost of execution plans?
a. Syntax errors in the SQL statements
b. The size of the query processor tree
c. The number of SQL statements in the batch
d. CPU processing, I/O time, and data statistics

Review Question 8.23
In SQL Server, when might the optimizer choose a less efficient execution plan?

a. When there are syntax errors in the SQL statement
b. When there are too many possible execution plans to evaluate
c. When there is no cost estimation for the execution plan
d. When the SQL statement is particularly complex

Review Question 8.24
Why is a deep understanding of the SQL Server query processing important for optimizing query performance?
a. To reduce the number of SQL statements in a batch
b. To improve the storage engine's efficiency
c. To enhance the data integrity of the database
d. To facilitate collaboration between the relational and storage engines

8.2 Graphical Execution Plan in SQL Server

In SQL Server, understanding how your queries are executed is crucial for optimizing performance. The graphical execution plan is a powerful tool that allows you to visualize and analyze the steps involved in query processing. It provides insights into how the database engine retrieves and manipulates data, helping you identify areas for improvement.

To display the execution plan graphically in Visual Studio, highlight the SQL statement, then, navigate to "SQL" in the menu and click on the "Display Estimated Execution Plan"

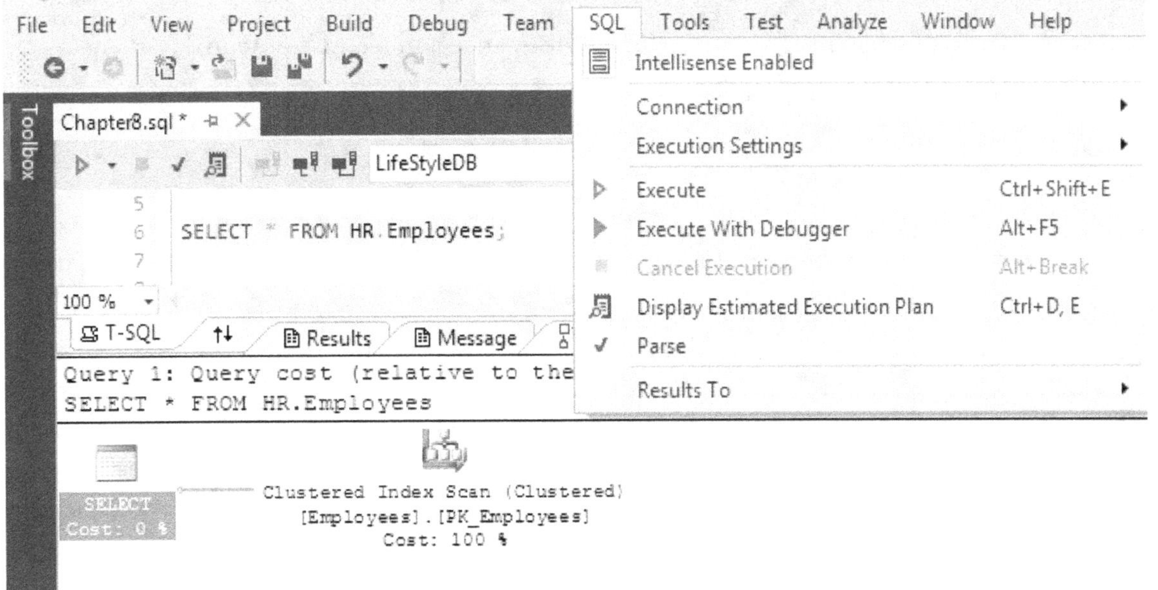

The graphical execution plan consists of a series of icons, each representing an operator. These operators represent specific actions performed during query execution. The plan should be read from left to right and top to bottom, with arrows indicating the flow of data between operators. The thickness of arrows reflects the amount of data being passed, with thicker arrows indicating larger data sets.

Each operator and arrow in the execution plan has an associated tooltip that provides detailed information.

For example, the following figure shows your mouse pointer is over the SELECT operator:

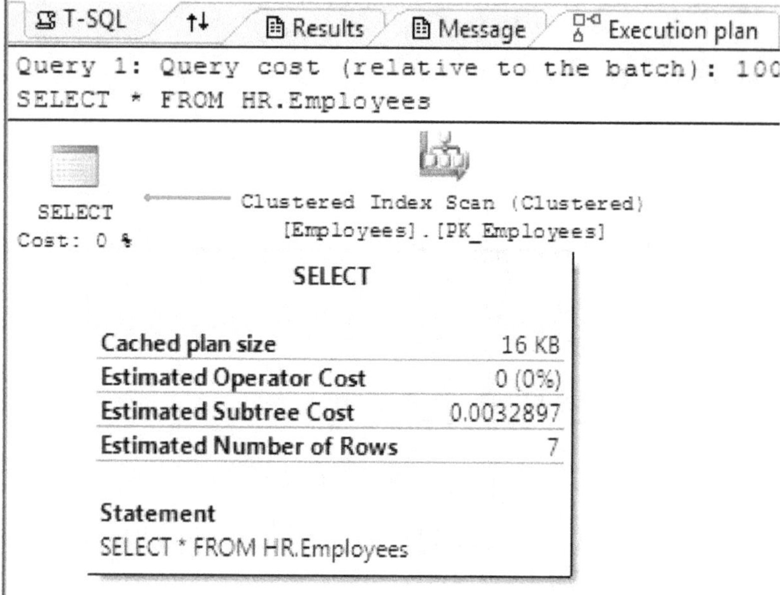

Some of the key details available in these tooltips include:

Cached Plan Size: This shows the amount of memory needed for the SQL statement.
Estimated Operator Cost: It represents the percentage of the cost of the operator compared to the entire batch.
Estimated Subtree Cost: This is the cumulative estimated cost up to the current node.
Estimated Number of Rows: It indicates the number of rows returned by an operator.

By analyzing these details, you can gain insights into query performance and identify potential bottlenecks.

For example, you can spot processes consuming excessive CPU, identify the need for additional indexes, or find unused indexes.

Let's explorer more of this, hover the mouse over the arrow to display the tooltip for the data flow from the "Clustered Index Scan" operator to the "SELECT" operator:

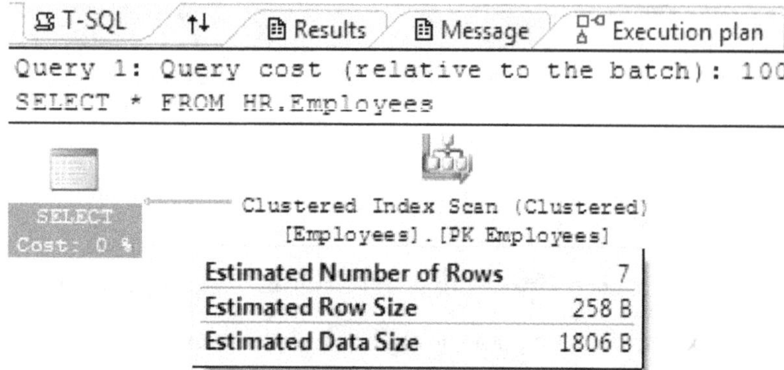

The "estimated number of rows" shows how many rows have passed from the Clustered Index Scan operator to the SELECT operator.

The estimated row size is the amount of data in each row.

The estimated data size is the total amount of data passed. In this case, it is 7 multiplied by 258B.

Let's explorer one more by pointing the mouse over the Clustered Index Scan operator to show the tooltip:

Clustered Index Scan (Clustered)

Scanning a clustered index, entirely or only a range.

Physical Operation	Clustered Index Scan
Logical Operation	Clustered Index Scan
Estimated Execution Mode	Row
Storage	RowStore
Estimated I/O Cost	0.003125
Estimated Operator Cost	0.0032897 (100%)
Estimated CPU Cost	0.0001647
Estimated Subtree Cost	0.0032897
Estimated Number of Executions	1
Estimated Number of Rows	7
Estimated Row Size	258 B
Ordered	False
Node ID	0

Object
[LifeStyleDB].[HR].[Employees].[PK_Employees]

Output List
[LifeStyleDB].[HR].[Employees].EmployeeId, [LifeStyleDB].
[HR].[Employees].FirstName, [LifeStyleDB].[HR].
[Employees].LastName, [LifeStyleDB].[HR].
[Employees].BirthDate, [LifeStyleDB].[HR].
[Employees].HireDate, [LifeStyleDB].[HR].
[Employees].HomeAddress, [LifeStyleDB].[HR].
[Employees].City, [LifeStyleDB].[HR].[Employees].State,
[LifeStyleDB].[HR].[Employees].PostalCode, [LifeStyleDB].
[HR].[Employees].Phone, [LifeStyleDB].[HR].
[Employees].ManagerId

The *Clustered Index Scan* is a different operator from the SELECT operator as displayed in the tooltip.

The *logical operation* gives the expected results calculated by the optimizer for what should happen when the query executes.

The *physical operation* represents what actually occurred.

The *estimated I/O cost* is the estimated processing time needed for file input and output.

The *estimated CPU cost* is the estimated amount of time needed from the CPU. All estimations are based on the statistics available on the columns and indexes in the tables.

The *ordered* indicates whether or not the data that this operator is working with is in an ordered state. For example, if you add ORDER BY EmployeeId to the SQL statement, the value will be changed to true.

The *node ID* is an ordinal number from left to right with 0 as the first number.

All of this information is at your disposal to gain a deeper understanding of the ongoing processes in your query. Armed with these insights, you'll be well-equipped to pinpoint CPU-intensive operations, recognize tables in need of additional indexes, and identify any unused indexes.

The following are some of the common operators used in SQL Server:

Image	Operator	Description	Example SQL with LifeStyleDB

	Table Scan	Search all rows of a table. Can be a costly operation if the number of rows is large.	`CREATE SCHEMA Chapter8 AUTHORIZATION dbo;`
			`GO`
			`SELECT * INTO Chapter8.Employees FROM HR.Employees;`
			`GO`
			`SELECT * FROM Chapter8.Employees;`

	Clustered Index Seek	Search by using index. Most optimized method to retrieve the data.	`SELECT FirstName + ' ' + LastName AS "Full Name"`
			`FROM HR.Employees`
			`WHERE EmployeeId = 3;`

	Clustered Index Scan	Scans most rows of a table, typically when the available index is insufficient.	`SELECT * FROM HR.Employees;`

	Nested Loops	Joins two sets of data by scanning the outer data set once for each row in the inner data set.	`SELECT *`
			`FROM HR.Employees AS E`
			`JOIN Sales.Orders AS O`
			`ON E.EmployeeId = O.EmployeeId;`

To explore a comprehensive list of operators and their descriptions, you can refer to Microsoft's official documentation: SQL Server Showplan Logical and Physical Operators Reference.

Review Question 8.25
The arrow in graphical execution plan represents the data being passed between the operators. The _______ of the arrow reflects the amount of data being passed.
a. length
b. thickness
c. direction
d. length and thinkness

Review Question 8.26
Which operator of execution plan does this describe? "Search all rows of a table. Can be a costly operation if the number of rows is large."
a. table scan
b. Clustered Index Seek
c. Clustered Index Scan
d. Nested Loops

Review Question 8.27
How can you display a graphical execution plan for a SQL statement in Visual Studio?
a. Click "Execute Query" in the menu
b. Select "Show Execution Plan" from the SQL statement's context menu
c. Highlight the SQL statement, then navigate to "SQL" in the menu and click on "Display Estimated Execution Plan"
d. It's automatically displayed when you run a SQL statement

Review Question 8.28
In a graphical execution plan, what does the thickness of the arrows between operators represent?
a. The number of operators
b. The estimated cost
c. The amount of data being passed
d. The execution time

Review Question 8.29
What does the "Cached Plan Size" in a tooltip of an operator's execution plan represent?
a. The number of rows returned by the operator
b. The percentage of the operator's cost compared to the entire batch
c. The amount of memory needed for the SQL statement
d. The cumulative estimated cost up to the current node

Review Question 8.30
What can you identify by analyzing the details in a graphical execution plan's tooltips?
a. SQL Server version
b. Hardware specifications
c. Query performance insights and potential bottlenecks
d. Administrator credentials

Review Question 8.31
When analyzing the estimated data size in a graphical execution plan, what does it represent?
a. The total number of rows in the table
b. The total size of the database
c. The total amount of data passed between operators
d. The average row size in the result set

Review Question 8.32
In a graphical execution plan, what does the "logical operation" in a tooltip represent?
a. The expected results calculated by the optimizer
b. The actual results achieved during query execution
c. The order of operators in the execution plan
d. The version of SQL Server used

Review Question 8.33
To change the "ordered" value in a graphical execution plan, what should you add to the SQL statement?
a. ORDER BY clause
b. GROUP BY clause
c. WHERE clause
d. HAVING clause

Review Question 8.34
What does the "node ID" in a graphical execution plan indicate?
a. The total number of nodes in the execution plan
b. The estimated processing time needed for file input and output
c. An ordinal number from left to right within the execution plan
d. The actual time taken by each operator

Review Question 8.35

Which operator is considered the most optimized method to retrieve data in SQL Server?
a. Table Scan
b. Clustered Index Seek
c. Clustered Index Scan
d. Nested Loops

Review Question 8.36
Which operator is considered to scans most rows of a table, typically when the available index is insufficient, to retrieve data in SQL Server?
a. Table Scan
b. Clustered Index Seek
c. Clustered Index Scan
d. Nested Loops

8.3 Estimated and Actual Execution Plan

In the previous section, you gained an understanding of how to display the estimated execution plan. This plan provides valuable insights into how the SQL Server's optimizer predicts the execution of SQL statements. Now, let's explore the actual execution plan, which reveals how SQL Server truly processes your queries.

Obtaining an actual execution plan is a straightforward process that involves the following two simple steps:

First, navigate to the "SQL" menu, select "Execution Settings," and finally, enable the "Include Actual Execution Plan" option, as illustrated in the following figure:

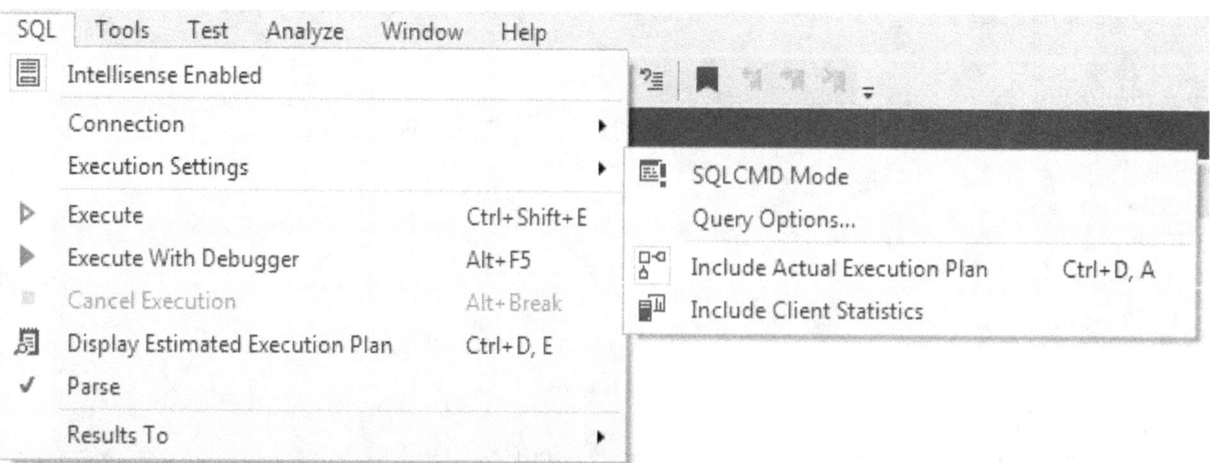

After enabling the "Include Actual Execution Plan" setting, highlight the query you wish to analyze and execute it. Then, click on the "Execution Plan" tab to view the actual execution plan, as shown in the image below:

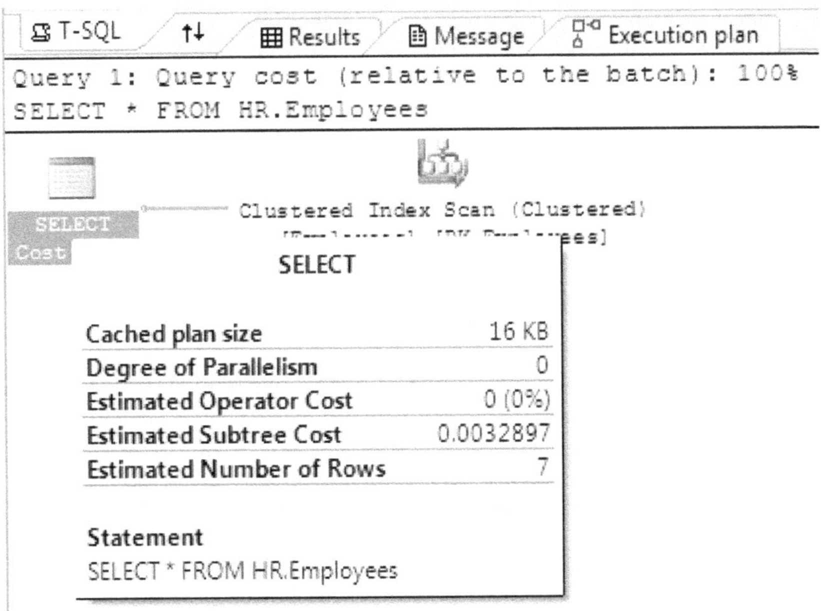

At first glance, you may not observe any significant differences between the estimated and actual execution plans. However, a closer inspection often reveals variations, with one notable distinction being the "Degree of Parallelism" in the Actual Execution Plan. This value indicates the extent to which parallel processing was utilized during query execution.

The "estimated execution plan" represents the SQL Server optimizer's prediction of how it will handle the SQL statements. It is a crucial tool for assessing query performance before actual execution. In contrast, the "actual execution plan" details the real steps and operations that the SQL Server undertakes when executing your queries. These differences between estimated and actual execution plans are primarily influenced by changes in statistics between the time when the estimated execution plan is generated and when the storage engine actually processes the query.

Previously, we discussed how some execution plans are stored in the plan cache for potential reuse. Which type of plan is saved in the plan cache—estimated or actual? It's the estimated execution plan. However, it's essential to note that even though the estimated plan is cached, it can still be affected by changes in statistics. This means that SQL Server's optimizer might adjust its approach based on the most up-to-date statistics to ensure optimal query performance.

Review Question 8.37

The storage engine _______ follow(s) the _______ plan provided by the _______ engine.
a. always, execution, storage
b. always, prediction, relational
c. does not always, execution, relational
d. does not always, prediction, storage

Review Question 8.38
What is the major reason for the differences between estimated and actual execution plan?
a. the programmer changes mind.
b. the database administrator changes mind.
c. statistics collected by the server.
d. the type of hardware on which the server runs.

Review Question 8.39
What is the purpose of an estimated execution plan in SQL Server?
a. To provide insights into the real execution of SQL statements.
b. To detail the actual steps taken by the storage engine.
c. To predict how SQL Server will process SQL statements.
d. To display statistics about the plan cache.

Review Question 8.40
How can you obtain an actual execution plan in Visual Studio?
a. By navigating to "SQL," selecting "Display Estimated Execution Plan."
b. By navigating to "Tools," selecting "Check Actual Execution Plan."
c. By navigating to "SQL," selecting "Execution Settings," and enabling "Include Actual Execution Plan."
d. By right-clicking the query and selecting "Plan Analysis."

Review Question 8.41
What is the primary difference between the estimated and actual execution plans in SQL Server?
a. The estimated plan displays actual steps, while the actual plan predicts SQL execution.
b. The estimated plan offers insights into parallel processing, while the actual plan does not.
c. The estimated plan provides statistics on the degree of parallelism, while the actual plan does not.
d. The estimated plan predicts SQL execution, while the actual plan details the real steps taken during execution.

Review Question 8.42
What is the "Degree of Parallelism" in the actual execution plan?
a. A measure of how many times the query has been executed.
b. An indicator of how many processors are used for query execution.
c. A metric for the number of rows returned by the query.
d. A measure of memory consumption by the query.

Review Question 8.43
Why is the estimated execution plan important for query optimization?
a. It reveals actual execution details.
b. It provides statistics on memory usage.
c. It allows you to analyze the plan cache.
d. It helps assess query performance before execution.

Review Question 8.44

Where is the "Include Actual Execution Plan" option located in Visual Studio?
a. Under "Query Analysis" in the "SQL" menu.
b. Under "Plan Settings" in the "Tools" menu.
c. Under "Execution Settings" in the "SQL" menu.
d. Under "Performance Metrics" in the "View" menu.

Review Question 8.45
What primarily influences the differences between estimated and actual execution plans in SQL Server?
a. The version of SQL Server being used.
b. The degree of parallelism set for a query.
c. Changes in statistics between estimation and execution.
d. The number of query operators in the plan.

Review Question 8.46
Which type of execution plan is saved in the plan cache for potential reuse?
a. Actual execution plan
b. Estimated execution plan
c. Visual execution plan
d. System execution plan

Review Question 8.47
What is the role of the "Degree of Parallelism" in SQL Server execution plans?
a. It indicates the number of data pages read during query execution.
b. It specifies the number of rows returned by the query.
c. It represents the number of processors used for parallel query execution.
d. It details the total CPU and I/O costs of the query.

Review Question 8.48
Why is it important for the SQL Server optimizer to adjust the estimated execution plan based on the most up-to-date statistics?
a. To reduce the degree of parallelism in the execution plan.
b. To minimize the number of query operators in the plan.
c. To optimize the query's logical operations.
d. To ensure optimal query performance as statistics change.

8.4 Query Optimization

Query optimization is a vast and vital topic in the world of database management. It involves fine-tuning your SQL queries to perform as efficiently as possible. In this section, we will delve into key strategies and concepts related to query optimization, with a particular focus on leveraging query execution plans to enhance performance. While the dataset used in this book is relatively small, and it may not always exhibit substantial performance differences, the principles we cover are applicable to larger databases.

One of the fundamental techniques for query optimization is the strategic use of indexes. Indexes are like the table of contents in a book, providing a quick way to locate specific information within your database. Here are some strategies to consider when working with indexes:

Choosing the Right Columns: Evaluate which columns are frequently used in search conditions, such as filtering, sorting, or joining tables. Indexing these columns can significantly speed up query execution. For instance, if your database frequently queries employees by their first name and phone number, it might be wise to create indexes on these columns.

Composite Indexing: In some cases, a single column index may not be enough. Composite indexing, which involves indexing multiple columns together, can be a powerful solution. Experiment with different sequences of columns within composite indexes to find the most efficient arrangement for your specific queries.

When your queries involve joining multiple tables, the order in which you perform these joins can influence query performance. The SQL Server optimizer needs to choose an execution plan, and this decision can be impacted by the sequence of table joins. It's essential to understand the different statistics and execution plans produced by varying join sequences. By experimenting with different join orders, you can gain insights into which sequence works best for your specific scenarios.

While SQL Server's query optimizer is highly intelligent and efficient at determining execution plans, there might be situations where you want to influence or even dictate the execution path. You can do this using the following methods:

The WITH Clause: The WITH clause allows you to specify query hints, indicating how the optimizer should approach your query. For instance, you can instruct it to use a particular index or optimization strategy.

The OPTION Clause with Hints: SQL Server provides a range of hints that you can use with the OPTION clause to give the optimizer guidance on query execution. These hints can influence join strategies, index usage, and more. It's a powerful but advanced technique, so use it judiciously.

Query optimization is a balancing act that involves leveraging indexing, optimizing join sequences, and occasionally using hints to fine-tune your queries. By understanding these principles and experimenting with different strategies in your specific database environment, you can significantly enhance query performance. Remember that the art of query optimization often involves trial and error to find the best approach for your unique data and query requirements.

Review Question 8.49

Which of the following activity is NOT recommended for query optimization?
a. indexing different columns
b. indexing as many columns as possible
c. joining tables in different sequences
d. forcing the use of a certain index

Review Question 8.50
Which of the following clause can be used to force the use of a certain index?
a. FORCE
b. FORCE INDEX
c. WITH
d. SET INDEX

Review Question 8.51
What is the primary goal of query optimization in database management?
a. To maximize storage efficiency
b. To minimize the number of tables in a database
c. To fine-tune SQL queries for optimal performance
d. To eliminate the use of indexes

Review Question 8.52
How are indexes compared to in a database?
a. They are like search engines
b. They are like table headers
c. They are like table of contents in a book
d. They are like folders in a file system

Review Question 8.53
When should you consider creating indexes on specific columns in your database?
a. When the columns are rarely used
b. When the columns are unrelated to each other
c. When the columns are frequently used in search conditions
d. When the columns contain long text data

Review Question 8.54
What is composite indexing in the context of query optimization?
a. Indexing only one column in a table
b. Indexing multiple columns together
c. Indexing columns in a random order
d. Indexing columns with the same data type

Review Question 8.55
Why is the order of table joins important in query optimization?
a. It has no impact on query performance
b. It can influence the SQL Server optimizer's execution plan
c. It only affects the readability of SQL queries
d. It helps in organizing the tables in the database

Review Question 8.56
What is the purpose of the WITH clause in SQL query optimization?

a. To specify query hints for the optimizer
b. To define complex SQL queries
c. To join tables together
d. To create new tables in the database

Review Question 8.57
When using the OPTION clause with hints, what aspect of query execution can be influenced?
a. The selection of database tables
b. The sequence of SQL statements
c. The join strategies and index usage
d. The style and formatting of query results

Review Question 8.58
What best describes the role of query optimization in database management?
a. A one-time task performed when creating a database
b. A recurring task needed to maintain database security
c. A continuous process to fine-tune SQL queries for optimal performance
d. A task that only database administrators can perform

Review Question 8.59
What should you expect when experimenting with query optimization techniques?
a. Instantly achieving optimal query performance
b. Frequent changes in the database structure
c. Trial and error to find the best approach for your data and queries
d. No impact on query performance

8.5 Project One:

Tiger State University (TSU) is embarking on the development of a new web application for their athletic department and is in need of a comprehensive database to support its functionality. Here's a breakdown of the various components and their characteristics:

Sports Teams:

Tiger State University (TSU) proudly hosts a wide variety of sports teams, catering to both men's and women's sports. While the majority of sports at TSU feature both men's and women's teams, there are notable exceptions. For instance, sports like football are exclusively male, while sports like golf exclusively field women's teams.

Each sports team at TSU is supported by a dedicated coaching staff. These coaching staff members are identified by their names, maintain individual office locations, and provide contact information for effective communication. It's also worth noting that some coaching staff members may serve multiple teams within the athletic department, reflecting the collaborative nature of coaching roles.

Seasons:

Each sport operates within a designated time frame referred to as a season. These seasons are intentionally designed with flexibility in mind, allowing for variations in start and end dates. It's important to note that many sports align their start and end dates with the school calendar, ensuring coordination and convenience for both athletes and academic schedules.

Game Schedules:

Each team has its own game schedule, which includes vital details such as the date, start time, day of the week, opponent, and game location (arena, city and state). Games played at TSU are categorized as "home games," while those at the opponent's location are "away games." Any games played elsewhere are labeled as "neutral." Games have different purposes, including regular season games, regional competitions, NCAA tournaments, and special events like fundraisers. Each school is represented by a mascot, complete with a name, an associated image file, and its head coach name.

Game Statistics:

For games that have already been played, statistics such as the final score, game outcome (win or lose), video recaps, and photo galleries will be recorded.

Player Rosters:

Each team maintains a roster of players, with each player having a photo, full name, position, height, weight, hometown, class, high school, uniform number, and a bio.

News Articles:

The athletic department also publishes news articles related to various sports. Each article includes a headline, date of posting, content, and relevant photos. Articles are tagged to specify the sports they are associated with, allowing for categorization and easy retrieval.

Ticket Sales:

The web application will facilitate the sale of tickets to both students and the public. Tickets are organized by sport and are available to two types of accounts: student, faculty, and staff accounts, and public accounts. Different account types will have varying prices for the same game. Both account types can purchase season tickets, single game tickets, and five-game packages. Some special events are exclusively accessible to student, faculty, and staff accounts. Each account includes details like the customer's name, email address, mailing address, phone number, and loyalty points (explained later).

Ticket Details:

Season tickets include information on seating type, price, donation, and availability. Individual game tickets encompass sale dates, opponents, game dates, seating types, and prices. Five-game packages specify the list of games included and their prices. The five games are pre-determined. The ticket-selling website provides information on seating availability for each seat type.

Online Store:

In addition to a physical store, the athletic department operates an online store that sells team merchandise. Shoppers can browse through Men's, Women's, and Kid's clothing, as well as t-shirts, sweatshirts, hats, jerseys, and collectibles. Each item for sale has a name, a brief description, an image, price, and sale price. The online store's checkout service is outsourced to a third party. While no customer payment information is stored, the department maintains purchase records, including details of what was purchased, its price, date of purchase, and whether it was made online or in-store. For anonymous in-store purchases, the department uses an anonymous account with the account ID 999999999.

Tiger Fund and Membership:

TSU's athletic department accepts donations through the Tiger Fund. Donors at different levels of contribution become members. Members are categorized as Scratch members (donating $1-$1000), Tigers ($1001 - $10,000), Pink Tigers ($10,001 - $100,000), and Elite Tigers ($100,000+). Each membership level comes with various benefits, such as tax deductions, access to pre-season parties, football signing day events, and loyalty points. Not all levels of membership enjoy the same benefits; higher-tier members enjoy more benefits than lower-tier members.

Loyalty Points:

The department operates a loyalty points system where customers earn one point for every dollar spent in the store or as donations towards membership. These points do not expire but cannot be transferred or sold. The primary benefit of loyalty points is the potential for ticket discounts, with the discount percentage determined on a season-by-season basis.

This comprehensive database will support TSU's athletic department in efficiently managing its operations and enhancing the experience for both teams and fans.

Your Task:

1. Write Business Rules: Document the specific rules and guidelines that govern the operation of the database and its components. Ensure clarity and comprehensiveness in defining how data should be handled and managed.

2. Create Logical ERD: Develop a Logical Entity-Relationship Diagram (ERD) that illustrates the essential entities, their attributes, and the relationships between them. Ensure that the ERD reflects the database's structure accurately. Include all primary keys for each entity.

3. List Relations Mapped from Logical ERD: Enumerate the relational tables that are derived from the Logical ERD. Specify the foreign keys that establish relationships between these tables.

4. Write SQL Code to Create the Database and Tables: Provide Data Definition Language (DDL) SQL statements to create the database and the necessary tables, including the appropriate keys and constraints.

5. Populate the Tables with Made-Up Data: Generate sample SQL statements to populate the tables with fictitious but meaningful data, ensuring that the data aligns with the defined structure.

6. Create Objects (Views, Indexes, Stored Procedures, Transactions, and Triggers): Develop at least one of each type of database object (view, index, stored procedure, transaction, and trigger) with clear explanations of their purposes and how they enhance the functionality of the database.

7. Write SQL Statements to Answer the Following Questions:
a. Display all sports for the current season, including both Men's and Women's sports.
b. Display all rosters for women's basketball.
c. Display the statistics for women's basketball played at a specific date in the past.
d. Display all news related to women's basketball.
e. Update a women's basketball schedule at a specific future date. Modify the play time due to the weather forecast.
f. Display all home games for women's basketball.
g. Display all women's basketball t-shirts.
h. Display tickets for women's basketball for a specific future date.
i. Display ticket info for women's basketball on a specific future date for a specific account.
j. Display account info for a specific account.
k. Display a customer's receipt/purchasing history.
l. Display all benefits by each type of membership.
m. Display all tiger fans with royalty points from high to low.

Ensure that the SQL statements are structured correctly and provide meaningful responses to the questions. Clearly define the rationale behind any complex SQL queries or operations.

8.6 Project Two:

The Tiger Movie Theatre (TMT) is a long-standing family-owned small business that embarked on its

journey in 1929. Over the years, it has seen both success and challenges. One notable challenge arose with

the introduction of cable TV, which prompted TMT to revamp its theater environment. This included investments in state-of-the-art audio systems and upgrading to deluxe seating.

Today, TMT faces a new major challenge, the Internet. However, the management has chosen to embrace this challenge rather than compete directly with online video streaming competitors. One of their plans is to create an online community for TMT, and for this purpose, they require a database to manage the data for this community.

The objective for TMT is to establish an online community where customers can share their movie ratings and provide detailed information about each movie, somewhat like IMDb but on a smaller scale. Visitors can peruse the content anonymously, but participation in the community, such as commenting and rating, as well as online ticket purchases, is reserved for registered users.

TMT comprises five distinct movie screening rooms, each with varying seat capacities, audio systems, and unique names, which will be given the honor of naming.

Visitors to the TMT web community can explore the list of movies scheduled for TMT, and they can refine this list based on TMT showtimes, theaters, or customer reviews. Clicking on a movie title will display detailed information about that movie on a separate page, along with a link to purchase tickets.

On the ticket purchase page, customers can see the price for the selected movie, showtime, and room. This page also offers options for purchasing popcorn, drinks, and souvenirs like t-shirts or keychains. Food and souvenir items are accompanied by names, photos, and prices. Customers can select their seat number if they buy any food or souvenirs, which will be delivered to their seats before the movie begins. Discounts on these souvenirs vary and are determined by the managers. The checkout process is outsourced to a third party, but TMT retains records of receipts, showing what was purchased, by whom, and at what time. A copy of the receipt is saved in the user's account and emailed to the user, with a reminder text sent within 24 hours between 10am and 8pm.

To register on the website, a user must provide the following information: first name, last name, a unique nickname, a list of movies they've watched, a watch-list, phone number, and email address. TMT is committed to not selling user data and will use this information solely for communication purposes.

Each movie in the database is characterized by a title, release date, age rating, genre, original country, runtime, language, production company, cast and crew, storyline, customer reviews, TMT screening date, time, and room.

The cast and crew data includes actors/actresses, characters, roles (e.g., actress, producer, director), dates of birth, and birthplaces (including state and country).

Customer reviews of a movie encompass a title/header, rating on a scale from 1 to 5, review date, review content, and the number of users who found the review helpful. Unhelpful votes are not permitted, and TMT's managers review user posts daily, removing any offensive content and potentially deactivating accounts if necessary.

Age ratings include Not Rated, G, PG, PG-13, R, and NC-17, and TMT's website provides a symbol with a question mark for each movie. Clicking on the question mark reveals the meaning of the age rating.

Movie genres, such as action, comedy, drama, and fantasy, may evolve over time, with new genres being added and old ones possibly being retired. A movie may have more than one genre.

Your Tasks:

Tasks 1 to 6 remain the same as Project One, with a focus on defining the structure and initial setup of the database. Here are the additional tasks for this project:

7. Write SQL Statements to Address the Following Queries:
a. Allow a user to edit a review they've previously written.
b. List all the movies that are on a customer's watch list.
c. Present all the movies that a customer has already watched.
d. Calculate and display the average customer rating for a specific movie.
e. Show all the reviews for a particular movie.
f. Display all movies associated with a specific cast or crew member.
g. List all the reviews written by a specific customer.
h. Display all the movies that TMT will be screening in the next seven days.
i. Present a list of all movies that will be playing between two given dates.
j. Allow users to add a helpful vote to a movie review.
k. Identify and display the customer(s) who have written the most reviews for fantasy movies.
l. Present the purchasing history and receipts for all customers.
m. Display the seat numbers for customers who require delivery within the next hour.

8.7 Project Three

The Vacation Inn (VI) is a charming family-owned hotel nestled in the Great Lake Resort area. Having previously created a database for their housekeeping tracking system in a prior project, they have now approached you with a request to expand the database to encompass room reservations and room service.

Online Reservation:

Customers visiting VI's website can easily initiate the reservation process. They select a check-in date and a check-out date, and with a simple click, the website displays the availability of each room type. For room types with more than five available rooms, only "available" is shown without specifying the exact number. Furthermore, the website provides an image, description, and price for each room type. Vacation Inn offers three room types: suites, rooms with one King-size bed, and rooms with two Queen-size beds.

Customers then proceed to select their preferred room type and the number of rooms required. Additionally, they specify the number of people in their party to comply with legal requirements (e.g., fire safety regulations, which limit each room to a maximum of four occupants). Importantly, this count does not affect the price, as long as it remains below four people per room.

At this stage, customers are prompted to enter their personal information, including first name, last name, middle initial, home address, phone number, and email. Customers have the option to register an account for convenience in future reservations, or they can proceed with a one-time reservation. If they choose to create an account, they must select a password, with their email address serving as their username.

Following this, customers proceed to the payment page, where VI exclusively accepts online credit/debit card payments. Customers provide the necessary payment information, and the website also accommodates coupons and gift cards issued by VI. These gift cards consist of random 16-digit numbers generated by the manager during the card's sale. The card numbers are stored in the database to facilitate validation and redemption.

Customers can also book rooms at VI through third-party services like Hotwire, Expedia, and hotel.com. These third-party reservations mirror customer data and room information, except for payment details. Third parties settle their payments on a weekly basis, with pre-agreed amounts for each room type per day.

Upon completing the reservation, a unique random confirmation number is emailed to the customer.
Check-in and Check-out:
Upon arrival, customers, whether they reserved directly via VI's website or through a third party, are assigned specific rooms by a manager. It's possible for customers to check in for fewer rooms or days than

originally reserved. In such cases, the manager can decide on any penalties to be applied. The actual check-in date may differ from the reserved check-in date. The checkout date is confirmed with the customer but may not necessarily align with the actual departure date.

During the actual checkout process, a date and time are entered into the database. These checkout dates can be earlier than the confirmed departure date, and any associated penalties are negotiated with the manager.

Customers arriving without a reservation go through an online reservation process, after which they are checked in. The checkout process is consistent for customers with or without reservations.

For customers with third-party reservations, credit card information is still requested, although VI doesn't charge for the room itself. Instead, this information is used for additional services like in-room dining, pay-per-view TV, phone charges, and potential expenses related to any damage or lost items.

The hotel comprises a single building with two floors. Room numbers for suites are 201 to 205, King-size bedrooms are 101, 103, 105, 107, 109, 111, 113, 115, and 117, and two Queen-size bedrooms are numbered from 102 to 118.

Housekeeping:

The management needs to stay informed about the condition of rooms at all times. Each housekeeper is equipped with an iPad. Every morning, upon arrival at work, housekeepers can log in to view the rooms that require cleaning. When they commence work on a room, they select the room number and start the timer. Upon completing the cleaning, they stop the timer and can report any missing items in the room. This information also tracks which housekeeper cleaned each room, allowing the management to address any performance concerns.

Employee Data:

While VI outsources accounting-related tasks such as payroll and taxes, they still need to maintain essential employee information. The hotel employs four types of workers: managers, who receive annual salaries, and housekeepers, staff, and AM food servers, who are paid hourly wages. The database retains data such as employee names, job titles, hiring dates, salary or wage information, and specialties. Importantly, historical data is preserved to account for changes in salary or wages and cases where employees may have left and later returned to work at VI.

Your Tasks:

Tasks 1 to 6 remain consistent with Project One, focusing on shaping the structure and initial setup of the database. In addition, you are tasked with the following new responsibilities for this project:

7. Write SQL Statements to Address the Following Queries:

a. Display all available rooms for a given check-in date and check-out date. If there are more than 5 rooms available, simply indicate availability without specifying the exact count. For room types with fewer than 5 available, show the number of rooms left.

b. Record a customer's reservation of one King room and two two-queen-bed rooms.

c. A customer who made a reservation through VI's website has arrived at the hotel, prepared to check in. A manager checks in the customer.

d. Display the name of the manager responsible for checking in a specific customer on a given date.

e. Document a customer's room service order for breakfast, which incurred a $40.00 charge to the room balance.

f. Display a list of rooms requiring housekeeping.

g. Report that two housekeepers have logged into two of the rooms in need of cleaning.

h. Confirm that one housekeeper has completed one of the aforementioned rooms after clocking in and then clocking out.

i. A manager checks which rooms are prepared for new customers to move into.

j. A customer with a third-party reservation arrives and is ready to check in.

k. Record the departure of one of the housekeepers from VI.

l. Acknowledge the return of the same housekeeper mentioned above, who has come back to work for VI again.

m. Display a list of rooms currently in the process of being cleaned.

n. Display the identity of the housekeeper who cleaned a specific room on a given date, along with the clock-in and clock-out times.

o. Document a scenario where a customer checks out one day earlier than anticipated, and the manager opts to issue a 70% refund for that particular day's rate.

8.8 Chapter Summary

We conclude the book with a final chapter dedicated to query performance. This chapter delves into a substantial and intricate subject, one often best grasped through practical experience as a database administrator. The primary focus of this chapter revolves around the three projects. We firmly believe that it is by actively engaging with these projects that you truly comprehend the mechanics of T-SQL

8.9 Solutions to the Review Questions

8.1 D; 8.2 C; 8.3 D; 8.4 A; 8.5 B; 8.6 B; 8.7 B; 8.8 B; 8.9 C; 8.10 C; 8.11 C; 8.12 C; 8.13 A; 8.14 B; 8.15 A; 8.16 B; 8.17 B; 8.18 B; 8.19 C; 8.20 D; 8.21 B; 8.22 D; 8.23 B; 8.24 D; 8.25 B; 8.26 A; 8.27 C; 8.28 C; 8.29 C; 8.30 C; 8.31 C; 8.32 A; 8.33 A; 8.34 C; 8.35 B; 8.36 C; 8.37 C; 8.38 C; 8.39 C; 8.40 C; 8.41 D; 8.42 B; 8.43 D; 8.44 C; 8.45 C; 8.46 B; 8.47 C; 8.48 D; 8.49 B; 8.50 C; 8.51 C; 8.52 C; 8.53 C; 8.54 B; 8.55 B; 8.56 A; 8.57 C; 8.58 C; 8.59 C;